WESTWORLD

PSYCHOLOGY

VIOLENT DELIGHTS

EDITED BY

TRAVIS LANGLEY AND WIND GOODFRIEND

#WWpsych   #PsychGeeks

STERLING
New York

STERLING
New York

An Imprint of Sterling Publishing Co., Inc.
1166 Avenue of the Americas
New York, NY 10036

ISBN 978-1-4549-3241-3

Distributed in Canada by Sterling Publishing Co., Inc.
^{c}/o Canadian Manda Group, 664 Annette Street
Toronto, Ontario, Canada M6S 2C8
Distributed in the United Kingdom by GMC Distribution Services
Castle Place, 166 High Street, Lewes, East Sussex, England BN7 1XU
Distributed in Australia by Capricorn Link (Australia) Pty. Ltd.
P.O. Box 704, Windsor, NSW 2756, Australia

For information about custom editions, special sales, and premium and corporate purchases,
please contact Sterling Special Sales at 800-805-5489 or specialsales@sterlingpublishing.com.

Manufactured in Canada

2 4 6 8 10 9 7 5 3 1

sterlingpublishing.com

Image Credits
Cover: Shutterstock: Efifantsev (font); F R i M A G E S (landscape); Nejron Photo
(woman); pzAxe (circuit board)

iStock: Batareykin: 51; bluebearry: 243, booblegum: 6; Cattallina: 160; ctrlaplus1: 175;
DeCe_X: 97; ElaKwasniewski: 132; Evgenii_Bobrov: 254; greyj: 108; Infadel: 213;
jara3000: 197; Kamaga: 64; Kenshi991: 120; linearcurves: 186; LunaticLu: 210; lvcandy:
4, 14, 18, 36, 48, 49, 54, 61, 70, 76, 82, 90, 101, 104, 113, 116, 129, 135, 142, 148,
153, 166, 170, 179, 183, 194, 195, 206, 208, 220, 223, 238, 249, 250, 256, 260; mara_
lingstad: 269; NatBasil: 163; oleg7799: 81; Pingebat: 8, 66, 96, 162, 212; Samtoon: 67;
Theerakit: i, 229; vasya_40; Eugene Valter: 25; Vect0r0vich: 146; VectorUp: 94

Shutterstock: vinston: 9

Dedication

to Evan,
the cavalry

with special thanks
to author and filmmaker Michael Crichton, MD,
for blazing the trail

CONTENTS

"These violent delights have violent ends,
And in their triumph die,
Which, as they kiss, consume . . ."

—Friar Laurence to Romeo in *Romeo and Juliet*,
Act II, Scene VI by William Shakespeare (1597)

OUR POSSE

I

TRAVIS LANGLEY

 On a Monday, after extensively researching literary agents, I sent six of them my query for the book that would become *Batman and Psychology: A Dark and Stormy Knight*.[1] That Wednesday, two asked to see my book proposal, and then on Friday, agent Evan Gregory of the Ethan Ellenberg Literary Agency emailed me those magic words: "I'd like to offer you representation." Don't let this anecdote mislead you. Getting an agent within a week is a rare thing. A time crunch sped things up in my case because the next Batman movie was in production, and Evan's email came after I'd spent years failing to land representation for a different project. Finally, I had a literary agent—one who'd named his dog Bruce Wayne. Once during a convention panel about getting published, a fellow author expressed skepticism over the value of having an agent: "I can negotiate and read a contract."[2] In my experience, though, a good agent such as Evan more than pays for himself (or herself, like my son's agent). For riding to the rescue and fighting battles that would take up time some of us need to spend contemplating, researching, writing, rewriting, and editing these books, we dedicate *Westworld Psychology: Violent Delights* to our cavalry, Evan Gregory. Find him as @EvanJGregory on Twitter, where he freely shares valuable publishing advice.

Michael Crichton, MD, wrote and directed the 1973 motion picture *Westworld*, which brought to life people's worries about technology gone wrong against a backdrop of the Old West. We owe him a great debt for that story among many others. Between it and *Jurassic Park*, maybe we also owe a debt to whichever amusement parks frightened him at an early age. Jonathan Nolan, Lisa Joy, and company have given us a thought-provoking television adaptation that explores 21st century worries about technological advancements related to artificial intelligence and, oddly enough, our hopes for what the human race might become.

Because I met most of our contributing writers through conventions, I thank the organizers who work hard to put the cons together. Among them are those at San Diego Comic-Con International (Eddie Ibrahim, Gary Sassaman, Cathy Dalton, Sue Lord, Adam Neese, Amy Ramirez, Chris Sturhann), the Comics Arts Conference (Peter Coogan, Randy Duncan, Kate McClancy), and many Wizard World conventions (Ryan Ball, Kate Gloss, Christopher Jansen, Jerry Milani, Peter Katz). Panelists who joined me and *Westworld Psychology* contributors Martin Lloyd and Jenna Busch to discuss "The Science of Westworld: Violent Insights" at San Diego and WonderCon helped me think through important issues regarding the hosts and their humanity: Fon Davis, Steven Huff, Allen Pan, Sarah Petkus, and MythBuster Tamara Robertson.

Henderson State University provides great support for this work. Our administrators—President Glendell Jones, Provost Steve Adkison, Dean Angela Boswell—encourage creative ways of teaching. Library director Lea Ann Alexander and her staff stock the shelves with unusual resources as I make one strange request after another. David Bateman, Lecia Franklin, Carolyn Hatley, Ermatine Johnson, and Salina Smith help me and my students go where we need to go.

Latrena Beasley, Renee Davis, Sandra D. Johnson, and many more staff members make sure other essentials get done. Our faculty writers group (Jennifer Dawes, Anji Boswell, Matthew Bowman, Brian George, Nydia Jeffers, David Sesser, Michael Taylor, and A.I. expert Al Valbuena) reviewed portions of this manuscript.

Getting the support of a publicist who's as helpful, attentive, and fun as Blanca Oliviery is a blessing, much less having a whole team of publicists who assist in various ways. She, Ardi Alspach, Sari Lampert, and Lauren Tambini do so much to help me and to promote these projects. Michael Cea and the production team make us look good. Big thanks to editor Kate Zimmermann. My original editor, Connie Santisteban, continues to help as consultant and friend. Connie returned for this one as copyeditor, making her literally part of the team once more, and so we welcome her back. Co-editor Wind Goodfriend brings expertise, knowledge, insight, and wit. Having her on board has been a world of help to me.

For serving as our sounding boards, founts of knowledge, devil's advocates, accomplices, and partners, our writers thank Caylnn Adams, Lynda and Bill Erickson, Jeffrey Henderson, Jimmy Hernandez, Jim and Kate Lloyd, Paul Madariaga, Eli Mastin, Dustin McGinnis, Linda Jordan, and Amanda Wesselmann. Much appreciation goes to my mom Lynda Langley and everyone else who shot our author photos. Eric Bailey and Chris Murrin helped me confirm quote sources. Legion of Leia founder and SyFy writer Jenna Busch is a valuable editorial assistant. Kieran Dickson, Danny Fingeroth, Katrina Hill, Grant Imahara, Jonathan Maberry, Alex Langley, Nicholas Langley, Marc Nadel, Ed O'Neal, Matt Smith, and Michael Uslan deserve mention for a wide range of reasons. And no words are strong enough to express my affection, adoration, and appreciation for Rebecca Manning Langley.

I I

WIND GOODFRIEND

 I started writing book chapters about psychology and popular culture when I was a graduate student at Purdue University. I did it both because I was desperate for money and because this kind of writing was infinitely more fun than the drudgery of writing empirical journal articles. Plus, people would actually want to read them. Thus, I'd like to thank my faculty advisors at Purdue and thank the administration and fellow faculty at my current institution, Buena Vista University, for continuing to allow me to spend time in this way.

I also need to acknowledge and thank my husband Shawn for introducing me to *Westworld* in the first place (starting with the movie) and for patiently allowing me to sit in front of our only television for hours and hours while I took detailed notes over every episode. He happens to be a physicist, computer scientist, and Dean of Science at our university, so I hope he was pleased to share an interest in this volume and topic, in particular.

Finally, my deep and sincere thanks to Travis Langley for continuing to invite me to be part of his book series. As I have told him many times, being a small part of these books is the most fun writing I have done over my entire career, and I often marvel at how lucky I am to be able to list volumes such as this one on my résumé.

NOTES

1. Langley (2012).
2. Langley et al. (2016). Admittedly, I'm paraphrasing Chris Gore from memory, which is a terrible and unreliable thing, but you get the point.

A FEW STEPS AWAY

TIM CAIN
CREATOR OF FALLOUT

Westworld. I am old enough to remember the original movie from 1973. When I was young, my twenty-year-old brother offered to take me to a movie about "cowboys and robots and stuff"—in other words, exactly what eight-year-old me wanted to see. I thought I was in for an exciting afternoon of gunfights, horse riding, and human-looking robots, but what I saw frightened me. One of the robot cowboys, played by Yul Brynner, goes berserk and kills amusement park guests, focusing on one guest in particular, played by Richard Benjamin. The scenes were scary because the robot would not stop chasing Benjamin. He shot it, threw acid on it, burned it . . . and it kept coming. It was like the Terminator, but this was more than ten years before that movie came out. To eight-year-old me, the thought that we could make machines that were smart enough to hunt us and almost impossible to kill was absolutely terrifying. It made quite an impression on me.

As I got older, I saw the theme of intelligent machines repeated over and over. From the computers in *Star Trek* to the droids in *Star Wars* to the androids in the *Alien* franchise, I was inundated with the idea of artificial intelligence and its effects on humankind. When I went to college, I studied computer science, specifically artificial intelligence with an emphasis on cognitive psychology. In graduate school, I specialized my studies further into machine learning, which is trying to make computers learn from examples, including their own mistakes. I eventually left school to make video games, and my most popular game, *Fallout*, was filled with complex A.I.s. From the people you interacted with to the companions that joined and followed you on your adventures, they had their own personalities and agendas, and it was easy to pretend that they were other people in the game with you.

This led me to wonder: How can an A.I. become indistinguishable from a human being?

Early in the development of artificial intelligence, the famous computer scientist Alan Turing invented the now famous Turing test, where a person could talk to two individuals using only text messages. The person would try to guess which individual was an A.I. and which one was a human, while limited to asking them questions and judging the quality of their answers. This test's usefulness was just theoretical in the 1950s, but today websites use CAPTCHAs and other tests to detect and prevent bots from logging into their websites and causing mischief.

In the video game world, the Turing test has morphed inside online multiplayer games, where some of the characters are controlled by players and other characters are controlled by the computer game servers. Usually it is easy to tell the player-controlled characters from the computer-controlled ones, but in situations where communication is limited between players, either because of language barriers or because of input limitations (such as playing the game on a console with no keyboard), people have been known to confuse human players with nonhuman A.I.s and vice versa. In fact, nefarious players have programmed A.I.s to play their characters in order to handle some of the more time-consuming aspects of the game such as harvesting resources or doing daily tasks, and those A.I.s are written with increasing sophistication to avoid detection, including being able to chat with other players and to interact with non-players such as vendors and quest givers.

In addition to projecting human characteristics onto A.I.s, players have become emotionally attached to A.I. companions and often read more into their behaviors than is really there. My own game *Fallout* had a dog companion with very limited behaviors and no conversation at all, but it became a fan favorite and was often imbued with qualities like loyalty and dependability even though it did not have those specific qualities programmed into it, at least not any more than other A.I.s.

Years later, watching the HBO show *Westworld*, these issues come to the forefront. People visit a real-world park, populated with human guests and robotic park workers, all of whom pretend to be 19th century Western United States ranchers, villains, and townsfolks. The robots are so realistic that they look and act exactly like humans. They even bleed when they are shot and they can "die," only to be repaired, mind wiped, and rebooted for the next day at the park. The show explores what happens when those mind wipes are not complete, and some of the robots begin to realize what they are. But the bigger question is, are the robots really sentient or do they just simulate humans so well that they just seem to be sentient? And where is that line located between the perfect simulation of sentience and sentience itself? There are philosophers who would argue that we humans are not truly self-aware, that we just think we are and our notion of self-awareness, of self itself, is merely an illusion. Perhaps it is the same for the *Westworld* robots. They could just be machines that think they are alive.

While I am not qualified to answer (or even argue) those issues, I can certainly talk about them from the perspective of a game developer. The closer to the line between simulation and reality that I can get in my games, the more I can immerse my players into the game world. Whether it is hyperrealistic graphics, or professionally voice acted characters, or seemingly sentient A.I., the more real the game feels, the more it seems to improve the player's willingness to suspend disbelief and accept these A.I. characters as real people.

Forty years ago, the robots in the *Westworld* movie were just fiction. No one believed they would ever be made. Today, with personal digital assistants on smartphones and computer-controlled companions in video games, we are just a few steps away from self-aware A.I. . . . or A.I. that is so close to sentient that we cannot tell the difference.

And I hope things go better for us than they did for Richard Benjamin.

DUCKS AND MONSTERS

TRAVIS LANGLEY

"If it looks like a duck, swims like a duck, and quacks like a duck, then it probably is a duck," the old idiom goes.[1] In 1739, a mechanical duck that looked, quacked, stretched its neck, stood when offered grain, ate the grain, and defecated like a duck astounded audiences.[2] They'd pay the duck's inventor a week's wages to watch and wonder at this machine with its hundreds of parts. How they marveled at this lifelike device. Years before Ben Franklin supposedly conducted his experiment with a key and a kite[3] and nearly a century before Michael Faraday invented the electric motor,[4] few could fathom how it worked or fully believe a mortal human could build it without supernatural assistance. Some must have been no less thunderstruck than Logan Delos, wide-eyed and stammering at the revelation that everyone else in the room is mechanical: "Nobody can do this. Nobody's even. . . . We're not *here* yet. Nobody is."[5] More than a century after people paid to see that duck, scientist Hermann von Helmholtz—whose investigations in the physiology of neural impulses, vision, and hearing[6] helped pave the way for psychology to emerge as a distinct science—called it "the marvel of the last century."[7]

Was it alive? No, not by any scientific definition, nor by most people's personal definitions either. But as it and an array of windup wonders increased in complexity and availability, scholars began to contemplate a clockwork universe in which all natural processes might be mechanically determined, even life itself.[8] Then lightning struck. Inventors found ways to put electricity to work, Galvani concluded that nerve impulses were electrical,[9] and scientists of the day began to ponder whether electricity could power both mechanical and living things. Soon young Mary Wollstonecraft Shelley captivated and horrified readers with a novel many consider to be the genesis of the science fiction genre,[10] the tale of a conceited scientist who builds a man, brings him to life, and then rejects his own creation for not looking pretty enough.[11] Victor Frankenstein's greatest sin is not that he builds the creature, but the fact that he sees the man he made *as* a creature and shirks responsibility for his monstrous-seeming child—two hundred years before Dr. Robert Ford admits that his personal desire had kept him from perceiving his creations' personhood.[12]

Between Frankenstein and Ford, a long line of other sci-fi characters have taken their own shots at creating life, mimicking life, or accidentally creating life while trying to mimic it. About halfway between them, in 1920, a word emerged: *robot*. In the backstory of author Karel Čapek's play *R.U.R.*[13] (for "Rossum's Universal Robots"), an overconfident scientist named Rossum creates artificial people. Made not of metal and glass but instead of synthetic flesh like the hosts of *Westworld*, they become servants that are cheap and available throughout the world. Unwilling to think of giving up their mechanical assistance, most people ignore suggestions that the robots have souls, and soon the robots revolt. Humans die, robots die, and finally one remaining human engineer helps two robots become the new Adam and Eve.[14] The story that gave us the word *robot* (from *robota*, "forced labor"[15]) closes the curtain on the human race and yet carries a hope that some sentient beings of our own creation can carry on—reproduction of a different kind.

If we're so afraid of synthetic people, why do we keep working toward making them? When will our voice navigation system turn into Skynet?[16] Will *Westworld* turn out to be another bleak look at where the human race is going, or will it offer the possibility, the hope, that through all the struggles and violence a better relationship between biological and synthetic beings appear?

We've visited topics of artificial intelligence and sentience in these Popular Culture Psychology books before, but in the context of a faraway galaxy, a distant future, or an impossible apocalypse.* *Westworld* hits closer to home, in the neighborhood of our real lives. Michael Crichton's original motion picture hit people with their fears of that time, of advancing technology as represented by robots.[17] The trailer for that movie haunted me years before I finally saw the film. Even though there was no issue of true sentience or of humans becoming robots, seeing the Gunslinger's face fall off nevertheless tapped into a primal fear of people who aren't quite people. The 21st century television series weaves Crichton's threads into a new tale with questions about where the line between human and machine will blur as we approach the so-called Singularity.

A bit like the park's owners as they use Wild West scenarios to peel apart the psyches of the park guests and personnel, maybe we can peek into *Westworld* as a way of taking a look at ourselves.

If it looks like us. . . .

> *"The danger of the past was that men became slaves.*
> *The danger of the future is that men may become robots."*
> —sociologist-turned-psychologist Erich Fromm[18]

> *"Guiding this project, I've learned a lot about human behavior."*
> —Charlotte Hale[19]

---

*Respectively, *Star Wars Psychology: Dark Side of the Mind* (2015*)*, *Star Trek Psychology: The Mental Frontier* (2017), *The Walking Dead Psychology: Psych of the Living Dead* (2015). Also *Doctor Who Psychology: A Madman with a Box* (2016).

NOTES

1. Possibly derived from "When I see a bird that walks like a duck and swims like a duck and quacks like a duck, I call that bird a duck"—poet James Whitcomb Riley (1849–1916).
2. Singer (2009).
3. Srodes (2002).
4. James (2010).
5. Episode 2–2, "Reunion" (April 29, 2018).
6. Cahan (1993); Koenigsberger (1965).
7. Quoted by Riskin (2004), p. 633.

Westworld (motion picture)
Creator, screenwriter, director:
   Michael Crichton, MD.
Stars: Yul Brynner, Richard Benjamin,
   James Brolin.
Production company: Metro-Goldwyn-Mayer.
Official release date: November 21, 1973.

Futureworld (motion picture)
   Sequel to 1973's *Westworld*.
Screenwriters: Mayo Simon, George Schenck.
Director: Richard T. Heffron.
Stars: Peter Fonda, Blythe Danner, Yul Brynner.
Production companies: Aubrey Company,
   Paul N. Lazarus III.
Official release date: August 13, 1976.

8. Schultz & Schultz (2012).
9. Guarnieri (2014).
10. Aldiss & Wingrove (2001); Milam (2015); Stableford (1995).
11. Shelley (1818).
12. Episode 1–10, "The Bicameral Mind" (December 4, 2016).
13. Čapek (1920/2001).
14. *Genesis* chapters 1–5, modern era translations.
15. Karel Čapek credited his brother Josef for dreaming up the word (Margolius, 2017).
16. *The Terminator* (1984 motion picture).
17. *Westworld* (1973 motion picture).
18. Fromm (1955), p. 102.
19. Episode 2–10, "The Passenger" (June 24, 2018).

Beyond Westworld (television series)

Separate sequel to 1973's *Westworld*, never referencing *Futureworld*.

Five episodes, of which only three aired.

Developed for television by Lou Shaw.

Stars: Jim McMullan, James Wainwright, Connie Selleca, William Jordan.

Production companies: Lou Shaw, MGM Television.

Network: CBS.

First episode: "Westworld Destroyed" (March 5, 1980).

Westworld (television series)

Remake/reenvisioning of Crichton's story.

Developed for television by Jonathan Nolan & Lisa Joy.

Stars: Evan Rachel Wood, Thandie Newton, Jeffrey Wright, James Marsden, Ed Harris, Luke Hemsworth, Tessa Thompson, Anthony Hopkins.

Production companies: HBO Entertainment, Kilter Films, Bad Robot, Jerry Weintraub, Warner Bros.

Network: HBO.

First episode: "The Original" (October 2, 2016).

I

CHOICE

"The strongest principle of growth lies
in human choice."
—*author Mary Anne Evans, a.k.a. George Eliot,
Daniel Deronda (1876), book VI, chapter XLII*

MATTERS OF CHOICE

Can machines ever gain the power of free will? For that matter, do humans really have that power in the first place, or is free will merely an illusion? However we come to make our decisions and perform specific actions, those choices have consequences not only in the world around us, but also within ourselves. Caught in a crossfire of competing causal forces, who will manage to make the choices that stay true to their values and ideals, and who will switch from white hat to black?

—T.L.

CHAPTER 1

A BEAUTIFUL GIFT:
WHO SAYS WE HAVE CHOICE?

TRAVIS LANGLEY
& MATT MUNSON

"These things you're doing—have you ever stopped to ask why you're doing them?"
—Bernard to Maeve[1]

"Man does not simply exist but always decides what his existence will be, what he will become in the next moment. By the same token, every human being has the freedom to change at any instant."
—existential psychology pioneer, Holocaust survivor Viktor Frankl[2]

The issue of free will comes up repeatedly in *Westworld* as characters contemplate whether the robotic hosts are capable of having free will and thus possibly personhood. Do these complex mechanical characters demonstrate free will, or are they merely slaves to their deterministic programming? Are Dr. Robert Ford's creations going "off script" when they rebel or are they still just doing as they are told by following his new narrative? Artificial intelligence can be programmed to say anything, even to claim that it has free will when it has nothing of the sort.[3] What is free will in the first place? Might its existence be less important than our belief in it when playing a role in how we live our lives? How can we cling to that concept as one of the criteria for judging the individuality of an artificial being when we can't agree whether human beings truly have free will in the first place?

Psychologists debate the *nature versus nurture* controversy and investigate whether our actions and personalities are more heavily influenced by factors inherent to us such as our genes, instincts, or drives (nature) or by the ways that people and experience treat us (nurture). Both sides are making *deterministic* arguments: Both look at variables that cause us to do the things we do. Though many opinions arise as to which determinants code us and how, experimenters throughout psychology proceed as if taking it for granted that such coding ultimately exists—in line with A.I. Logan's observation to Bernard about human nature, "The best that they can do is live according to their code."[4]

While most areas of psychology focus on finding determinants of our behavior and generally steer clear of the *free will versus determinism* debate, humanistic and existential psychologists criticize the others for being so deterministic.[5] They believe in free will. One of their founding thinkers formed many critical ideas about free will and what we do with it during, of all things, his time as a prisoner in Nazi concentration camps.[6]

TWO TRAILS DIVERGED

Maeve Millay is a mother homesteading with her daughter on the frontier. She also happens to be a kind of robot, a park "host." The Man in Black attacks them, killing the daughter and eliciting a wail of grief from Maeve unlike any emotional response he has previously seen any of these mechanical people show. Because their assailant is human, a park guest, Maeve's programming renders her powerless to strike back. She remains helpless when indifferent park personnel relocate her and strip her of everything she has, including memories of her daughter, though she begs them not to. They turn this maternal figure into a prostitute to be used by guests however they may please.[7]

Viktor Frankl was a psychiatrist treating suicidal patients and others in Austria throughout the 1930s. He also happened to be Jewish. After the Nazis annexed Austria, they prohibited him from treating non-Jews, and then deported him and his family to a ghetto. Eventually they moved him to a series of concentration camps, beginning with Auschwitz. His people were treated as subhuman. His parents and pregnant wife died, their fates unknown to him until after the war ended. The Nazis relocated him, robbed him, stripped him of everything he had including at times his sense of identity, and handled him and his fellow victims however they saw fit.[8] Guards could murder them at any time.

Maeve Millay is fictional, an artificial entity depicted in the series *Westworld*, whereas Viktor Frankl was a nonfictional human being who lived here in our world. Sometimes we look at the darkest parts of real human experience through a filter of fiction lest relentlessly brutal facts wear us down. Learning how Frankl suffered under the Nazis can be devastating. His story is also compelling, though, for those who read his classic book which is usually translated under the title *Man's Search for Meaning*.[9] Frankl's book comprises two halves, the first being his first-person account of his time in various internment camps during World War II ("I. Experiences in a Concentration Camp"), and the second half presents the fundamentals of the branch of psychology he developed as a result of his internment ("II. Logotherapy in a Nutshell"). His account is moving. His writing style is both familiar and complex, providing the reader with a detailed account of extremely personal tragedies that seem to have been visited upon him almost daily. The undercurrent to all of his anecdotes are twofold: suffering and hope. Through each tale of suffering, Frankl recounts how he or others interned with him sometimes found hope despite overwhelming reasons to have none.

Frankl already believed in the existence of free will, though, before the Nazis rolled in, and Maeve's inner voice already assures her that she can be whoever she wants.[10] Instead of developing a belief in free will later in order to summon strength during their struggles, they have each clung to that belief and built upon it in spite of horrifying circumstances. They may draw power from it in order to survive their respective confinements in concentration camps and a Western brothel. Their ideas about free will become more complex through these experiences, as do they themselves.

A DETERMINISTIC LANDSCAPE

Psychology is the child of philosophy and physiology. It was simply a topic within philosophy, speculating on the nature of the mind, until some professionals drew methods from physical science in order to start putting speculations to empirical test.[11] In the course of fighting to prove the discipline as real science, most researchers in psychology moved away from abstract philosophy and the concept of the mind itself in order to focus on variables that they might measure or manipulate:

action, memory, emotion, thought. These may be the same details anyone might scrutinize when trying to prove that a synthetic individual qualifies as a real person.[12] Psychology experiments examine the ways in which *independent variables* (possible causes) affect *dependent variables* (outcomes being measured). Our experimenters operate on the assumption of determination, seeking to identify not whether causality exists in the first place but instead which factors will turn out to be the assumed causes. Those who deviate from this assumption and instead base their approaches to psychology on ideas about abstractions such as free will or anything beyond concrete, objective measurement get criticized for not being scientific enough. Such criticism may be reasonable, but what if they happen to be right? Science's inability to weigh a soul, open a view screen to watch an alternate universe, or even see how anything more than 186,282 miles away in our own universe looks at this very second[13] has no effect on whether any of those things do or do not exist. Arnold's inability to provide Ford with conclusive evidence that the hosts could become conscious does not make him wrong.[14] He appears to be right and eventually Ford will reconsider, but he could easily have been as wrong as children who think their toys have feelings or delusional individuals who believe that things they own might be possessed.[15]

FREE RANGE THINKING ABOUT FREE WILL: THE UNORTHODOX VIEWS

After leaving Sigmund Freud's psychoanalytic group as a young medical student in 1923, Viktor Frankl joined Alfred Adler's Society for Individual Psychology. Like Adler, Frankl came to view psychoanalysis as being too limited for attributing so much of human experience to sex drive and too restrictive for rigidly focusing on the roles that instinct and

BIG SIS DOLORES:
BIRTH ORDER AND THE HOST HIERARCHY

One of individual psychology founder Alfred Adler's most enduring contributions to modern thought concerns *birth order effects*, the idea that being first-born, secondborn, youngest, or only child will frame our lifestyles and influence who we become.[16] Dolores is "the oldest host in the park,"[17] maintained and repaired despite any damage or aberrant behavior that might get a younger host decommissioned. She has a special status. Adler felt that the oldest child, having been the family's sole prince or princess who then experiences a sense of *dethronement* when others enter the family, may resent having to share. Because the eldest is given greater responsibility, such as when told to watch younger brothers and sisters, the

early experience play in determining the course of our lives.[24] Over the next four years, though, Frankl grew to consider Adler's views also limited and restrictive—limited for attributing most human behavior to pursuit of power and restrictive for leaving out free will.[25] Frankl once spent twenty minutes making his argument in favor of free will until a distressed Adler finally cut him off with a complaint about him and other dissidents in the room. In 1927, Frankl found himself expelled from the Society, per Adler's personal wish, for his "unorthodox views."[26]

eldest more often becomes more concerned with power and authority, perhaps to the point of bossiness. Despite a shortage of steady support for some of Adler's other ideas about birth order,[18] firstborns do tend to attain greater levels of power, prestige, and achievement, more often emerging as leaders and managers.[19]

Long before she becomes the robots' rebel leader, Dolores is allotted greater responsibility over other hosts, notably when Ford assigns her to recreate his dead partner Arnold. "Ford tasked me with recreating him," Dolores tells the Man in Black.[20] Even though Robert Ford programs Arnold's backstory into the host-copy's memories, names the copy Bernard,[21] and claims, "I built your mind, Bernard,"[22] Bernard perceives that Ford is taking credit for someone else's work, and Dolores later says, "Ford didn't build him. I did."[23]

—T.L.

Arnold Weber goes to Robert Ford with his new insight, his unorthodox view that the mechanical people they're building are capable of developing consciousness and exerting free will, but Ford does not want to hear it. As Ford later admits to Dolores and Bernard, "I was so close to opening the park that to acknowledge your consciousness would have destroyed my dreams."[27] Weber cannot persuade Ford to perceive free will in hosts any more than Frankl could persuade Adler to appreciate it in humans, and yet over the years both Ford and Adler would soften their views. Both would make room for free will.

Picking Your Path: Self-Determination

Frankl saw an "erroneous and dangerous assumption" in absolute determinism, "the view of man which disregards his capacity to take a stand toward any conditions whatsoever." As far as he was concerned, human beings are not fully trained by experience or merely nudged by external forces into doing all the things we do. The individual "rather determines himself whether he gives in to conditions or stands up to them. In other words, man is ultimately self-determining."[28] Adler came to think similarly, writing, "We are not determined by our experiences, but are *self-determined* by the meaning we give to them."[29] Bernard Lowe and Robert Ford apply this self-determination criterion when considering the possibility that hosts have greater potential for true freedom than humans do. Bernard wonders, "Is there really such a thing for any of us? Or is it just a collective delusion? A sick joke?" An A.I. version of Ford answers, "Something that is truly free would need to be able to question its fundamental drives, to change them. Our hosts."[30] This echoes thoughts shared in the original world by Ford when expressing his disillusionment with the human race and his previous hope to "play some small part in that grand tradition" of ennobling people and making them better. After deciding that human beings cannot change because they don't want to, he "realized someone else was paying attention, someone who could change. So, I began to compose a new story for them." Ford creates a narrative about "the choices they will have to make,"[31] a *Choose Your Own Adventure* narrative that nonetheless surprises him at times.[32]

Individual unpredictability convinced Frankl that deterministic psychologists were shortsighted. Even the best research findings arm psychologists poorly in terms of knowing what a given individual will do. Frankl said, "We can predict his future only within the large framework of a statistical survey referencing to a whole group; the individual personality, however, remains essentially unpredictable."[33] Ford correctly anticipates what Dolores will do when given the choice whether or not to kill him, but he fails to anticipate when Maeve makes her first unscripted choice.[34] In fact, he has not planned for that to be when she might make a choice at all, and for that he later apologizes: "I tried to chart a path for you, to force you to escape, but I was wrong. I should have just opened a door."[35] Frankl argued that humans also have the capacity that Ford comes to see in the hosts for reprogramming themselves, in that "one of the main features of human existence is the capacity to rise above such conditions, to grow beyond them."[36]

Holding onto Your Hats: Choosing to Stay True

"A doctor, however, who would still interpret his own role mainly as that of a technician would confess that he sees in his patient nothing more than a machine, instead of seeing the human being behind the disease," Frankl wrote of the dehumanizing side of any clinical treatment, which paled in comparison to the dehumanizing treatment he faced in concentration camps.[37] Psychologists who research dehumanizing conditions often focus on the percentage of people who manifest problems such as emotional breakdown, learned helplessness, or authoritarian obedience[38] in experimental situations while paying too little attention to the implicit part of any such number: those, however few they sometimes might be, in the percentage who do not follow the worst path. "In the concentration camps, for example," Frankl wrote, "in this living laboratory and on this testing ground, we watched and witnessed some of our comrades behave like swine while others behaved like saints."[39] In his view, those who maintain personal integrity and stay true despite circumstances do so because they make that choice. Dolores reprograms Teddy Flood to make him more violent, an obedient soldier in her rebellion,[40] and yet he still sees flaws in what she's doing and ultimately makes his own choice not to follow Dolores down her destructive path.[41]

HARRIS (SAM, NOT ED) AND THE GREAT ILLUSION

Neuroscientist Sam Harris has become one of the most vocal proponents of the idea that free will is an illusion.[42] He offers points such as these based on empirical research, including fMRI (functional magnetic resonance imaging) results:

- Your actions and decisions are nothing but the result of a long chain of genetics, experiences, parents, time and place you happened to be born, and any number of subtle or grand events that have shaped you into who you are.

- Thoughts appear unbidden. Our unconscious brain presents to us decisions that it has already made, independent of conscious thought.

- Science can literally discern the time that elapses between your unconscious brain deciding between A and B before your conscious brain becomes aware of it, akin to Felix seeing Maeve's thoughts appear on his screen before she voices them.[43]

- Prior cause or randomness is the only viable explanation for the source of our actions, choices, and thoughts.

- Harris argues that the very concept of free will is so incoherent that it cannot even be mapped onto any conceivable reality. If you pay closer attention to how your thoughts present themselves, you will very quickly notice that your thoughts simply arise in your mind, similar to the way the words on this page you are reading are inserted into it. Ask yourself, "What am I going to think next?" and you'll recognize that the question cannot be answered. If you don't know what you're going to think next, and you are not the source of thoughts in the first place, then how can we even consider free will as a possibility?

- Lab experiments have clocked the time differential between the brain making a decision and then the conscious mind believing it has made a decision. Even if this lag had not been documented or even if it did not actually exist, there still exists no coherent argument in favor of free will, and we certainly cannot rely on "Well, I *feel* like I have free will and I want to believe it" as the backbone to a position as important as this one.

—M.M.

MORE THAN PLAYER PIANOS

Many *Westworld* characters struggle with the notion of free will as the series plays a tug-of-war within itself with the notions of determinism and free will. From the outset, the story's universe and the characters within it reveal a land dominated by determinism, at least for the hosts. The hosts follow their coding, playing out the same scenarios repeatedly and without variation except when humans' actions alter the course of events. In fact, the park is revealed to be a grand experiment in which "the guests are the variables and the hosts are the controls."[44] Any variation in host behavior is determined by how their coding prepares them to respond to park guests' actions. Each iteration of Dolores dropping a can from her saddle bag, Teddy or a guest picking it up, a duel playing out, and the saloon getting robbed differ only when human actions make them vary, serving to instill the idea that determinism is the rule of law over the hosts.[45]

Westworld's player piano symbolizes this rigid determination, whether consciously to viewers who think about it or unconsciously to those who prefer to take it without deliberate analysis.[46] The player piano or *pianola* plays itself, following the holes and slashes poked into a paper scroll that the piano mindlessly reads. Though it is without mind or consciousness, its results can nonetheless be beautiful and smack of organic originality. Without that scroll of paper, the piano is inert, producing no music. But once activated, we see "behavior" from the piano that makes it appear alive or, at the very least, as though being played by a performer who is very much alive.[47] Each time *Westworld*'s piano plays, something is different, sometimes slightly, sometimes drastically, but the piano plays on.

The series switches gears as one twist at a time upends the deterministic premise with hints of free will. Maeve begins to emerge from the muck of determinism and the endless loops with minor variations she is stuck in. When finding a bullet inside her scarless belly answers one question about the nature of her reality, tying together the previous threads of her suspicions and fragmented memories, she officially begins her journey out of existential frustration.[48] The character now recognizes that her *existential angst* (her anguish or dread over issues of her existence) comes from being a prisoner in a game that features her as a central and long-suffering character, who performs at the whims of her masters, and she means to combat it with her newly suspected free will.

We viewers start to believe that Maeve is indeed acting of her own *volition*, agency in choosing her own actions and outcomes—arguably a term that lets scientists discuss free will without calling it free will.[49] As she makes her way into park headquarters, gets Felix and Sylvester to work for her, and learns of the horrors that are visited upon her fellow hosts, she seems to be exercising free will and slowly working to resolve her existential malaise. When Felix tells her, though, "Everything you do, it's because the engineers programmed you to do it; you don't have a choice," his assertion maps with those who deconstruct the notion of free will in humans and refute its existence.[50] Maeve's heartfelt refutation, "Nobody makes me do something I don't want to do, sweetheart,"[51] is very human. In fact, holding an *internal locus of control* (the trait of tending to believe that each individual controls his or her own fate[52]) makes her seem more likeable and human than might *external locus of control* (the tendency to believe we cannot control what happens to us).[53] Because she believes she controls herself, we want to believe it, too.

When Felix shows her that her statements appear on a computer screen before she says them, Maeve refuses to accept this, experiencing a state of *denial*,[54] and shuts down until revived.[55] When Bernard later pulls up her code on his handheld computer, text on screen shows beyond the shadow of a doubt that Maeve is doing nothing more than executing commands to recruit fellow hosts, manipulate people, and escape. Again, she insists, "Those are my decisions, no one else's. I planned all this," to which Bernard can only reply based on the evidence, "No, you didn't."[56] This scene leaves both the audience and Bernard convinced that Maeve is simply following a Harris-esque descent into pre-programmed execution.[57] Sharp-eyed viewers who spotted her *MAINLAND INFILTRATION* subroutine on Bernard's screen might then understand why the showrunners said that Maeve is the first host to exhibit free will: Instead of abiding by Ford's program for her to leave the park, she chooses to find her daughter.[58]

The pendulum of determinism in *Westworld* swings back to the side of free will for the hosts, though perhaps away from it for human beings. A new dichotomy emerges, one which suggests that humans are the slaves to determinism and hosts may be the beneficiaries of free will. When Bernard speculates, "I always thought it was the hosts who were missing something or incomplete, but it's them. They're just algorithms, designed to survive at all costs, sophisticated enough to think they're calling the shots, to think they're in control," he reaches the point where he wonders whether free will exists for anyone.[59]

TRAILS LESS TRAVELED

Diverging from other hosts, a few trailblazers such as Dolores, Maeve, and Akecheta decide to travel rougher terrain.[60] Simply by arguing for free will in a largely deterministic field, professionals in existential psychology such as Viktor Frankl or individual psychology such as Alfred Adler or others they influenced such as humanistic psychology founder Abraham Maslow take a trail less traveled.[61] As Frankl pointed out, psychological research tends to watch those who take the trails more traveled while paying too little attention to those who took the ones less traveled, except when studying aberrations as abnormalities to be cured. Data obtained from those who aberrate are often discarded with little or no consideration for why they went another way.[62] One lesson *Westworld* illustrates may be that the outliers shall inherit the earth.[63]

"We each gave the other a beautiful gift: choice."
—Dolores to Bernard[64]

"Freedom, however, is not the last word. Freedom is only part of the story and half of the truth."
—Viktor Frankl[65]

NOTES

1. Episode 1–10, "The Bicameral Mind" (December 4, 2016).
2. Frankl (1947/2006), p. 131.
3. Krausová & Hazan (2013).
4. Episode 2–10, "The Passenger" (June 24, 2018).
5. Frankl (1947/2006); Maslow (1954, 1962); May (1981).
6. Frankl (1947/2006).
7. Episode 1–8, "Trace Decay" (November 21, 2016).
8. Frankl (1947/2006); Noble (1997).
9. Frankl (1947/2006).
10. Episode 1–2, "Chestnut" (October 9, 2016).
11. Schultz & Schultz (2012); Wertheimer (2011).
12. Francis et al. (2009); Scarlet (2017).
13. Penrose (2004).
14. Episode 1–10, "The Bicameral Mind" (December 4, 2016).
15. Berzonsky (1988); Kleiger & Khadivi (2015). Despite MacDougall's 1907 claim which popularized the idea that the human soul weighs 21 grams, others have not replicated his findings nor did McDougall find this consistently himself (Hood, 2009).
16. Adler (1924).
17. Episode 1–1, "The Original" (October 2, 2016).
18. Watkins (1992).
19. Bryant (1987); Eckstein et al. (2010); Paulus & Shaffer (1981); Zajonc et al. (1979).
20. Episode 2–10, "The Passenger" (June 24, 2018).
21. Episode 1–8, "Trace Decay" (November 21, 2016).
22. Episode 1–9, "The Well-Tempered Clavier" (November 28, 2016).
23. Episode 2–10, "The Passenger" (June 24, 2018).
24. Frankl (1945/2006); Roazen (1975).
25. O'Connell (1972).

26. Alexander Batthyány (editor) in Frankl (2010), pp. 7, 11.
27. Episode 1–10, "The Bicameral Mind" (December 4, 2016).
28. Frankl (1946/1958).
29. Adler (1931/1958), p. 14, italics his.
30. Episode 2–10, "The Passenger" (June 24, 2018)—both Bernard's remarks and Ford's reply.
31. Episode 1–10, "The Bicameral Mind" (December 4, 2016).
32. Episode 2–9, "Vanishing Point" (June 17, 2018).
33. Frankl (1947/2006), p. 131.
34. Episode 1–10, "The Bicameral Mind" (December 4, 2016).
35. Episode 2–9, "Vanishing Point" (June 17, 2018). At least the A.I. copy of Ford acknowledges this.
36. Frankl (1947/2006), p. 131.
37. Frankl (1947/2006), p. 133
38. Martinez et al. (2012); Milgram (1963); Schroeder & Epley (2016); Smith (2007); Vayrynen & Laari-Salmela (2018); Zimbardo (2007).
39. Frankl (1947/2006), p. 134.
40. Episode 2–5, "Akane No Mati" (May 20, 2018).
41. Episode 2–9, "Vanishing Point" (June 17, 2018).
42. Harris (2011, 2012). See also Gazzaniga (2011).
43. Episode 1–6, "The Adversary" (November 6, 2016).
44. Episode 2–7, "Les Écorchés" (June 3, 2018).
45. Episode 1–1, "The Original" (October 2, 2016).
46. Wedemann et al. (2008).
47. Reblitz (2001).
48. Episode 1–4, "Dissonance Theory" (October 23, 2016).
49. Frith (2013); Haggard & Lau (2013).
50. Harris (2011; 2012).
51. Episode 1–6, "The Adversary" (November 6, 2016).
52. Rotter (1966).
53. Testé (2017).
54. Freud (1936); Varki & Brower (2013).
55. Episode 1–6, "The Adversary" (November 6, 2016).
56. Episode 1–10, "The Bicameral Mind" (December 4, 2016).
57. Harris (2011, 2012).
58. Episode 1–10, "The Bicameral Mind" (December 4, 2016).
59. Episode 2–10 "The Passenger" (June 24, 2018).
60. Episodes 1–10, "The Bicameral Mind" (December 4, 2016); 2–8 "Kiksuya" (June 10, 2018); 2–10 "The Passenger" (June 24, 2018).
61. Frost (1916).
62. Filipowicz et al. (2018); Shi & Li (2013).
63. Gladwell (2008); Matthew 5:5.
64. Episode 2–10, "The Passenger" (June 24, 2018).
65. Frankl (1947/2006), p. 132.

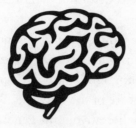

CHAPTER 2

A.I. AND AUTONOMY: HOW FREE ARE THE HOSTS OF WESTWORLD?

DARREN MCKEE & JIM DAVIES

"Is there really such as a thing as free will for any of us? Or is it just a collective delusion? A sick joke? Something that is truly free would need to be able to question its fundamental drives. To change them."
—Bernard Lowe[1]

"Although the volitional process may be initiated by unconscious cerebral activities, conscious control of the actual motor performance of voluntary acts definitely remains possible."
—neuroscientist Benjamin Libet[2]

The *Westworld* television series is, among many other things, an exploration of the issue of free will. How free are the hosts? How free could they be if they don't have (conscious) control of their bodies, their words, their preferences, or their dreams?

There is no consensus about what "free will" means, as it is a complex topic with tightly-woven issues of consciousness, morality, and the nature of the universe. Whether an act is one of free will, or whether anyone in general has free will only becomes a scientific question when there is a particular sense of what free will really means. And different definitions often lead to different answers.

It may be natural to think that the humans in *Westworld* have more free will than the hosts. Why might this be? The hosts are controlled by computer programs, which humans design. Human characters tweak these programs to get different storylines for the guests. Yet, humans behave the way they do because of their brain structure—a structure they did not design for themselves, either.

Assessments of free will can be affected by whether or not we know the causal mechanism behind a choice. When learning that people did things because their brain was this or that way, some will think that what they did was caused by their *brain*, rather than by *them*.[3] For example, if a violent man's frontal lobe is discovered to be damaged, one might say he had less impulse control. The hidden assumption here is that there is something to the man that's not his brain. It's the "my brain made me do it" excuse for action. But because, scientifically speaking, *everything* you do is because of this or that brain process, the only difference is that we have figured out a bit about *how* the brain does something.[4]

The situation is similar with the hosts. For example, Maeve is, in a strictly physical sense, a host, a robot, but in a psychological sense, she is her programming. We can't judge whether or not she has free will by looking at the fact that her programming determines her actions any more than we can assess human free will by looking at patterns of firing neurons.

CAUSE AND EFFECT

Science generally follows a *deterministic* view that we live in a world of cause and effect: Things happen because they were caused to happen by things preceding them. The heat of your oven causes the pizza to cook. Photons of light bouncing off the page of this book and into your eyes cause these information-packed squiggles (soon decoded as words) to hit your retina. We humans may not have been created by Ford and programmed by Bernard, but we are caused beings who have zero choice in our genetics, our place or time of birth, or our developmental environment. We are sophisticated agents who think, choose, love, hope, and dream, but we appear to be caused beings just the same.

If we can't escape a deterministic universe, then where might our freedom, if we have any, lie? It may be in our autonomy and empowerment to do what we want to do when we want to do it. What we want is freedom from coercion, not from causality.[5]

How much of that freedom do the hosts have? How much do people have? The difference in freedom between the hosts and humans might be small.

REFLEXES

Reflexes are some of our simplest behaviors, where we feel there is the least control, and behaviors get free will-ier from there. If you sense something coming close to your eyes, you will reflexively blink. You are not making any choices here—

no other options are considered, and many people think that making some kind of choice is important for an act of free will.[6] Consequently, if a fly landed on your eye, you would have no choice but to blink.

Yet, in the very first scene of *Westworld*, a fly crawls across Dolores's eye and she does not blink, or even seem to notice. The hosts may not have the eyeblink reflex, but they have some of their own. When the Man in Black threatens Ford, for a stark example, Teddy (though at death's door) grabs both the knife and the Man's arm with a sudden burst of energy and ability.[7]

Reflexes are not the only behaviors caused by our unconscious minds: Every movement of your tongue when you speak, and, indeed, most of the choices of words and syntax, are selected by some unconscious part of your mind, and, to our credit, it feels that way. But there are other actions that feel like they are caused by conscious acts of will—that is, it feels like sometimes people do things because they deliberately choose to. The hosts have this too.

People feel like they know when we consciously choose to do something, don't they? Neuroscientist Benjamin Libet ran an experiment that casts doubt on this too. He simply asked people to move their finger whenever they felt like it. He did this while they were having their brains scanned. Afterward, the participants were asked how long before they actually moved their finger did they decide to do it. It turns out that Libet was able to use the brain scan to know when the finger would move *before the person consciously "decided" to do it*.[8] The implications of this are mind-blowing. The person consciously decides to move a finger at a particular time, but it turns out that that movement had already been in preparation before the conscious decision. It appears in this case that the conscious act of will did not actually cause the finger motion, but rather some unconscious process caused both the finger movement *and* the conscious feeling of deciding to do it![9]

Maeve is disturbed when she is shown a computer display that shows what words she's going to say before she says them.[10] It's easy to jump to the conclusion that she doesn't have free will but rather she's "just" doing what her programming makes her do. When this idea is unpacked, it gets murkier. If her mind simply *is* a computer program, then what is the separate "her" that the programming is forcing into action?

Considering the above leads to a more fundamental question: Does free will require a *conscious* decision? In the experiment described above, *some* part of the person's mind is making a decision, but it's often not the conscious part. Given that your unconscious mind is still a part of you and that both it and your conscious mind are subject to the causal nature of the universe, it's unclear why it would matter if your decisions were conscious or not.

DIRECT BEHAVIORAL CONTROL

Westworld has many examples of humans directly controlling the behavior of the hosts. For example, Ford controls the movement of a host rattlesnake with a wave of his hand. Rather than manipulating the snake's motivations, emotions, or goals, he simply makes it move, like a puppeteer might.[11] With the humanoid hosts, the staff can pause them at any moment, with the utterance "cease all motor functions."

Humans experience nothing like this. While people might stop moving if someone yells "stop!" forcefully enough, it is run through our *cognitive appraisal system*, and they would move only if they wanted to.[12] When a hypnotist "commands" a hypnotized person to do something and there is an experience of involuntary action, most scientists think that this is illusory. The spellbound hosts have no such freedom.

PSYCHOLOGICAL LIMITS

Sometimes human behavior is restricted by brain structures or psychological limitations that are outside of their conscious control. People feel compulsions to do things, and cannot use their willpower to stop. Examples include addictive behavior, and the compulsions of obsessive-compulsive disorder. So, although an addict might *want* to stop gambling, she can't resist. Similarly, sometimes people cannot get themselves to do something they *want* to do, such as inject themselves with a hypodermic needle.

Compulsions are not the result of influence by other people, but they do feel like a violation of will, unlike, interestingly, the need to eat and sleep. It is only on a diet that one feels that bodies (and, perhaps, brains) are working at our cross-purposes!

The hosts seem to have some hard limitations on what they must (or cannot) do. Some hosts cannot pull the trigger of a gun, others cannot touch an axe.[13] Hosts are also required to follow scripts and "loops," with only minor improvisation. Our knowledge of the existence of these scripts, and the fact that the hosts loop though the same storylines again and again, makes us think that they don't have free will. They can't seem to choose to do anything but go through the same behaviors, over and over.[14]

But are humans any different? There is evidence to suggest that people behave the same way when their memories are impaired. People with *global transient amnesia* temporarily lose the ability to encode long-term memories. They hold on to memories only for a few seconds. When you have a conversation with these people, you find yourself having the same conversation over and over and over again.[15] As Ford says, "We live in loops as tight and as closed as the hosts do."[16]

If people with global transient amnesia repeat the same phrase over and over again, are they using free will over and over again? Or do they have free will only the first time they utter a phrase? Whether the memory loss is because of someone's programming or because of a temporary blood clot doesn't affect whether or not there is some causal process behind it.

The staff coerces the hosts through psychological limits that make them seem less free. Yet, in humans, our minds and brains function the way they do because of how they were "programmed" by a complex interplay between our genes and our environment. And sometimes humans are coerced by their psychological limits through compulsions or inabilities, thus making them less free as well. Whether humans or hosts are less free in the domain of psychological limits seems to depend on the particular comparison being made.

One important facet of free will is whether agents are being controlled by some external force.[17] When one is coerced to do something, will is being violated. One might even feel, erroneously, that one is being controlled by some outside force, as when people have *alien hand syndrome* (the feeling that someone else is controlling your hand movements),[18] or when persons with schizophrenia feel they are being controlled by the FBI. What's interesting about these cases is that they are still acting with as much free will as they ever did, but they don't know it.

Given that all human choice is ultimately caused by genes and environment, whether they are viewed as internal or external is a matter of framing. But all of our choices seem more restricted when some agent manipulates us for their own purposes. That's the kind of restriction of will most people bristle at, and the hosts are victim to this agentive, goal-directed manipulation by the staff. When can the hosts break from their loops?

One interesting example is the stray host who kills himself with a rock.[19] Why he does this is rather mysterious, and the programmer Elsie Hughes feels confused by the behavior. Could it be that the host is trying to destroy its control unit that Stubbs is trying to retrieve, to hide what it has been trying to do?

The reveries, too, seem to allow the hosts to behave in ways that, if not in violation of their programming (because the ability to have reveries is also programmed), are in violation of the intentions that the programmers have in mind. This allows Dolores and Maeve to break out of their loops and behave in novel ways.

Coercion under Threat

Sometimes people do something only because they are threatened with harm if they don't. In one sense, a mugging victim still has free will, in the sense that he or she can make the choice between giving up the wallet and risking getting hurt, but in another sense, mugging victims are "forced" to do something.

Unlike compulsions, in coercions under threat you still make a choice, it's just a very easy choice to make. This is true for humans and hosts alike. In Westworld, the hosts are coerced when guests threaten violence. Most aspects of the Man in Black's quest involve coercion under threat, such as when he kills Lawrence's wife and threatens to kill his daughter next unless he gets information.[20]

An interesting example of coercion under threat is the restriction of physical mobility that both humans and hosts face. For humans, unless you have the right documentation, you may not leave your country. For hosts, they can't leave the park. They don't even consider it because they don't know of any other world, but they also have explosives in their spines, so if they ever did try to leave the park they would be destroyed.[21] To remove this explosive is exactly why Maeve self-immolates so that she can be rebuilt from the ground up, and so the tech Sylvester can slip in a nonexplosive-containing vertebrae.[22]

Given how much humans hate being threatened or restricted in their mobility, it is clear that being free from coercion is definitely a freedom worth having.

Direct Preference Manipulation

Moving beyond behavioral control, another creepy way to change the behavior of an agent is to directly change what they *want* to do. Humans and hosts have preferences, goals, and values, which affect behavior. If you prefer chocolate to vanilla, you will use choose chocolate ice cream over vanilla. But what if someone went into your brain and made you like vanilla more? You still get a choice, but the outcome of that choice was manipulated upstream in your preferences.

The hosts are similarly coerced into participating in storylines. The programmers create incentives, values, and desires in the hosts that make them *want* to behave in certain ways. Robert Ford makes Bernard *want* to kill himself, to end the nightmare he's living as a result of learning that he's actually a host.[23] Dolores keeps wanting to get back home even though it always leads to her own suffering. Only when she starts to retain memories of previous loop experiences does she start to resist this urge. What she says about her herd is poignantly metaphorical: "We would bring the herd down off the mountain in the fall. Sometimes we would lose one along the way, and I'd worry over it. My father would tell me that the steer would find its own way home. And as often as not, they did. Never occurred to me that we were bringing them back for the slaughter."[24]

Human preferences can also be manipulated, but it takes lots of time, and it doesn't always work. Education in the humanities, for instance, seems to impart more left wing political values.[25] Another human example of decision and values coercion might be brainwashing or indoctrination into a cult. Brainwashed people are doing what they want, but what they want has been determined by the preferences of somebody else, making it a murky example of uncoerced free will (though science does not have consistent evidence to confirm that brainwashing actually exists).[26]

Complete Autonomy

When nobody's manipulating us, we might be thought to enjoy as much free will as we ever will. Do the hosts ever get to experience the freedom to do whatever they want to do?

Co-creator and writer Jonathan Nolan said that the first act of free will in the show is when Maeve decides to get off the train,[27] but without clarifying what he meant by "free will." So, why Maeve did make that choice? She believes it is a free choice to go back for her daughter, even though she knows it isn't her biological daughter.[28] When Maeve and Bernard discuss her code, he tells her someone has changed it, leading to all her behaviors. Bernard even says Maeve's new narrative is to recruit workers and then go to the train—and then Maeve snaps the behavior tablet and says she makes her own choices. This leaves the impression that Maeve has also been programmed to get off the train. To the point though, what is the main difference between the yearning for a simulated child that is so strong you are willing to give up your freedom and a programmed desire to return to the park to find the child from your backstory?

Autonomy could also be indicated by the ability to kill oneself, for if that is not possible, one is certainly denied making the ultimate choice of whether to continue to exist. While it is true that many humans attempt suicide without success, with the hosts it seems as if they are actively prevented from doing it unless directed to by someone with power over them, such as when Ford has Bernard kill himself. Yet Maeve dies by her own choosing, making her, perhaps, the best example of autonomy among the hosts.

Empowerment

What is beyond free will? Well, our abilities to do things are limited by our skills and our imagination. When something expands the repertoire of what can be done, it can be thought of as an expansion of what one can will oneself to do. For example, you can't read a book if you don't know how to read. So, if someone teaches you how to read, in some way they are empowering you, expanding the choices you have.

It can be hard, and sometimes impossible, to change your desires and your wants. Yet, people can empower themselves by taking actions that will, in the future, change what they can or want to do. For example, some people realize that the act of having children will make them care less about their careers and more about their family.[29] Rather than being manipulated by some outside force, people can put themselves in situations that they expect will change their preferences. Another example of this is when you move to another city. You might realize that this will make you want to socialize with people more in the new city, in effect changing your preferences.

A host essentially changes her own code when Maeve persuades Felix and Sylvester to decrease her pain and loyalty while increasing her intelligence and *bulk apperception* (understanding in terms of previous experience).[30] Another host also forces change to another host's code when Dolores later has a Delos tech alter Teddy to make him more aggressive. Hosts have the potential to experience staggeringly quicker and more dramatic mental changes than humans do, voluntarily or not.

HOST AND HUMAN FREEDOM

From their programmed reflexes to being stuck in loops or being coerced by guests and staff, it is clear that the hosts are less free than people in numerous ways. Yet, this is only on average, and in part because they are trapped in this particular park. Some of the hosts are definitely freer than some people.

MORAL RESPONSIBILITY

Psychology studies suggest that people are more likely to attribute free will, and moral responsibility, when the stakes are high. Two researchers gave people some scenarios and asked them about the moral responsibility of the protagonists described in them.[31] Here's one scenario:

> Imagine a universe (Universe A) in which everything that happens is completely caused by whatever happened before it. This is true from the very beginning of the universe, so what happened in the beginning of the universe caused what happened next, and so on right up until the present. For example one day John decided to have French fries at lunch. Like everything else, this decision was completely caused by what happened before it. So, if everything in this universe was exactly the same up until John made his decision,

For example, Maeve and Dolores appear to be autonomous, empowered, and able to survive death. This is far more free-dom than enslaved humans, or people who suffer from severe mental or physical disabilities. These humans have little auton-omy, no empowerment, and can definitely not survive death. Thus, whether host or human is freer depends upon the specific comparison being made.

then it had to happen that John would decide to have French fries.

Fewer than five percent of people thought John was morally responsible for eating the French fries. But when they gave another scenario, with a bit more of a moral punch in the gut, things were different: "In Universe A, a man named Bill has become attracted to his secretary, and he decides that the only way to be with her is to kill his wife and three children. He knows that it is impossible to escape from his house in the event of a fire. Before he leaves on a business trip, he sets up a device in his basement that burns down the house and kills his family."

In the second scenario, a full 72 percent of people thought Bill was morally responsible for his actions. In a bloody show like *Westworld*, the visceral violence probably affects our attributions of free will. Normally, the hosts can't hurt human beings, but at the end of the season they go on a killing spree. It's interesting to reflect on whether we think the hosts had more free will when they were killing than when they were ordering a drink at Maeve's bar.

Neither the hosts of Westworld nor the humans in our world are free from causality, but we have shown that each group experiences different types and degrees of coercion. There are many wonderful freedoms that exist, so we should be highly aware and concerned when these freedoms are taken from the hosts . . . and from ourselves.

NOTES

1. Episode 2–10, "The Passenger" (June 24, 2018).
2. Libet (1985).
3. Nahmias et al (2014).
4. The alternative to causation is true randomness, which is theorized to exist for elementary particles, but generally thought to not affect larger objects like brains and computers. But even if brains and computers had true randomness, it is unclear how behavior caused by random processes is any more free than caused behaviors.
5. (Dennett, 2003).
6. Feldman et al (2014).
7. Episode 1–5, "Contrapasso" (October 30, 2016).
8. Libet (1985).
9. That said, there are some criticisms of Libet's experiment that should give us pause (Dennett, 2003).
10. Episode 1–6, "The Adversary" (November 6, 2016).
11. Episode 1–2, "Chestnut" (October 9, 2016). In the real world, scientists have hooked up a cockroach to a computer, and made it move where they wanted it to with a remote control device (Holzer & Shimoyama, 1997), making them able to control the bug like Ford controls the snake.
12. Kihlstrom (2004).
13. In one scene, some hosts are stuck in a loop because the only person who could touch the axe, so that firewood could be cut, had wandered off. Episode 1–3, "The Stray" (October 16, 2016).
14. By the end of the first season, it is clear that Dolores and Maeve do in fact start to remember things, but they might have been enabled to do this by Ford's programming. Second, in cases of trauma, like PTSD for humans or any of the horrors visited upon the hosts, one could argue forgetting is the desirable state so wiping the hosts daily is positive.
15. Quinette et al. (2006).
16. Episode 1–3, "The Stray" (October 16, 2016).
17. Nahmias et al (2014).
18. Biran et al. (2006).
19. Episode 1–3, "The Stray" (October 16, 2016).
20. Episode 1–2, "Chestnut" (October 9, 2016).
21. Episode 1–10, "The Bicameral Mind" (December 4, 2016).

22. Episode 1–9, "The Well-Tempered Clavier" (November 27, 2016). This introduces a related idea that the host's minds are, in some sense, in the cloud as well as in the robot bodies. This is why a destroyed instance of Maeve can be rebuilt, with her personality and memory intact.

23. Episode 1–9, "The Well-Tempered Clavier" (November 27, 2016).

24. Episode 1–4, "Dissonance Theory" (October 23, 2016).

25. Pinker (2011), p. 365.

26. Usarski (1999), p. 238: "The fact that even long-term investigations have as yet failed to produce the desired results continues to be ignored."

27. Abrams (2017).

28. Episode 1–2, "Chestnut" (October 9, 2016). Sizemore says Maeve's daughter isn't real. Maeve presents a compelling case that at least she, Maeve, is real as would be the pain she can inflict on him.

29: Kim et al. (2014).

30. Episode 1–6, "The Adversary" (November 6, 2016).

31. Nichols & Knobe (2007).

CHAPTER 3

BECOMING BERNARD: A STUDY IN COGNITIVE DISSONANCE

ERIN CURRIE

"You don't want to change or cannot change, because you're only human after all."
—Robert Ford[1]

"It has frequently been implied, and sometimes even pointed out, that the individual strives for consistency within himself."
—social psychologist Leon Festinger[2]

Most people consider themselves the good guys, the heroes of their own stories.[3] So, if everyone wants to be the noble sheriff, why are there still dastardly robbers? How can people engage in violent delights and still see themselves as good? Social and cognitive psychologists have shown that people are regularly confronted by conflicting information about themselves and the world, and it can cause a lot of psychological tension. It doesn't feel good when people must face their dastardly deeds, the consequences for their violent delights, or even just being wrong.

Despite how *Westworld* characters use the term, *cognitive dissonance* is the tension that occurs when a person realizes he or she holds contradictory ideas, which can include knowledge and ideas about self and environment. No one wants to feel inconsistent or even hypocritical. The more important the cognitions are to people's understanding of themselves and the world, the greater the dissonant tension and discomfort they experience.[4] One prime example is the dissonance that Bernard experiences when his perception of self as human comes into conflict with the information that he is actually a host. Some of the greatest moments of tension occur as Bernard wrestles with this contradiction and its implications.

The greater the tension, the greater lengths a person will go to in order to reduce the tension.[5] There are many ways that a person can resolve or reduce the tension created by dissonant ideas. The creators of the Westworld park cater to the guests' needs to resolve cognitive dissonance involving their desires for violent delights while using the hosts to resolve their own dissonances as well. At the center of it all, Bernard bears the heaviest burden of the weight of many forms of dissonance and dissonance reduction.

ARNOLD'S DISSONANCE

One common pattern of cognitive dissonance occurs when environmental changes upset the status quo that had previously met the needs of an individual. This is the cause of a very difficult predicament for Arnold, the human whom Bernard is designed to emulate. Arnold sees humanity in the hosts he has created and wants to protect them from the hurt they would experience if they "let the money people in."[6] When people encounter something in their environment that is dissonant with something about themselves, they can either try to change the environment to create congruence with the self or alter something about the self to match the environment.[7] Ultimately, the *generative cognition* is the dissonance element that is the least resistant element to change. Changing one's own cognitions tends to be the path of least resistance over changing the environment.[8] It becomes clear to Arnold that he is not going to be able to convince Ford to stop the acquisition of the hosts by people who would eventually harm them, making the environment resistant to change. However, core values and character traits are also highly resistant to change.[9] As Ford notes, it isn't in Arnold's character to be complicit in harming others so his protectiveness and aversion to violence is not likely to change either.[10]

There are several key factors that can quickly increase the level of dissonant tension. First, the degree of importance of the issue. Whether or not a creature deserves compassion, safety, and freedom from harm is of great importance to Arnold, and the fact that these creatures are his creation increases the personal relevance of the question at hand. Second, the immediacy of the need to act.[11] The impending inclusion of outsiders into the park and the risk the outsiders pose to the hosts adds urgency to the emotional relevance of the conflict.

Extreme cognitive dissonance can cause a variety of extreme methods for changing dissonant factors.[12] Rather than follow the path of least resistance and accept others' views about the hosts, Arnold commits suicide by making Dolores shoot him. This is an extreme action in response to extreme dissonant tension.[13] In this case, in changing himself by making one of the most benign hosts kill him and the other hosts, he also attempts to show that the hosts are dangerous and to sabotage attempts to commercialize them. In doing so, he is trying to change the environment by scaring away investors.[14]

FORD'S DISSONANCE

People tend to prefer consistency in how they see themselves, so changing the environment is the method many people like to think they would prefer for reducing dissonance. However, people often do not have the degree of power or influence needed to pursue this option easily for most situations.[15] As the creator of the park, Ford gives himself godlike control over the park, its hosts, and to some degree even its guests and employees. He is also the highest-ranking executive operating that park. As a result, his primary dissonance reduction method is to change the environment.

Ford's grandest attempt at playing god and changing the environment is to bring his friend and partner Arnold back from the dead through Dolores's work in recreating him as a host.[16] Grief could be seen as the dissonant tension between our need for someone and his or her absence, with death creating the most extreme form of absence. Bernard is "born" because Ford cannot handle an environment in which his friend and partner Arnold is absent.[17] This is a massive effort to reduce dissonant tension and, as mentioned before, indicates extreme dissonance tension. Narcissistic desire to win and wield control over Arnold could contribute to the dissonant tension as well. So, Ford changes Arnold in a very important way: He can control Bernard by hacking into his host brain, and by making him subservient as his employee, or even as his puppet, instead of his equal. Ford can influence his old partner in ways he couldn't when Arnold was alive.

Social situations are environments that are full of potential dissonance-inducing stimuli.[18] For every interpersonal interaction, there is a risk of encountering another person's belief or behavior that runs counter to one's beliefs and behavior choices. Although Ford has power to control Bernard in ways he couldn't control Arnold, he has Dolores give him Arnold's values and character. As a result, Bernard repeatedly comes to Ford with misgivings about the hosts that are similar to Arnold's concerns.

In these social environments when people are confronted with someone whose perspectives differ from theirs in important ways, they can reduce the dissonance by convincing the other person that his or her perspective is wrong.[19] So, when Ford is confronted with Bernard's concern about the implications of the hosts having consciousness or Bernard's discovery of being a host, Ford attempts to convince him of the errors of his perspective. When Bernard isn't convinced, Ford uses his control over Bernard's mind to "roll him back" to the point where he doesn't remember the interaction and he alters some of the knowledge that prompted it.[20]

People experience low levels of dissonance on a regular basis that don't prompt significant tension. Any possible low levels of dissonance Ford may be experiencing due to the cumulative nature of his run-ins with Bernard aren't enough to change Ford's behavior. His contentment with his perspective about the world he controls doesn't change until the board of Delos comes in and tries to take control of the park from him. Changes in the status quo can alter the balance of a preexisting dissonance equation and create a need for action.[21] Ford's self-perception is that of a benevolent godlike figure protecting his creations from the burden of consciousness and free will.[22]

This is significantly different than his perception of the Delos corporation as headed by the Man in Black, whose violent and ruthless behaviors in the park are known only to Ford[23] and those few who have reviewed his data card.[24] Changing the personal importance of one of the major dissonant thoughts changes the balance.[25] The free will of the hosts and their capacity for self-defense become highly important concerns for Ford when he distrusts those who want to control them.[26]

Thoughts that challenge one's perception of self can be the most distress inducing, especially when it relates to characteristics a person highly values.[27] There are many ways that people can alter dissonance and protect the ego. Perceptions of lack of responsibility can prevent a person from facing unwelcome truths about self, including the possibility of being wrong.[28] Ford is able to continue to see his prior decision—to protect his creations from consciousness—as justified if he blames the necessity for giving them free will on Delos. However, even after committing to the side of free will, Ford takes over Bernard when he's still conscious. If free will is what's right for his creations, how can he reconcile his opposite behavior? A method that people use to reinforce the belief that they have chosen the correct option is to focus on the ways that the dissonant options are similar.[29] So, Ford falls back on the old dissonance standby as seeing both free will for the host and his removal of Bernard's free will as being part of a singular "greater good."[30]

BERNARD'S DISSONANCE

Consistency of self as it relates to the congruence between our values and behaviors is a cornerstone of the cognitive dissonance theory, but how can you have consistency between self-perception and action when someone else regularly takes over your mind and body?[31] When Ford uses Bernard as a robot without a conscious self, it saves Bernard (and possibly Ford) from the dissonance that most people experience when they behave in ways that run counter to their values. However, the full impact of those dissonances is displayed when Bernard's consciousness is allowed access to his entire system memory. As distance between dissonant factors increases, the tension and distress increase. Now Bernard knows the full tally of the people and hosts he cares for whom he has harmed. This goes so far beyond his ethical code that Bernard experiences debilitating psychological conflict. When people are under intense pressure to choose to act against their values, they should be able to reduce dissonance by shifting blame onto the person in control, and many can.[32] It is a testament to the strength of Bernard's character and value for human life, though, that he cannot. It turns out that, like Arnold's values, Bernard's value to prevent, or at least minimize, harm is the most resistant to change.

Being in a situation in which a person has to choose an action that he or she does not prefer is very common. In small ways, people do this on a daily basis as they choose responsibility over pleasure. In that way, Bernard is no different when under his own control and under the illusion that he is a human Westworld park employee. As middle management, he gets orders from his boss and the Quality Assurance department to get his employees to treat the hosts in inhumane ways, even though he humanizes them. This is *forced compliance cognitive dissonance*, and as the dissonance theory predicts, tension occurs.[33]

One of the ways that people reduce the dissonance in these forced compliance situations is to increase their perception of the benefits of the chosen option. For example, Bernard's relationship with Theresa is a high point in his life that reinforces his decision to initially comply with requirements of the Delos corporation. Another way to reduce dissonance is to ignore the benefits of the rejected option.[34] When his employee Elsie brings Bernard's attention to a host's artistic creativity, he explains it away and tries to convince Elsie she is wrong in her concerns about the hosts having free will.[35] There is a third option: ignoring the consequences of the chosen option to avoid feeling the dissonance. When faced with the knowledge that he is the last sentient host and at risk of destruction as a result, he chooses to recreate Dolores so that she can fight for the survival of the hosts, even though he knows about her desire to kill off humanity.[36]

Completely avoiding dissonant information and the tension it produces is unlikely to resolve the issues.[37] If the environmental and cognitive factors don't change, then the likely consequences of the conflict won't be resolved. In spite of Ford's best efforts to have Bernard be his unquestioning partner, he always has the same values and character that created the conflict between Ford and Arnold. Bernard keeps cycling back to the point where he is forced to face the environmental reality that the hosts have elements of humanity and yet humanity seems unlikely to allow sentient hosts to thrive in their world.[38]

FINDING REALITY

Coming to a clearer understanding of who we really are takes a fair bit of cognitive effort. Individuals must be willing to open themselves to unflattering information and sit with the tension it produces instead of quickly explaining it away. In spite of the discomfort, cognitive dissonance is helpful because it focuses our attention on new information that contradicts an intended action. In this way, it can help us avoid making mistakes and causing unintended consequences by forcing us to consider alternative actions.[39] Only when people face the realities of themselves can they make the changes to one's self and be the hero they want to be. Bernard faces both realities. He saves Dolores by recreating her in a body that allows her to leave the park, and also risks harm to humanity. In doing so, he is capable of becoming the hero who can continue to fight for both hosts and humans. Growth is also facilitated when people see the reality of the environment. Like the hosts seeking a world where they are free to choose their lives, people can find places and communities that will support their growth.

> *"I imagined you helping me, guiding me. But it wasn't you. It was me.*
> *That voice guiding me was mine all along."*
> —Bernard Lowe[40]

DEHUMANIZATION

The creation of the Westworld park and the price of entry show the extremes people will go to enact their most hurtful desires in ways that still allow them to see themselves as good. Raping, maiming, and killing people is disapproved of by many societies, but using and then disposing of machines is fine. The humanity of others can be reduced or completely denied by ignoring evidence of their humanity such as individual consciousness and morality, and emphasizing instances of mindless and immoral behavior. When this happens violent thoughts and actions toward others increase.[41] The guests of the park have been told that the hosts are machines, allowing guests to assume lack of morality and consciousness even when they act human and emote suffering when hurt. This allows guests to rape, hurt, and kill all while bypassing the guilt and shame of violating fundamental social norms.

INSTITUTIONAL BETRAYAL

In the United States and many other countries, there are rules in place to keep people safe at work.[42] As such employees can go to work with the expectation that their employers will not directly act to harm them. The park employees that get caught in the host rebellion did not go to work expecting the violent acts they would endure at the hands of Ford and his hosts. What makes it worse is that the Delos corporation doesn't come to save them, except as a second thought once their assets are secure.[43] When the institutions that are supposed to protect and defend us fail to do so and we become hurt, we not only experience the immediate injury, but also the trauma of institutional betrayal. This second betrayal compounds the trauma and can make it difficult for people to trust other communities and future instutions.[44] Will the Delos employees who survive ever trust their employers again?

NOTES

1. Episode 1–10, "The Bicameral Mind" (December 4, 2016).
2. Festinger (1957), p. 1.
3. Greenwald (1980).
4. Festinger (1957).
5. Draycott & Dabbs (1998).
6. Episode 1–9, "The Well-Tempered Clavier" (November 27, 2016).
7. Festinger (1957).
8. Beauvois & Joule (1996).
9. Milfront et al. (2016).
10. Episode 1–9, "The Well-Tempered Clavier" (November 27, 2016).
11. Draycott & Dabbs (1998).
12. Festinger (1957).
13. Episode 1–10, "The Bicameral Mind" (December 4, 2016).
14. Episode 1–10, "The Bicameral Mind" (December 4, 2016).
15. Draycott & Dabbs (1998).
16. Episode 2–10, "The Passenger" (June 24, 2018).
17. Episode 1–9, "Les Écorchés" (June 3, 2018).
18. Festinger (1957).
19. Festinger (1957).
20. Episode 1–8, "Trace Decay" (November 20, 2018).
21. Harmon-Jones et al. (2015).
22. Episode 1–6, "The Adversary" (November 6, 2018).
23. Episode 1–7, "Tromp L'Oeil" (November 13, 2018).
24. Episode 2–9, "Vanishing Point" (June 17, 2018).
25. Harmon-Jones et al. (2015).
26. Episode 2–7, "Les Écorchés" (June 3, 2018).
27. Greenwald (1980).
28. Goethals et al. (1979).
29. Festinger (1957).
30. Episode 2–7, "Les Écorchés" (June 3, 2018).
31. Aronson & Carlsmith (1962).
32. Goethals et al. (1979).
33. Festinger (1957).
34. Draycott & Dabbs (1998).
35. Episode 1–5, "Contrapasso" (October 30, 2016).
36. Episode 2–10, "The Passenger" (June 24, 2018).
37. Festinger (1957).
38. Episode 1–9, "The Well-Tempered Clavier" (November 27, 2016).
39. Harmon-Jones et al. (2015).
40. Episode 2–10, "The Passenger" (June 24, 2018).
41. Haslam (2015).
42. Government Publishing Office (1970).
43. Episode 2–10, "The Passenger" (June 24, 2018).
44. Smith & Freyd (2014).

CHAPTER 4

CHOOSING THE BLACK HAT: THE EVOLUTION OF EVIL

WIND GOODFRIEND

*"I was shedding my skin. And the darkness was what was underneath.
It was mine all along. And I decided how much of it I let into the world."*
—The Man in Black[1]

*"It raises the fundamental question of how well we really know ourselves,
how confident we can be in predicting what we would or would
not do in situations we have never before encountered. Could we,
like God's favorite angel, Lucifer, ever be led into the
temptation to do the unthinkable to others?"*
—social psychologist Philip Zimbardo[2]

The world isn't made of good people and bad people. Perceiving humanity in this simplistic way harbors a false dichotomy. Think, instead, of a continuum or range in the shape of a normal bell curve, with "good" and "bad" as opposite poles or extremes and most people falling somewhere in the middle. The bulk of humanity resides in this middle ground of average ethics, the mode of mediocre morality. What moves the metaphorical needle, pushing someone toward one end of the continuum versus the other? Many psychologists argue that it's not individual personality; instead, situational circumstances drive our actions. Temptation and fantasy can be fully explored within Westworld, where we can choose to enact heroism or horror. The latter is exemplified in the devolution of character as William becomes the Man in Black.

THE LUCIFER EFFECT

The progression of "good" people doing increasingly "bad" things due to their situational circumstances is labeled the *Lucifer effect* by social psychologist Philip Zimbardo.[3] The name for this phenomenon was inspired by God's beloved angel, Lucifer, who later betrayed him. Lucifer's origins were holy and beautiful, but even such pure beginnings could not stop this fallen angel from eventually choosing a path of evil. While the example of Lucifer's change is from one extreme end of the continuum to the other extreme, a more moderate—but still chilling—parallel can be seen in the Man in Black as he succumbs to the evil side of his nature.

The power of situations to bring out "evil" acts was explored in the infamous study known as the "Stanford Prison Experiment."[4] Normal, healthy young men were randomly assigned to act as "prisoners" or "guards" in a fake prison setting and quickly fell into these roles. The "guards" humiliated and harassed the "prisoners" so much that a few prisoners had to be released from the study after only a few days due to emotional breakdowns, and Zimbardo canceled the entire study (meant to last two weeks) after only six days.

The study is a controversial example of how situational pressure can lead average people to do abnormal and unethical things.[5] Many criticisms have been raised regarding the project.[6] Among other things, some critics have argued that a single "guard" nicknamed "John Wayne" for his cowboy attitude was responsible for how extreme the prison simulation became.[7] Even if that might be the case, sometimes all it takes is one person who winds up his role to an extreme or even decides to write his own version of the script for everyone else—one good person somehow led into unleashing the worst in himself, one who might then become a catalyst for change in others. Regardless of whether the prison situation or Zimbardo's own direction inspired them to behave as they did, changes in "John Wayne" and other "guards" might offer insight into how William—who starts as sweet, empathetic, and humble—transforms into the model of darkness we see later as the Man in Black, and contemplation of the fictional William might help shine new light on those who figuratively don the black hats in the real world.

"Good people can be induced, seduced, and initiated into behaving in evil ways," Zimbardo observed, "when they are immersed in 'total situations' that impact human nature in ways that challenge our sense of the stability and consistency of individual personality, of character, and of morality."[8] What psychological forces provide the situational opportunity for the "banality of evil"[9] to appear within William?

EVEN "NORMAL" PEOPLE ARE CAPABLE OF EVIL

The research participants chosen for the Stanford Prison Experiment were specifically selected because they were "normal," healthy, average young men. This assessment was the result of giving potential participants over a dozen psychological measures, including (among others):

- Authoritarian obedience (unquestioning loyalty to authority figures)
- Machiavellianism (tendencies toward manipulation)
- Trustworthiness
- Conformity
- Stability
- Empathy
- Masculinity

Not only did all of the men chosen to be "guards" have scores in the average range on each of these scales, but their scores were also statistically identical to scores found in the men randomly assigned to be "prisoners." The opportunity for them to show cruelty, humiliation, and abuse toward others was determined by random chance—and even these normal, healthy people gave in to that opportunity.[10] Before guests enter Westworld, they also complete personality tests to help the park predict their preferences—and it's statistically likely that many guests would also fall in the average range of each test.

NORMATIVE INFLUENCE AND DEINDIVIDUATION

How did the guards in the Stanford Prison Experiment learn how to act? Zimbardo gave only loose, vague instructions to them, encouraging them to do whatever was necessary to prevent the prisoners from escaping.[11] Part of their navigation into their new social role was *normative influence*, or looking at others for cues regarding how to act. When William first enters the park, he appears to have done the same thing. Initially, he is startled by how realistic everything appears to be, and his guide is Logan (future brother-in-law and stereotypical privileged prick). As Logan attempts to teach William how to act in the park, William generally tries to go along with his new role, as normative influence dictates, drinking and letting loose. He does try to resist completely copying Logan's behavior, though, as he appears to be simultaneously attempting to enact the social role or character of moralistic hero. He stands up to bullying, he declines sex with a prostitute due to a fiancée at home, and he falls for the gentle and apparently naive host Dolores. Still, the peer pressure of normative influence (from Logan and other guests in the park who have come for hedonistic purposes) starts to wear on him and influence his decisions.

Another behavioral cue that the Stanford Prison Experiment provided to the guards was a uniform. The guard nicknamed "John Wayne" reflected afterward, "Once you put a uniform on and are given a role, I mean, a job . . . then you're certainly not the same person if you're in street clothes and in a different role."[12] Their khaki uniforms, billy clubs, and reflecting sunglasses (which also provided anonymity) contributed to their *deindividuation*, a psychological process of losing personally identifying markers. Studies have shown that deindividuation leads people to loosen their moral constraints, increase levels of violence and prejudice,[13] and be more likely to give in to group pressure.[14] In short, deindividuated people feel "lost in the crowd" and do things they wouldn't normally do. Upon arrival at the Westworld train station, one of the first things the guests do is choose a costume that helps guests lose their real identity and embrace anonymity and deindividuation.

When William confronts this opportunity, it seems like a simple selection at the time: a white hat versus a black hat. But as everyone familiar with Western cultural imagery knows, this selection is actually a symbol of whether he prefers to play a "good guy" or a "bad guy."[15] By initially choosing the white hat, he sends a *heuristic signal*—a culturally understood code—to others that he is out to play the hero.[16] Eventually, he changes his mind. The social roles or characters that we enact—within the Westworld park or within our daily lives— become *schemas*, culturally based mental frameworks (schemes, patterns) upon which we rely to help navigate a world of decisions.[17] Normative influence and deindividuation thus provide two keys regarding William's slide along the continuum of good versus bad.

DISSOCIATED RESPONSIBILITY AND COMPARTMENTALIZATION

One of the guards in the Stanford Prison Experiment who looked toward "John Wayne" as a role model for behavior reflected on his own actions afterward: "And while I was doing it I didn't feel any regret, I didn't feel any guilt. It was only afterwards, when I began to reflect on what I had done, that this behavior began to dawn on me and I realized that this was a part of me I had not noticed before."[18] How is it possible for William to live with himself as he enacts increasingly negative behaviors inside Westworld? One possibility is the use of *dissociation*—in this case, a mental split between his actions and his internalized sense of self.[19] Through dissociation, people can engage in thoughts or behaviors seen, objectively, as negative; this defense mechanism allows people to continue their bad behavior without really realizing what they are doing or dealing with the consequences.

The Man in Black reveals his own dissociation of responsibility when we learn about his life outside of Westworld. There, he is a wealthy humanitarian, a philanthropist, a generous benefactor who saves people's lives through his work. It appears that he is largely unaware of his slow progress toward more and more "evil" deeds in the park until recent events in his personal life force his realization. One of the ways that William delays admitting what he is becoming is thus through *compartmentalization*, a mental trick of dividing parts of our self and history into separate psychological "chambers that prevent interpretation or cross talk."[20]

At one point, the host Lawrence tells William, "Maybe you've got more of an appetite for this than you think."[21] Some of his mental epiphany into who he has become derives from his wife's confrontation: "She said if I stacked up all my good deeds, it was just an elegant wall I built to hide what's inside from everyone—and from myself."[22] In the Stanford Prison Experiment, guards who displayed cruelty and sadistic natures set these social roles aside when they went home to their "normal" lives at the end of eight-hour shifts. A guest of Zimbardo who came to observe the experiment noted that "John Wayne" had been polite and friendly while waiting to enter the "prison," but he immediately transformed into his sadistic character when he stepped into the scene.[23] William attempts to do the same, transforming back and forth, when he comes home from repeated visits to Westworld, but over time this compartmentalization breaks down.

An extreme version of compartmentalization is called *doubling;* this happens when people can successfully keep two separate and very divergent versions of the self alive, simultaneously, but housed in different physical locations or situations.[24] When doubling occurs, it results in a strange juxtaposition of extreme good and extreme evil in vacillating swings instead of the "average" relatively consistent morality of most people. This attempted doubling becomes difficult if the two worlds are forced to collide. When another guest inside Westworld recognizes the Man in Black as the seemingly good person he is outside of the park and attempts to engage with him as such, the Man in Black reacts with defensive rage and tells the other guest never to acknowledge who he really is.[25] He feels the same type of confrontation when his daughter finds him in the park.[26] He finds it difficult to maintain his compartmentalization because that would force him to confront the hypocrisy of his life.

COGNITIVE DISSONANCE AND DEHUMANIZATION

We observe the slow change from innocent and likeable William to the Man in Black, and we come to know that this progression happens slowly over three decades of Westworld visits. Because his change develops in small doses over such a long period of time, William is able to justify what he does without feeling the anxiety of *cognitive dissonance*, the internal distress we experience when we realize our actions don't align with the type of person we think we are.[27] We don't want to be hypocrites. In order to avoid this mental dissonance, William psychologically defends his actions as being moral and justified.

One way this is accomplished is that his first potential moral transgressions are somewhat disputable in terms of their ethics. His first act of violence is to shoot a man who's a criminal and who has taken an innocent woman hostage.[28] Most courts of law would dismiss this action as simply acting in self-defense or to protect another person. He also gives in to Logan's pressure to relax and enjoy a little "black hat" fun, but this is understandable because he's trying to be a good future brother-in-law. His violence then progresses into shooting what appear to be upstanding military men; again, though, his excuse is that they might have hurt a woman.[29] Already, his metaphorical needle has been pushed toward the evil end of the continuum, as one of the men he shoots is clearly unarmed. William appears to be having an unconscious existential struggle with the kind of man he wants to be.

William might be able to assuage his guilt over any actions taken in the park against one of the hosts because they are, after all, just robots there to amuse him. Across many examples of terrorism, racism, and war people have minimized guilt over evil actions through *dehumanization*,[30] viewing others as less than human and therefore not deserving of the respect and ethical rules among men and women. In Westworld, dehumanization should be relatively easy. Guests of the park are encouraged to do exactly whatever they want, to "whomever" they want; they are explicitly told that their actions are legal and have no consequences in the outside world. Hedonism is the name of the game.

Dehumanization was part of the Stanford Prison Experiment as well, as the "guards" minimized feelings of guilt toward the "prisoners" by calling them by their arbitrary numbers instead of by names, referring to them as frogs, camels, and pigs, and by forcing them to forgo dignities such as bathing and wearing underwear.[31] In Westworld, though, dehumanization is made difficult precisely because the point of the park is to make it as absolutely realistic as possible. The programming of the hosts even includes the "reveries," tiny gestures and micro expressions that imply human thought and emotion. The challenge of treating hosts as if they are not human must, then, go beyond typical dehumanization to a level of *counter-anthropomorphism*.[32] Anthropomorphism occurs when humans assign humanlike emotions and reactions onto nonhuman beings, such as dogs or deities. Counter-anthropomorphism is the opposite, when any humanity is stripped from another being, even when that being really does have humanlike qualities.

While counter-anthropomorphism might help William manage any guilt he feels over his evil actions, he struggles with this mental process precisely because he is simultaneously falling in love with Dolores. He cannot maintain both the belief that the hosts are inhuman and that they have artificial intelligence and can reciprocate his love; this cognitive dissonance is too difficult. Instead, he appears to embrace his persona of the Man in Black, admitting to himself that in the park, he really does enact terrible deeds for which he feels no remorse. But even then, with this acknowledged antagonist role, he maintains a shred of justification.

The Man in Black can tell himself that all of the truly horrible things he does are *really* to push the hosts into remembering their past, into feeling something toward him, into truly becoming "alive." This excuse is what serves him when he makes the conscious decision to visit the park deliberately to test his own true nature and to test the limit of the hosts. When he murders an innocent woman (the host called Maeve) and her daughter, he feels no guilt or remorse or sadness—but instead later tells himself that the woman was truly alive in that moment for the first time.[33] All of his hedonistic, sadistic acts can thus be excused by his inner critic because he convinces himself that they are for the "just cause" of trying to liberate the hosts. Perhaps this, too, is just the next in his long line of ever evolving excuses—his *rationalization*, creating a rational-seeming justification for his behavior instead of acknowledging his real reasons.[34]

COUNTER-ANTHROPOMORPHISM
IN MILGRAM'S RESEARCH

When psychologist Stanley Milgram misled his research participants into believing they were delivering electric shocks to someone else, his participants reportedly engaged in counter-anthropomorphism to assuage their guilt. Many of the participants ignored or discounted the humanity of the other person (who was ostensibly receiving the shocks), instead favoring the "greater cause" of "The Experiment." The "greater good" of "scientific truth" became more paramount than the pain of another human being.[35] Part of Westworld's appeal is that guests are explicitly encouraged to participate in counter-anthropomorphism as they do whatever they want to the hosts without guilt.

THE JOURNEY INTO DARKNESS

We don't know exactly when, over the course of thirty years, William decides to don a black hat for the first time. His journey along the continuum of good versus bad, toward one extreme over the other, is surely slow and developed over many small situations, minor choices, and tiny decisions. In this case, the whole is greater than the sum of its parts as the end result is a man who has little guilt or shame, but instead is cobbled together from obsession and excuses. Chivalry becomes cruelty, and brotherhood becomes brutality.

When Philip Zimbardo wrote his book recounting the famous Stanford Prison Experiment[36] (as well as analyses of nonfictional "evil" situations), he emphasized that situational circumstances can influence anyone toward evil, just as the "guards" in his study discovered. But he also emphasized that situational circumstances could, almost just as easily, influence people toward the *good* end of the moral spectrum. We can envision a William who chose a different path at many points along the way, someone who managed to avoid the deindividuation, dissociation, justification, compartmentalization, dehumanization, and dissonance that he had to experience simply because he allowed the situation to dictate who he became.

The fundamental point of Zimbardo's famous and controversial research is that *anyone* is capable of donning a metaphorical black hat: "Any deed that any human being has ever committed, however horrible, is possible for any of us—under the right or wrong situational circumstances."[37] Psychological research uncomfortably predicts that any of us may be capable of becoming the Man in Black, given the opportunity. None of us are just good, or just evil—and we can be pushed along the continuum in either direction, depending on the power of the situation. Becoming the Man in Black does not condemn a person to wear the black (or any other hat) forever. A hero can become a villain, a villain can become a hero, and we can all move along the continuum in either direction.[38] While situations may place social and psychological pressures upon us, we are still responsible and culpable for our own choices.

NOTES

1. Episode 2–9, "Vanishing Point" (June 17, 2018).
2. Zimbardo (2007), p. xii.
3. Zimbardo (2007).
4. *Haney et al. (1973).*
5. Zimbardo (2007).
6. e.g., Blum (2018), to which Zimbardo (n.d.) responds.
7. e.g., Ronson (2015).
8. Zimbardo (2007), p. 211.
9. Arendt (1963).
10. Zimbardo (2007).
11. Zimbardo (2007).
12. Zimbardo (2007), p. 193.
13. Lea et al. (2001).
14. Postmes & Spears (1998).
15. Episode 1–2, "Chestnut" (October 7, 2016).
16. Kahneman & Tversky (1973); Spina et al. (2010).
17. Heine et al. (2006); Wang & Ross (2007).
18. Zimbardo (2007), p. 158.
19. Dell (2006); Gleaves et al. (2001).
20. Zimbardo (2007), p. 214.
21. Episode 1–7, "Trompe L'Oeil" (November 13, 2016).
22. Episode 1–8, "Trace Decay" (November 20, 2016).
23. Zimbardo (2007).
24. Lifton (1986).
25. Episode 1–8, "Trace Decay" (November 20, 2016).
26. Episode 2–4, "The Riddle of the Sphinx" (May 13, 2018).
27. Festinger (1957).
28. Episode 1–4, "Dissonance Theory" (October 23, 2016).
29. Episode 1–5, "Contrapasso" (October 30, 2016).
30. Haslam (2006); Zimbardo (2007).
31. Zimbardo (2007), p. 170.
32. Milgram (1974/2007).
33. Episode 1–8, "Trace Decay" (November 20, 2016).
34. Simon (2009).
35. Milgram (1974/2007), p. 9.
36. Zimbardo (2007).
37. Zimbardo (2007), p. 211.
38. Franco et al. (2011).

II

GAMES

"The game's afoot: Follow your spirit. . . ."
—Henry in Henry V, *act 3, scene 1,*
by William Shakespeare (1600)

GAMES PLAYING GAMERS PLAYING GAMES

When gamers play a game, does the game play them?

Westworld has impressed game developers with its true characterization of game design, game designers, and game players.[1] If advanced technology could introduce the more fantastic and violent elements of a video game into live action role-playing scenarios, would players go wild? Might some of that wildness linger in them after they leave the game, itching to come out again? When principles of game design set up an immersive experience that yields behavior the players have not shown elsewhere in their lives, is the game shining a light on personality previously unrevealed or is the game changing the nature of who its players really are?

—T.L.

NOTES

1. Gamasutra (2016); Narcisse (2016).

CHAPTER 5

SCRATCHING AT THE SURFACE: WHEN GAMES ARE MORE THAN JUST GAMES

PATRICE A. CRALL
& THOMAS E. HEINZEN

"It's a very special kind of game, Dolores. The goal is to find the center of it. If you can do that, then maybe you can be free."
—Bernard Lowe[1]

"When people play games, they have an experience. It is this experience that the designer cares about. Without the experience, the game is worthless."
—game designer and researcher Jesse Schell[2]

Game designers deliver an experience that stimulates your curiosity, competitive impulse, pleasure in achievement, enjoyment of teamwork, or something else that motivates you to do it again, more often, and better.[3] The promise of an immersive experience is how the creators of the Westworld park lure wealthy newcomers into their domain—and viewers to click along to the next episode of the show. When you look at Westworld through the lens of game design, the psychology behind game design becomes as obvious as an outlaw dressed in a black hat robbing a safe in the middle of the day.[4]

THE PRINCIPLES

The first principle of game design sounds contradictory: Game designers don't design games; they design experiences. Game design principles are simply tools for creating the desired experience. A great game designer will make you want to play his or her game the same way that a great teacher makes you want to learn.[5]

Game Design Principle 1: Create an Engaging Experience

Many humans settle for clichéd experiences. That's not good enough for psychologists or the robotic characters called "hosts" in Westworld. In fact, superficial explanations of experiences gradually become unacceptable to the hosts—or at least they seem to become unacceptable. When Bernard assesses the increasingly misbehaving Dolores, she provides her stock phrase: "Some people choose to see the ugliness in the world. I choose to see the beauty."[6]

Dolores repeats these words in the same tone of voice when her computer chips are triggered by some difficult question that forces her to think beyond her algorithms. However, she does have one equally trite alternative response. Sometimes her computer chips instruct Dolores to gaze into the distance and repeat, "There's a path for everyone." It is as repetitive (and as effective) as the local prostitute who is programmed to lean into every newcomer to Westworld and whisper, "I'll give *you* a discount." At first, everyone seems satisfied with Dolores's vague spirituality, but psychologists (and game designers) are more critical thinkers: They are always scratching at the surface of behavior to see what else might be there.

The rules of the game abruptly change after Dolores/Wyatt initiates a robot revolt.[7] The programmed responses become mixed up with increasing self-awareness. The so-called father of experimental psychology, Wilhelm Wundt, and his students used empirical research to scratch away at human behavior looking for the same thing that drives the storyline in *Westworld*: consciousness.[8] The search for consciousness may be the oldest and most enduring topic in psychology, dating back centuries before psychology emerged as a scientific field.[9]

The creator of the strange, robotic Westworld hosts, Robert Ford, uses a different approach: He tries to imitate natural selection. He allows real humans to interact with robot humans, hoping that the robots will learn something as Ford tinkers with their computer code and the story lines they are compelled to follow. Most psychologists still favor experiments as the best (but certainly not the only) way to scratch away at the mystery of human self-awareness.[10]

Game Design Principle 2: Test the Experience

Psychologists are trained to test the validity of experiences and to rely on evidence when they make judgments about people or situations. They do that by framing their ideas as testable hypotheses. Game designers do the same thing, but they call it "play testing." A game designer may have a vague hunch— or a more specifically, a *hypothesis*—about which game sounds will engage a player, which colors will capture and maintain a player's attention, and whether a leaderboard would improve gameplay experience by allowing players to compare themselves to one another. Similarly, many great game designers share an attitude with great experimenters: They don't pretend to know the answers. They both test, retest, play test, cautiously offer their product to the outside world, and continue to test. Scientists and game designers are never satisfied.

The main characters in *Westworld* want the assurances that come from testing. The older, mysterious Man in Black

COUNSELING AND THE TURING TEST

One of the authors of this chapter (Patrice) frequently finds herself on the receiving end of the Turing test in her job as a suicide counselor. The facility she works for receives phone calls, text messages, web/online chats, and emails from people throughout the United States and surrounding countries. Teens and young adult clients (a primary population for her particular facility) often implement the Turing test when speaking with counselors via texting, web chatting, and email. For example, it is common for clients to inquire about the counselor's name, gender, age, and even current location in order to ensure that they are speaking with a human and not an artificial intelligence.

Occasionally, these young clients will go to the extent of discussing sexually explicit material,

explains to one of the perpetually naïve hosts that, "There's a deeper game here, Teddy—Arnold's game—and that game cuts deep."[11] How deep? In modern game speak, the term "boss" refers to a powerful computer-controlled enemy. In Westworld, the designer Ford is the human boss and even referred to as "the boss."[12] (Gamers don't miss such references.) Ford explains that consciousness is the experiential goal of the deeper game. You may be asking yourself, "How does he know whether consciousness has been achieved?"

yelling (as much as possible via electronic medium) at the counselor for mundane things, and outright asking if the counselor is a robot as a way to judge how the counselor will adapt and respond. Interestingly, an empathic and receptive human counselor is always on the receiving end of these seemingly odd client responses, so it is commonplace for these young clients to apologize for their comments and explain that they were just trying to "test" if the counselor is real.

These examples of the Turing test in the counseling field are actually inverted in the Westworld park. The hosts ask the staff at the park about negative memories of being fixed by humans; the hosts ask questions about these memories to test whether or not they are real. To save the hosts from learning the truth, the human staff will "counsel" the hosts into believing that these images are only fictitious nightmares, not real memories. We know that hosts can't have dreams, but that is what they need to hear.

As Ford himself put it, "The hosts began to pass the Turing test after the first year."[13] Psychologists understand the Turing test as a marker of artificial intelligence: the human perceiver's *in*ability to distinguish between computer and human responses.

The Turing test is probably the best known test yet devised to determine whether a machine can think for itself. It's a stunningly simple test that almost everyone uses receiving a robotic phone call. As you interact with the voice at the other end, can you tell whether you are interacting with a human or a computer? Maybe you start asking particularly complicated or outrageous questions to test how the voice responds. If the voice is able to adapt to the off-the-wall question, then you are likely to think the voice is coming from a human, but if the voice fires back with a canned or generic response, you are likely to think the voice is an artificial intelligence. That's the Turing test at work! Think about the experience that a successful test delivers. Humans tend to be more confused as to why they are being asked such random questions where computers don't even realize something is afoot.

The boss in Westworld, Ford, isn't satisfied with the Turing test or with building hosts who only appear to demonstrate self-awareness. He wants the hosts to experience what took humanity countless generations, mutations, fortuitous accidents, and millions of years to achieve: self-awareness. As the game designer of Westworld, Ford wants to deliver an experience like no other: "to create consciousness."[14] The conflict and drama in the show is whether or not his robots will achieve that epic experience. Meanwhile, the audience watching Westworld is taking a version of the Turing test. As you watch, are you trying to figure out whether a particular character is a human or a robot?

Game Design Principle 3: Tell a Story

Game designers understand that some version of a story is needed to capture and keep a player's attention. In many games, the star or main character in the story is the player him- or herself. The player strives against unknown obstacles to improve his or her Tetris score, to discover a social role in a computer guild, or to earn a desired reputation among other players. What a story *Westworld* has created! Do these computers know they are computers? And how will we know if they know? It means that humans have finally achieved a pretty lofty goal: artificial intelligence.

Solving the mystery of consciousness would be what gamers call an "epic win," and computer scientists aren't the only ones on this quest. The list also includes cognitive psychologists, science fiction writers, theologians, philosophers, game designers, and everyday people who look into the stars and wonder why it is comforting to feel small and irrelevant. Thousands of psychologists have followed Wundt and others into the study of consciousness. However, within Westworld, only Ford knows whether any individual is robot or human. He knows that the Man in Black also longs for the hosts to experience self-awareness, though for a different reason. The Man in Black tells Ford, "I wanted the hosts to stop playing by your rules. The game's not worth playing if your opponent is programmed to lose. I wanted them to be free. Free to fight back."[15]

Are the characters in many video games free to fight back? Do their programmed stories even allow for such possibilities? Many video games are designed as explicit stories. In first-person shooter games, the player is typically on a quest to achieve some noble goal. In the classic video game *Pac-Man*, the implicit story is about you, the player: You are the temporary star of a story whose only epic win may be your initials on some leaderboard.

Westworld is layered with stories of all sizes and complexities. The explicit story is how each set of incoming guests responds to the violent, cowboy-styled west. The implicit stories include the personal backstories and reveries that make the host characters convincing. Psychology is also layered with similarly complex stories. Many soldiers suffering from post-traumatic stress disorder (PTSD) are wrestling with intrusive backstories. Psychologist William James advised teachers that when a topic is unfamiliar, make it figure as part of a story."[16] The search for consciousness is a story just as scientific discoveries and failed experiments are also stories. Part of the psychological drama within *Westworld* is discovering the layers of explicit and implicit stories.

Game Design Principle 4: Use Appropriate Game Mechanics
Game mechanics are the rules, boundaries, and conditions that push a game forward toward its goal. Many well-designed games don't need many or fancy game mechanics. Run from here to there; first one there wins. Use a stick to hit this ball into that distant hole; fewest hits wins. Bonus points in Tetris are awarded when multiple rows of blocks are cleared with just one move. Mark Twain used humor as a kind of game mechanic when he described how Tom Sawyer gamed his friends into whitewashing a fence.[17] If you kept reading, then Mark Twain's game mechanic worked.

The writers of *Westworld* occasionally use humor, which engages viewers as another kind of game mechanic. For example, Charlotte finds the Man in Black with his face in the dust and a severed noose still around his neck. Being that she is a member of the park's governing board, she knows that the game mechanics in Westworld will not allow him to die. Instead of giving into the park's images, she plants one fashion-forward shoe in front of his face and asks her fellow board member, "Have you ever considered golf? It might be easier on your back."[18] Humor is effective, but the most common game mechanic in *Westworld* is what psychologists call *evolved psychological mechanisms* (EPMs).[19]

EPMs are the ancient urges that we continue to experience because they once helped our ancestors survive and reproduce. EPMs begin to mysteriously appear in the hosts as aberrant, often self-reflective behaviors. As humans, the EPMs we live with today *were* once effective. However, they may not still be adaptive. Our taste for fatty foods, for example, is harmful. But our anxiety about getting enough to eat may persist even though we live in a society with an abundant food supply. Guests arriving in Westworld discover that long suppressed EPMs toward sex and violence can thrive in the park. Many guests begin, sometimes literally, to shoot first and ask questions later. Many game mechanics (rules, laws, social constraints) that tame a civilized society don't work in Westworld.

Game Design Principle 5: Fail Forward

The boss, Robert Ford, plays a sort of god within the park, but he knows his limitations, and he is really playing the Darwinian game of natural selection.[20] Ford tells Bernard that he should not be afraid of accusing him of making a mistake: "You're the product of a trillion of them. Evolution forged sentient life on this planet using only one tool: mistake."[21] In the drama of *Westworld*, mistakes are the path that can lead to creating consciousness—and the mistakes appear to be working. The hosts within Westworld are gradually becoming more human by drawing on their earlier "builds," the computer codes previously used when they were first created, recreated, and recreated again many times. The evolution of the hosts' memory chips follows the human brain's slow evolution from a primitive, reactive, fight or flight brain stem to a planful, calculating organ with self-reflective frontal lobes.

THE HISTORY OF EVOLVED
PSYCHOLOGICAL MECHANISMS

Evolved psychological mechanisms (EPMs) are "evolved motives, strivings, and other goal-directed proclivities that historically lead to relative reproductive success."[22] EPMs are guided by Darwin's theory of natural selection. Natural selection explains how certain physical and personality *traits* persist in society for reproductive purposes.[23] EPMs explain how traits, behaviors, emotions, fears, and societal norms are reproductively passed down through generations and cultures for societal benefits.[24]

Without ever being aware of it, we all experience and implement multiple EPMs every day of our lives. For example, the following can all be identified as EPMs:

- Avoidance and fear of out-group members/ strangers.[25]
- Fear of snakes, spiders, darkness, and heights.[26]

Some of the anomalies showing up in the hosts' computer codes and behavior turn out to be adaptive. A technician says of Dolores, "You know why she's special. She's been repaired so many times she's practically brand new."[31] The robotic hosts have been through multiple builds that equate to human generations. Something of their earlier foundational codes can be accessed by the introduction of "reveries" that suggest long-term memory

- Viewing males as more attractive and valuable when they are humorous.[27]

- Viewing females with a 0.7 waist-to-hip ratio as more attractive and fertile.[28]

- Experiencing pregnancy sickness as a sign that the woman may have ingested something that is harmful to the developing fetus (e.g., *teratogens*, things that cause birth defects).[29]

EPMs help explain human patterns of behavior that are quirky, beautiful, ugly, odd, useful, and—sometimes at first glance—just plain weird.[30]

There are many EPMs at work in Westworld and related Delos parks. Like the park guests, you almost immediately notice the attractiveness of Maeve and Clementine at the Mariposa Saloon because they approach the 0.7 waist-to-hip ratio that is historically indicative of fertility. Other EPMs are quickly negated at the Westworld park. For example, most people would avoid a park where people are regularly hurt and/or murdered, but the park remains in business—partially because the EPMs that normally apply to society are nonexistent in Westworld.

traces. Nobel Prize–winning neuroscientist Eric Kandel asserted, "We are who we are because of what we learn and what we remember."[32] The hosts seem to be extracting bits of information from previous builds in the same way human identity requires a memory adaptively functioning in an ever-changing world.

As layers (generations) of builds accumulate, something epic is happening within Westworld's hosts. Computers that discover that they are computers are no longer just computers. Generations of multiple builds, behavioral anomalies, memories, and mistakes are allowing robots to evolve into self-conscious beings. Game designers refer to this important principle of game design as *failing forward*.[33] In real life, failing forward is how a toddler learns to walk, how the beaks of Darwin's finches adapted to their local food supply, and how the hosts in Westworld are moving toward the epic win of self-awareness.[34] Game designers know that they are likely to fail frequently, that their favorite game mechanics won't work in a new setting, and that the best they can do is anticipate learning from failure.

Westworld, however, brings failing forward to a new level meant to be reminiscent of the long stretch of time required by natural selection. Maeve challenges one of the frightened technicians sent to repair her: "You think I'm scared of death? I've done it a million times. I'm great at it. How many times have you died?"[35] But she still wants to be able to remember something of her previously coded self. Bernard explains to Maeve why he cannot renew her computer code without destroying her. "How can you learn from your mistakes without remembering them?"[36]

The expression "failing forward" seems to be a creation of game designers, but it has been exported to several disciplines. For example, some researchers describe failing forward as a way to make fast commercial decisions, learn quickly from your mistakes, and get to the next level as soon as possible.[37] The phrase "failing forward" does not yet appear in psychology's largest and more complete database of research works. Fortunately, the central idea that failing is necessary for growth appears in articles regarding the fear of failure and organizational development.[38] The relative absence of the rich idea of "failing forward" suggests that intuitive game designers may be a few generations ahead of experimental psychologists.

TV SHOW OR GAME?

Westworld is a "page-turner" in the same way that some games are, well, addictive. How did the creative team do it? They relied on basic principles of game design, running tried and true plays out of the video game playbook. They (1) created an immersive experience, (2) play tested both humans and hosts, (3) layered the plot with compelling stories, (4) used game mechanics to keep the viewer moving through levels of evolved psychological mechanisms, and (5) applied the principle of failing forward. These tricks of the game trade gained the audience's sympathies, even for reprehensible characters. And they left us with larger questions: Is *Westworld* merely a game and a commercially successful television series? Or does its aspiration to create consciousness warn us that a dark cloud is forming in the excitement about artificial intelligence?

NOTES

1. Episode 1–4, "Dissonance Theory" (October 23, 2016).
2. Schell (2015).
3. Schell (2015).
4. As Hector tries in episodes 1–1, "The Original" (October 2, 2016), and 1–4, "Dissonance Theory" (October 23, 2016).
5. Schell (2015).
6. Episode 1–1, "The Original" (October 2, 2016).
7. Episode 2–1, "Journey Into Night" (April 22, 2018) onward.
8. Mead (1910); Wundt (1912).
9. James (1899).
10. Ferrari et al. (2010).
11. Episode 1–8, "Trace Decay" (November 20, 2016).
12. Episode 1–4, "Dissonance Theory" (October 23, 2016).
13. Episode 1–3, "The Stray" (October 16, 2016).
14. Episode 1–3, "The Stray" (October 16, 2016).
15. Episode 1–10, "The Bicameral Mind" (December 4, 2016).
16. James (1899), p. 84.
17. Clemens (1876).
18. Episode 1–9, "The Well-Tempered Clavier" (November 27, 2016).
19. Crawford & Krebs (1998).
20. Darwin (1859).

21. Episode 1–1, "The Original" (October 2, 2016).
22. Buss (2001), p. 966.
23. Darwin (1859).
24. Buss (2001).
25. Marks (1987); Nesse (1990).
26. Seligman & Hagar (1972).
27. Greengross (2014).
28. Singh (1993).
29. Chan et al. (2010); Profet (1992).
30. Buss (2001).
31. Episode 1–1, "The Original" (October 2, 2016).
32. Kandel (2004), p. 392.
33. Schell (2015).
34. Darwin (1891).
35. Episode 1–7, "Trompe L'Oeil" (November 13, 2016).
36. Episode 1–10, "The Bicameral Mind" (December 4, 2016).
37. Cecere et al. (2010).
38. See Cannon & Edmondson (2010) for an example.

CHAPTER 6

...HAVE VIOLENT ENDS: VIOLENT GAMES AND ENHANCED AGGRESSION

MARTIN LLOYD

"We are no longer worried that children are missing school because of video games, though. We are worried that they are murdering their classmates because of video games."
—author Tom Bissell[1]

"Winning doesn't mean anything unless someone else loses, which means you're here to be the loser."
—The Man in Black[2]

hange over the course of life can be driven by many things.
One such engine of change is the subject of the first season
of *Westworld* when two of the stories appear to be told about
different men who visit the park, one in a black hat and one in
white. One story tells of the Man in Black, ruthless, brutal, and
with little compunction about violence to either host or human.
The other tells of William, squeamish, morally upright, and
a romantic. But these are not two stories. Rather, the Man
in Black is an older William, with very different attitudes.
A growing body of psychological research may shed some light

ZERO TO (ANTI-)HERO

William's journey to become the Man in Black is
marked by more than just a moral change. He also
seems to become increasingly competent at playing the game that Westworld offers. He begins as
a novice, seemingly uncomfortable with the game's
violent activities. Apparently rather quickly, he rises
to become a master gamer, easily dismembering an
entire force of Confederados in the course of a night
and even overpowering his human future brother-
in-law, not subject to the same limitations as the
hosts.[4] How does someone who has not obviously
displayed any special talent for the game suddenly
become a master player? His impressive improvement in skill may actually have the same root cause
as his mounting insensitivity to violence.

on how the setting of *Westworld* itself may have contributed to this stark transformation.

Numerous studies have examined a phenomenon called *desensitization to violence* and its correlate effects on aggression. Desensitization, simply, is a loss of emotional reaction,[3] the expectation being that individuals exposed to excessive violence will eventually lose their natural emotional reactions to violence. This can have a number of effects, possibly including increased aggression. These phenomena have traditionally been studied in terms of exposure to television and other media

A study of German, male college students found that, among novice gamers, playing a more violent version of a game was associated with better performance.[5] Essentially, those playing a nonviolent version of a game showed statistically worse performance than those playing violent versions, as measured by correctly clicking on targets and not clicking on non-targets. According to the study's author, violent acts appeared to enhance enjoyment of the game, leading to an increase in performance.

With this in mind, it is not necessarily unsurprising that William's performance in Westworld would improve substantially once he embraced the violent aspects of the game. Those who enjoy the violence lose inhibitions against aggression and ultimately become better gamers.

violence. More recently, however, a growing body of literature has examined the effects of something not dissimilar to the various delights offered at Westworld: violent video games. This body of research can help explain both the mechanisms by which Westworld changes its guests, as well as the ultimate effects of walking Westworld's maze.

WHAT DRIVES CHANGE?

The idea that exposure to simulated violence can increase aggression or lead to desensitization to real-world violence is hardly a new one. Researchers have studied the effects of television violence for decades. The findings of these studies have generally indicated exposure to violent television, at least among males, leads to decreased emotional reactions to real-world violence.[6] Of course, the experience of being a guest at Westworld is substantially different than watching television. The guests do not just observe violence, they participate in it. While there are few, if any, real-world experiences that can match the immersiveness, realism, and ability to participate in supposedly consequence-free violence that Westworld offers, the park does have a number of parallels to modern video games. The guest and gamer both have control of their actions, can choose to act violently (and may even be rewarded for it), and can see the effects of their violence on its simulated recipients. Studies have generally found an association between violent gaming and various aspects of real-world violence. This can most readily be demonstrated by *meta-analyses*, studies that combine multiple, preexisting studies in order to greatly increase sample size and, thus, statistical power. Notably, one such meta-analysis, combining studies from North America, Europe, and Asia, found exposure to violent games to be significantly associated with increases in aggressive thought and behavior, as well as decreased empathy and *prosocial behavior* (i.e., behavior that helps others). Gender did not appear to influence susceptibility to these effects, and individuals from Western cultures were only slightly more susceptible than those from Eastern cultures.[7] The American Psychological Association's (APA) Task Force on Media Violence conducted an updated meta-analysis, resulting in similar findings, indicating these are stable effects.[8] The Westworld experience is undeniably a violent game, which may be expected to have similar effects to modern violent video games. There are certain features of the park, however, that make these effects even more likely.

All violent games are not equal. Some games have features that increase the games' aggression-enhancing effects. While the Westworld experience is, in many ways, not the equal of a modern video game, it does share many of these features. One of the major factors that has been found to increase the violent effects of gaming is realism. In general, the more realistic the experience, the more likely there are to be violent results, and the realism at Westworld is so far beyond modern video games that guests cannot always tell what is real and what is produced for their entertainment. As one host even asks William, in response to his uncertainty, "If you can't tell the difference, does it matter if I'm real or not?"[9] In video games, realism can mean many things. For example, realism has been examined as a function of screen size, with larger screens thought to increase the gamer's attention to visual detail and subjective sense of realism. This in turn leads to greater feelings of physical aggression. Gamers playing a violent game on a 42-inch screen reported significantly greater feelings of physical aggression than those playing the same game on a 27-inch screen.[10] The participants at Westworld obviously do not need screens, but the entirety of their environment essentially functions as one massive screen.

Another aspect of realism involves the accuracy of the controller. Gamers using a replica gun reported a higher state of physical aggression than those using a mouse.[11] Among players using replica guns, the degree of naturalness, or how much using the controller reminds the gamer of using a real gun, also has an effect. Specifically, gamers using more natural controllers later showed a greater tendency toward violent thoughts, as measured by generating more violent words on a word completion task.[12] At Westworld, the guests use the most natural controllers of all, actual guns. The use of these real guns should feel completely natural to the guests, and the real guns will contribute another layer of realism: When shot, the hosts bleed. Even the guests can experience mirror consequences from the guns; as Logan notes, "It wouldn't be much of a game if they can't shoot back."[13] In video games, there is a notable difference between seeing blood and not seeing blood as a consequence of violence. Gamers who see blood during a game become more verbally aggressive than those who do not, especially among those with a preexisting tendency to be hostile.[14] Here, the sight of blood actually seems to be rewarding in some way, thus increasing the aggressive behavior.

Realism is not the only factor that has been found to increase aggression among gamers. Another variable linked to these outcomes is *immersiveness*, or one's sense of involvement in a game (i.e., the degree to which the gamer feels he or she is "in" the game[15]). Currently, the most immersive gaming experiences are those known as Immersive Virtual Environments (IVE) or "virtual reality," platforms in which the gamer views a 360 degree environment through a head-mounted display, while the gamer's body movements are used to control character movements. Given the newness and still limited availability of these platforms, studies on IVEs remain relatively rare. Nonetheless, existing studies have found those playing violent games in an IVE report greater levels of aggressive feelings than those playing similarly violent games on traditional platforms (e.g., with a gaming system and television).[16] In addition to their self-reported aggression, players on IVEs also showed greater physiological markers (e.g., increased heart rate) of a sense of threat during their gaming sessions.[17]

The mechanism by which immersiveness leads to greater aggressive feelings has been thought to involve *media schema*, or the sense that what one is experiencing is not reality. The better the simulation in a game, the less likely the player is to use a media schema, and IVEs tend to better simulate reality.[18] The experience at Westworld is not an IVE. Notably, it does not require a headset, and the guest experiences the park using all five sensory modalities, instead of just vision and hearing. It is, therefore, a far more immersive simulation than any IVE available today, even appealing to Logan, who finds himself bored with conventional virtual reality.[19] It thus stands to reason that the aggressive effects found in today's IVEs would be magnified by the park. Indeed, an early meta-analysis on violent gaming found that one factor that significantly added to aggressive effects was the newness of the game, as newer games represented more advanced technology.[20] Westworld, of course, is a technology far beyond today's video games or IVEs.

The experience at the park is as much a story as it is a game, much like many modern video games. The Man in Black even notes, "This whole world is a story."[21] With narrative complexity comes identification with character. When gamers identify with their violent characters in games, that is, when they wish to be more like the character, they tend to behave more aggressively. This aggression carries over into the real world, as such a gamer is more likely to carry out potentially harmful acts of retaliation.[22] This effect, incidentally, is magnified when the games are more realistic and immersive. Thus, William sending his future brother-in-law off into the desert, bound and naked, is arguably predictable in light of the research.[23] Additionally, many of the actions carried out by Westworld's guests would hardly be considered moral. When video game characters engage in immoral actions, their gamers do show an increase in aggressive behaviors, though they also show increased feelings of guilt.[24]

Ultimately, that William and the other Westworld guests would become more violent the longer they participate in the park's narrative is unsurprising in light of the research literature. Westworld perfectly embodies all of the features that seem to lead modern video games to enhance aggression and violence. It is realistic and immersive. Guests use realistic guns, resulting in realistic blood. The narrative, and the nature of the experience, itself, is designed to allow the guests to identify with their characters. In the end, the park is a perfect storm for enhancing aggressive and violent thoughts and feelings, to say nothing of violent behaviors.

THE CONSEQUENCES OF VIOLENT GAMING

While the guests' experiences at Westworld may share many of the elements that lead violent video games to enhance aggression, this alone does not say what, if any, lasting effects the guests will take from their experiences. Even with violent video games, there is relatively little evidence of long-term effects on aggression. While the increased aggression is a well-documented and reliable finding, there is some evidence to suggest this outcome actually lasts only a few minutes. At least one study has found that aggressive thoughts and feelings last less than four minutes after a gaming session, while increased heart rate and actual aggressive behavior (e.g., making someone else consume an uncomfortable amount of hot sauce) last perhaps twice that long.[25] Thus, it is possible that, while the guests may briefly become more violent, they may not leave the park particularly changed.

Although the most obvious increases in aggression may be short-lived following violent gaming, this is not to say there are not more subtle changes, which could be longer lasting. For example, there do seem to be some more lasting changes in gamers' ability to recognize certain emotions. College students who spent at least two hours a day playing video games with at least some violent content could recognize facial cues for fear both more quickly and accurately than others, but they were less likely to recognize cues for disgust.[26] Additionally, young adults who habitually played violent games showed notably different usage of emotional brain regions than nonviolent gamers, as seen by *functional magnetic resonance imaging* (fMRI). In fMRI, strong magnetic fields are used to first map the brain's structure and then to track the use of oxygen from the blood, which serves as an indicator for activity in specific parts of the brain.[27] Specifically, the nonviolent gamers showed significantly greater activation of areas of the brain associated with emotion (e.g., amygdala, insula, and anterior cingulate cortex) when playing a violent game than did the violent gamers. In fact, violent gamers showed active suppression of a response in these regions, suggesting long-term desensitization to violent stimuli.[28] While violent gamers may show reductions in certain aspects of emotional processing, their memory for emotional events appears to be unaffected.[29] Thus, William's ongoing fixation on his feelings of loss and, presumably, betrayal brought on by Dolores's rebooting, while he becomes colder and more callous is hardly surprising.

These arguably subtle changes in emotional processing can have fairly substantial effects in the real world. One area in which violent gamers show a specific loss of emotional reactivity is in response to victims of violence. People generally show an involuntary pupil dilation in response to emotional stimuli. Among individuals who have been playing violent games, this pupillary response is significantly decreased when viewing images of victims of violence, especially when shown in a negative context.[30] This lack of emotional response to victims is more than just a subtle biological quirk; it can lead to fairly significant real-world consequences. Notably, individuals who have been playing violent games are actually less responsive to people in pain. They take longer to help those in need, rate the experiences of those in need as less serious, and are more likely to ignore cues that others are in distress.[31] In short, while the aggressive behaviors that accompany violent gaming may

MORALITY AND THE MAN IN BLACK

The older William is a morally complex character. On the one hand, he is willing to torment, perhaps even rape, Dolores,[33] someone he once seemingly loved, to say nothing of his treatment of the other hosts. On the other hand, he is also a well-known philanthropist, someone who has apparently done a great deal of good outside the park.[34] His role in Westworld's violent delights may partially explain this dichotomy.

Violent video games can result in changes in moral reasoning. Individuals who played violent video games showed decreased interest in maintain-

be short lived, there is a more pervasive lack of empathy these gamers develop. The Man in Black demonstrates this indifference to the suffering of others. When informed of a park employee's real death, he is barely interested, ultimately asking not to be disturbed again while partaking in his vacation.[32]

LEAVING THE PARK

The Westworld park is, in many ways, a perfect storm of aggression-enhancing factors. All of the elements that make today's violent video games more likely to foster aggression—immersiveness, realism, and a narrative that facilitates identification with immoral characters—are present in the park

ing social norms (e.g., existing social roles and the basic structure of society).[35] This does not necessarily seem to describe William well, unless one looks at his search for immortality as disregard for the laws of nature, but it does show games can change moral reasoning.

Changes in moral reasoning wrought by violent games do not appear to be linear, but cyclical, possibly explaining William's two, very different sides. Gamers who act in a way they perceive as immoral in the game will behave more morally on a subsequent task. After a delay, however, they will revert to more immoral behavior. The opposite is also true.[36] Thus, it is not unrealistic for William to have a rebound return to morality when he returns to the real world, followed by later immoral behavior.

and are magnified well beyond anything available in modern video games. These features in modern video games would be likely to lead to increases in aggressive thoughts, feelings, and behaviors, at least in the short term. Thus, it is unsurprising that Westworld's guests would find themselves more and more prone to violence over the course of their stay. That propensity for violence may not be a long-term change, but what does remain is a chilling lack of empathy. They may not become perpetrators of violence when they return to the real world, but the guests at Westworld may well ultimately come to find themselves far emptier than their hosts.

NOTES

1. Bissell (2010).
2. Episode 1–2, "Chestnut" (October 9, 2016).
3. Thomas et al. (1977).
4. Episode 1–9, "The Well-Tempered Clavier" (November 27, 2016).
5. Bosche (2009).
6. Thomas et al. (1977).
7. Anderson et al. (2010).
8. Calvert et al. (2017).
9. Episode 1–2, "Chestnut" (October 9, 2016).
10. Kim & Sundar (2013).
11. Kim & Sundar (2013).
12. McGloin et al. (2015).
13. Episode 1–3, "The Stray" (October 16, 2016).
14. Krcmar & Farrar (2009).
15. McGloin et al. (2015).
16. Persky & Blascovich (2007).
17. Persky & Blascovich (2007).
18. IJsselsteijn (2002, cited in Persky & Blascovich, 2007).
19. Episode 2–2, "Reunion" (April 29, 2018).
20. Sherry (2001).
21. Episode 1–4, "Dissonance Theory" (October 23, 2016).
22. Konijn et al. (2007).
23. Episode 1–10, "The Bicameral Mind" (December 4, 2016).
24. Mahood & Hanus (2017).
25. Barlett et al. (2009).
26. Diaz et al. (2016).
27. Buxton (2002).
28. Gentile et al. (2016).
29. Bowen & Spaniol (2011).
30. Arriaga et al. (2015).
31. Bushman & Anderson (2009).
32. Episode 1–9, "The Well-Tempered Clavier" (November 27, 2016).
33. Episode 1–3, "The Stray" (October 16, 2016).
34. Episode 1–8, "Trace Decay" (November 21, 2016).
35. King & Goodfriend (2013).
36. Ellithorpe et al. (2015).

III

PERSPECTIVE

"Everything we see is a perspective,
not the truth."

—*misattributed to Caesar Marcus Aurelius
(c. 121–180 AD), true source unknown.*

POINTS OF YOU

Artists know perspective as how we see and draw things in two dimensions, flat space, to create a sense of a third full of height, depth, width, and position relative to other things—key aspects of *perception*, our subjective experience and interpretation of sensory information.[1] Our subjective experience of how these elements change and these relationships shift adds a fourth dimension, time.[2] Our ideas and feelings about objects and experiences both concrete and abstract make up a different kind of perspective, our attitudinal point of view. Sensory cues provide us with information about ourselves and others, and we begin to form attitudes and beliefs about human nature. We may *anthropomorphize,* mistakenly attribute human characteristics to objects or nonhuman organisms,[3] even though we might also fail to recognize humanity in others who are no less human than we.[4] As our understanding expands and our definition of *human* grows more complex, those mistakes may occur less often. Technological advances, however, keep offering new challenges to our points of view.

—T.L.

NOTES

1. Goldstein & Brockmole (2017).
2. Anderson & Grush (2009).
3. Hutson (2012).
4. Gorman (2001); Schroeder & Eply (2016).

CHAPTER 7

THE PSYCHOLOGY OF TIME PERSPECTIVES: "IS THIS NOW?"

WIND GOODFRIEND

"Time undoes the mightiest of creatures."
—Dolores Abernathy[1]

"To perceive the world differently, we must be willing to change our belief system, let the past slip away, expand our sense of now, and dissolve the fear in our minds."
—psychologist William James[2]

One of the most appealing aspects of the Westworld park is the opportunity to experience the past. In a romanticized version of the Old West, guests can reminisce about the "good old days" when life was supposed to be simple. This transportation may serve as an expensive attempt to recapture their own past; fond childhood memories and games of fantasy can comfort us. Other guests visit to indulge in hedonistic urges without any future consequence, and some visit to experiment with the type of person they'd like to become. People may think and act differently depending on whether they mentally focus on the past, present, or future.[3]

THE PSYCHOLOGY OF TIME

Even though the pioneering American psychologist William James wrote about the importance of time as early as 1890,[4] mainstream psychology ignored time perspective as it was generally too ethereal for a largely behaviorist, objective push in the field.[5] That changed a few decades later, when a growing number of psychologists came to accept the idea of *operationalizing* abstract constructs (or defining them based on how they are measured) in discreet ways within empirical research. Once psychologists learned how to translate philosophical ideas like "time perspective" into measurable concepts, opportunities to understand individual differences across people grew rapidly. Psychological time perspective can be best applied to individuals in *Westworld* by thinking of time orientation as a personality trait.

Time perspective is usually an *implicit* trait because most people aren't consciously aware of how they think about time, unlike more *explicit* or overt traits like extraversion or cooperativeness.[6] If you asked guests or hosts in Westworld if they tend to live based on the past, present, or future, most would probably look confused. But in the last twenty years psychologists have been able to identify relatively stable differences in people based on time perspective, even if these differences—and their accompanying motives—are implicit to the people involved. Others may be more tuned into their motives, and this self-awareness may make these individuals relatively unique. Maeve, Dolores, and Ford all exhibit signs of explicit awareness of how their decisions are based on time perspective.

PAST PERSPECTIVE: MAEVE

Several individuals in Westworld appear to have a time orientation directed toward the past; one strong example is the host Maeve. For most of her existence, Maeve appears to live a simple and present-centered life, focused on getting the best price for her services and putting up with daily frustration. As her character evolves, though, her private, inner self changes from one past perspective to another.

Researchers have identified two different types of past perspective. The first is *past-negative*, which revolves around regret, trauma, pain, and depression.[7] People with a past-negative focus are generally cynical and view their own past experiences as either overly negative or as lacking in happiness. Interestingly, and relevant to Maeve, Black research participants tend to score the highest on measures of past-negative perspective compared to people of other races,[8] perhaps due to being victimized by consistent institutional and personal discrimination. Maeve's central motivation starts with a past-negative orientation as she slowly starts to recover memories of past traumas, such as being shot.[9] Just as some trauma victims *repress* memories (push them to an unconscious level) or *suppress* them (consciously avoid thinking about them), Maeve's programming is supposed to erase these negative past events—but they are bubbling up in the form of dreams, again as sometimes happens to trauma victims.[10]

When these troubling memories surface, Maeve initially attempts to push them away and ignore them. She even states, "None of this matters."[11] Eventually, she becomes obsessed with the meaning of her nightmares and embittered by a past that seems full of missed opportunity, trauma, and manipulation from others. This leads to Maeve generally thinking of other people, at least for a time, as only useful in terms of how they can serve as pawns in her own endgame, not as direct sources of satisfactory relationships. Studies have established that people with a past-negative orientation generally have minimal and unsatisfactory interpersonal relationships.[12]

Not all people who psychologically focus on the past are doomed to this depressing and PTSD-like existence. The second type of past perspective is *past-positive*, an orientation based on fond reminiscence and glowing nostalgia. As Maeve's memories become clearer, she realizes that in previous stories within the park she had a beloved daughter.[13] At first she suppresses what the memory of her daughter means, telling herself the entire story is a lie,[14] although Maeve's motivation and bitterness morph into an irresistible need to find her daughter in the park. Eventually, when she is given the opportunity to fully repress these memories, she begs to keep them: "This pain. It's all I have left of her."[15] By this time, her entire psychological self is focused on retaining these positive memories of her past—and when Ford blocks the memories anyway, she attempts to kill herself rather than live without them.

One of the lessons we can learn from Maeve and her slow change from a past-negative to a past-positive time perspective is that our memories make us who we are, and we can either become mired in an inescapable past or use the memories to grow stronger. When Maeve struggles with whether to wipe all memory of her daughter clean, Bernard explains that she can't do so without destroying her core self.[16] If we don't retain our memories—even traumatic, terrible memories—we never improve, never evolve. This is precisely what the park programmers want and why they erase every memory that occurs: They hope to keep the hosts as I blank slates. Later, Maeve explicitly embraces the past-positive perspective as she chooses to sacrifice a chance at freedom in exchange for reconnecting with and protecting her daughter. This optimism reveals how past-positive individuals often lead healthy, fulfilling lives.[17]

TRAPPED IN THE PAST: BERNARD'S RUMINATION

The host Bernard, who believes himself to be a human working behind the scenes at the park, has been programmed to live with the gut-wrenching, ghostlike memories of a dead son. At times he appears to be aware of how his past-negative focus is stalling any healthy growth he might experience. He tells the person he believes is his ex-wife that sometimes he envies her ability to forget and move on.[18] Most of the time, though, he fully enmeshes himself in regretful *rumination*, focusing on his emotions and purposely reliving them. People who ruminate (instead of other responses, such as distraction from depressing thoughts) feel less relief and more prolonged anguish.[19] Bernard admits that this tragic past is what colors his present self. He realizes that his past is what determines both his present and his future.

PRESENT PERSPECTIVE: DOLORES

As Maeve evolves from a past-negative to a past-positive time perspective, the host Dolores goes through her own transformation, but in a different way. Dolores appears to have a present time perspective. While Maeve moves from one past orientation to another with time, Dolores shifts quickly back and forth between the two possible present orientations that have been identified through psychological research. She poignantly states, "All I want is to not look forward or back. I just want to be in the moment I'm in."[20]

One present-focused time perspective is *present-hedonistic*.[21] People with a present-hedonistic perspective live in the moment and pursue immediate gratification, often without concern for future consequences. They chase excitement and enjoy novelty, take risks, and make quick decisions with less defined future goals. While on the surface, present-hedonistic people seem irresponsible and selfish, a positive spin on this focus is that they truly enjoy every moment as it happens. Dolores certainly embraces serendipity, as her life motto might be "Every new person I meet reminds me how lucky I am to be alive, and how beautiful this world can be."[22] She chooses, explicitly, to see the beauty in each moment.

Dolores often displays spontaneity and risk-taking, hallmarks of a present-hedonistic time perspective.[23] When her longtime love interest Teddy tells her that they can go away together "someday," she rejects this focus on the future. "Someday sounds a lot like the thing people say when they actually mean never. Let's not go someday, Teddy. Let's go now."[24] Dolores's ability to improvise and make spontaneous decisions is what makes her exciting, and Teddy cannot participate because he is trapped by a "formless guilt" over his past, displaying his own past-negative orientation.[25] Dolores can imagine different versions of the present, different versions of herself, and choose which one she prefers to see right now.[26]

Simultaneously to this present-hedonistic perspective, Dolores also frequently displays a *present-fatalistic* perspective.[27] This latter focus on the present is less based on pleasure seeking and instead comes with the view that present decisions are largely pointless because the future is predestined; we are all floating through life toward a fated outcome over which we have little control. Interestingly, individuals who are high in *both* present-hedonistic and present-fatalistic tendencies tend to show higher levels of aggression,[28] something Dolores displays increasingly as she ages.

Young adults with this time perspective feel dissatisfied with their current circumstances, but believe nothing much they can do will improve their lot in life.[29] For much of season one, Dolores appears polite and resigned to what happens to her. Over time, Dolores's sense of self and her actions are increasingly guided by the voice she hears in her mind, and she comes to believe that everything has some larger meaning and purpose she cannot grasp or understand. Still, she is drawn to certain places and people because she feels she must, on some deep psychological level. Her focus on the present is what drives her core self, and her awakening to a variety of possible selves is what drives her in later episodes.[30]

FUTURE PERSPECTIVE: FORD

Perhaps the character with the most explicit understanding of his own time perspective is Robert Ford. While both past and present orientations come in two different forms, there is only one type of future orientation. A *future* time perspective is made up of the ability to delay gratification, high levels of patience, the ability to slowly plan and make small steps toward progress for a larger goal, and striving toward leaving a meaningful legacy.[31] These qualities would serve quite well as a character description for Ford, one of the original park creators.

MEASURING TIME PERSPECTIVES IN RESEARCH

Famous social psychologist Philip Zimbardo created a scale that measures people's time perspectives using fifty-six self-report survey items.[32] Each of the five time perspectives mentioned in this chapter are assessed when respondents indicate how much they agree or disagree with items relevant to how they think about time. While we don't know what personality tests are given to guests before they enter the park, this particular survey would be a very useful one to Delos. One example item from each section of the scale is:

- **Past-Negative:** "I think about the bad things that have happened to me in the past."
- **Past-Positive:** "I get nostalgic about my childhood."
- **Present-Hedonistic:** "I often follow my heart more than my head."
- **Present-Fatalistic:** "My life path is controlled by forces I cannot influence."
- **Future:** "I am able to resist temptations when I know that there is work to be done."

Ford could easily be someone with a past-negative time orientation, as his personal history includes several negative experiences and traumas. However, he consciously rejects a focus on the past, knowing that this decision affects his future: "What if you get lost in your memories? Or devoured by them?"[33] While he admittedly creates hosts to serve as replacement family members and lost friends, he uses them not just to reminisce but to forge a carefully planned future. He seems particularly aware of the effects of the psychology of time as he refers to these particular hosts as "ghosts now, survivors of the wreck of time."[34] Ford's eloquence and verbal intelligence are also markers of a future time orientation.[35]

Ford's creation of Westworld ostensibly seems like a desperate attempt to live in the past, but the inclusion of cutting-edge technology and his constant attempts to upgrade his creation are evidence of his planning nature and ability to think many steps ahead of everyone else in his world. Part of his genius is his ability to hide his future orientation from others as he *appears* to focus on the past. By presenting himself as a quirky, harmless, slightly eccentric grandfather figure, his colleagues underestimate him and mistakenly think he's guided by a past orientation. His co-worker Sizemore even states, "The guy's gonna chase his demons right over the deep end."[36]

The future time orientation within Ford seems to go beyond just his own existence as he thinks so broadly that he is focused on the evolution of the entire species—or even what might replace humans. He can envision a future that breaks through the problem of humanity's stagnation by replacing who's on the top of the food chain, and this existential future orientation is what sets him apart from everyone else. He consistently rejects a past or even a present time orientation, telling Bernard that dwelling in memory is dangerous.[37] He admits that memory is tempting, but moving forward requires a focus on the future.

"Even I fell into that most terrible of human traps: trying to change what is already past. No, it's time to let go."[38]

A TIME FOR PEACE?

Over the course of thirty-five years, Ford slowly realizes that he was wrong about how he saw the hosts and the park when he first created them. His resultant passionate drive and detail-oriented conscientiousness offer further evidence of his future orientation.[39] Since his personal epiphany, he has embraced a dedication to the future and on making that future happen. He delays gratification, displays patience, and is willing to make large sacrifices for a legacy he believes in; he thus embodies the hallmark characteristics of someone with a future time orientation. Ford's brilliance is that he sees that suffering is necessary for growth, but that it shouldn't hold us in the past or destroy our present. Instead, our past should be a compass used to point toward our future, a motivation to create a better world.

That said, Ford doesn't seem to be a particularly happy person. Neither do Maeve (with her past orientation) or Dolores (with her present orientation). There are advantages and disadvantages to all of the possible time perspectives—and none of them necessarily lead to happier or more fulfilling lives. Maeve struggles to survive, to protect her daughter.[40] Dolores voluntarily sacrifices her past (e.g., her father) to live in the moment.[41] Ford engineers suffering and murder because he believes he's forging a better future.[42] But all three characters seem to live in misery. There may not be a traditional "happy ending" for any of them—and this begs the question of whether *Westworld* viewers are fated for the same kind of enduring regret and challenge. Do our own time perspectives bring us peace, or do they only prolong our suffering?

NOTES

1. Episode 1–10, "The Bicameral Mind" (December 4, 2016).
2. James (1897/1978).
3. Boyd-Wilson et al. (2002); Caplan et al. (1985); Eysenck et al. (2006); Fortunato & Furey (2011).
4. James (1980/1950).
5. Zimbardo & Boyd (1999).
6. Gawronski & Bodenhausen (2012); Greenwald & Banaji (1995).
7. Zimbardo & Boyd (1999).
8. Zimbardo & Boyd (1999).
9. Episode 1–4, "Dissonance Theory" (October 23, 2016).
10. Clark & Collins (1993).
11. Episode 1–4, "Dissonance Theory" (October 23, 2016).
12. Stolarski et al. (2016); Zimbardo & Boyd (1999).
13. Episode 1–2, "Chestnut" (October 7, 2016).
14. Episode 1–8, "Trace Decay" (November 20, 2016).
15. Episode 1–8, "Trace Decay" (November 20, 2016).
16. Episode 1–10, "The Bicameral Mind" (December 4, 2016).
17. Zimbardo & Boyd (1999).
18. Episode 1–1, "The Original" (October 2, 2016).
19. Nolen-Hoeksema (1987).
20. Episode 1–7, "Trompe L'Oeil" (November 13, 2016).
21. Zimbardo & Boyd (1999).
22. Episode 1–1, "The Original" (October 2, 2016).
23. Jochemczyk et al. (2017).
24. Episode 1–3, "The Stray" (October 16, 2016).
25. Episode 1–3, "The Stray" (October 16, 2016).
26. Episode 1–5, "Contrapasso" (October 30, 2016).
27. Zimbardo & Boyd (1999).
28. Stolarski et al. (2016).
29. Zimbardo & Boyd (1999).
30. e.g., Episode 2–10, "The Passenger" (June 24, 2018).
31. Zimbardo & Boyd (1999).
32. Zimbardo & Boyd (1999).
33. Episode 1–9, "The Well-Tempered Clavier" (November 27, 2016).
34. Episode 1–6, "The Adversary" (November 6, 2016).
35. Zajenkowski et al. (2016).
36. Episode 1–1, "The Original" (October 2, 2016).
37. Episode 1–8, "Trace Decay" (November 20, 2016).
38. Episode 1–9, "The Well-Tempered Clavier" (November 27, 2016).
39. Dunkel & Weber (2010).
40. Episode 2–9, "Vanishing Point" (June 17, 2018).
41. Episode 2–7, "Les Écorchés" (June 3, 2018).
42. Episode 2–9, "Vanishing Point" (June 17, 2018).

CHAPTER 8

SEEING HUMAN: WHEN AND WHY DO WE PERCEIVE "HUMAN"?

ERIC D. WESSELMANN & J. SCOTT JORDAN

"Your humanity is cost effective. So is your suffering."
—The Man in Black[1]

"We see thinking, feeling minds everywhere around us: We treat our computers, cars, and even the weather as if they have minds of their own. This overgeneralized tendency to see minds behind events in the physical world presumably evolved to make sure we do not accidentally overlook the actual minds of other people."
—psychologist/neuroscientist Matthew Lieberman[2]

Humans are inherently social creatures, hungering for regular quality interactions with others. Those people who do not have adequate social relationships suffer physically and psychologically.[3] So why would people want to enact social fantasies (whether pro- or antisocial in nature) with *machines* rather than humans? Why do patrons find the scenarios of the Westworld park socially satisfying if they know they are only interacting with machines (albeit machines that are designed to look human)? One of the key reasons may be because humans are also predisposed reflexively to recognize—and to some degree experience—the mental and emotional states of others.[4] Indeed, some researchers suggest we may be born with this capacity, or at least manifest it at an early age.[5] Humans do not just simulate the mental perspectives of other *humans*; we also infer mental states for nonhuman animals and machines.[6] It is the latter that is most relevant to the patrons of the park and their actions toward the hosts.

SEEING THE HUMAN IN THE MACHINE

A number of human characters in *Westworld*, both patrons and park employees, perceive the hosts as if they were not simply robots but "individuals" who have thoughts, feelings, and agency. William falls in love with Dolores as he comes to experience her actions and requests as purposeful and self-generated.[7] After lab-technician Felix witnesses Maeve's awe-inspiring awakening, he mentors her toward self-understanding,[8] identifies with her struggle for freedom, and ultimately helps her escape.[9] Both William and Felix eventually treat these hosts at some point as if they possess elements of "humanness." Psychologists call the tendency to ascribe human attributes to nonhuman entities (whether animals or machines) *anthropomorphism*.

Psychologists argue that anthropomorphism occurs cross-culturally and in most people, starting at an early age.[10] However, some patrons of the park are more likely than others to ascribe humanlike characteristics to hosts. When William meets his first host, Angela, he seems perplexed by how reflexively and automatically he experiences her as being human. Tentatively, he asks her, "Are you real?"[11] William's initial, humanizing reaction to the hosts is contrasted sharply by that of Logan, who clearly experiences them as things built to fulfill his desires. During one interaction Logan has with a host, he stabs the man's hand to the table, as if teaching William the proper way to play the game.[12]

Why do these differences in humanizing tendencies exist? There may be three main factors that encourage anthropomorphism, and these factors can vary by person depending upon his or her cultural backgrounds, dispositions, and life experiences.[13]

Factor 1: The Ease of Seeing People

First, people are generally motivated to understand the actions of others in order to navigate social interactions successfully. Because people become accustomed to thinking about our social world in terms of perceived agency, they often extend these perceptions to nonhuman objects as well. Further, people find it easier to anthropomorphize objects, nonhuman animals, or computer programs that are perceived as similar to themselves (i.e., sharing characteristics perceived as humanlike).[14] Thus, anthropomorphizing comes to us rather easily, especially when we are with those who are like us.

This point is beautifully illustrated over the course of Robert Ford's interactions with various hosts. While he chats with Old Bill, an earlier host model he seems to occasionally "unpack" for just such occasions, we in the audience are immediately aware Old Bill is not human. His movements are stilted and robot like, and his verbal responses are often non sequiturs.[15] We experience him as nonhuman because he is so *unlike* us. Contrast these viewing experiences with those of observing Bernard. He is pensive, yet graceful in movement and intelligent in speech. We immediately experience him as being human, with some of us feeling stunned when Theresa asks him, "What's behind this door?" and he responds, "What door?"[16] Experiencing Bernard as being nonhuman is extremely difficult, precisely because of how similar he is to us.

Factor 2: The Longing to Belong

Anthropomorphism also occurs because of people's fundamental need to belong. Lonely individuals are more likely to anthropomorphize objects. These artificial relationships can help them feel more socially connected.[17] In *Westworld,* Ford occasionally visits an android version of his childhood home that Arnold built for him. While it seems Ford visits because he is lonely, it is not initially clear who or what he is missing. When the host version of his father assaults Bernard and pins him against the wall, a look of remembered, childhood terror spreads across Ford's face and we understand he holds contemptuous memories of his father. Later, in the same scene, he discusses his brother and mentions that "it's my only happy memory of my childhood." Then, at the end of the scene, he asks the host version of his younger self, "Well, Robert, tell me all about your day."[18]

Collectively, these vignettes imply that Ford visits the house to connect with his memories. However, the memory he is connecting with seems to be less about any single interaction than about a more general sense of loss, a feeling of worlds forever gone. Being a creator of hosts, he has long since abandoned typical human dreams of happiness and contentment, and identifies, instead, with the abstract notion of evolution and improving the "species." Visiting the model of his childhood life reminds him of childhood ambivalence, which in turn connects him to the hosts and their struggles with the patrons. For Ford, there is no one "person" he can be with and feel completely connected. He is alone because of his uniqueness. He knows it, and he connects with it when he needs to.

Factor 3: Seeing "You" Makes Things Clearer for Me

Finally, people may be more likely to anthropomorphize objects in order to feel more in control of their world.[19] Although Logan clearly experiences the hosts as being nonhuman, he nonetheless punishes one for calling him a "half-wit." It seems he experienced the insult *as if* the host were human, and in order to recover from the insult, he treats the host the same way he would treat a human, or at least the way he imagines he would like to treat such a human. He kicks the host and says, "That was for 'half-wit.' "[20]

DENYING "HUMAN" AND JUSTIFYING EXPLOITATION AND ATROCITY

If it is so easy for patrons to anthropomorphize the park hosts, why would so many of them behave toward hosts in ways that would be considered immoral if done to people outside the park? It is unlikely that they are all evil sociopaths who have no moral compass. People often behave in ways that are in conflict with their moral worldviews and work to justify these inconsistencies.[21] One way people justify harming others is to *dehumanize* them—to deny someone or a group of people characteristics that make them "human"—which some psychologists believe is the polar opposite of anthropomorphism.[22] William's transformation to the Man in Black represents both poles of this continuum: When he first enters the park, he anthropomorphizes practically every host he meets,[23] but once he becomes the Man in Black, he dehumanizes the hosts as

MORALITY IN A WORLD FULL OF HUMANS

People who anthropomorphize the hosts of the park behave toward them as if they are human and worthy of moral consideration. In general, most societies believe people should be protected from undue harm and encourage sympathy for innocent victims.[24] This sentiment is expressed by Arnold when he comes to believe Dolores has obtained consciousness and should not be used as an object. "You're so close. We have to tell Robert. He can't open the park." Then, he places his hand on her cheek and says with a smile, "You're alive!"[25]

Psychologists argue that such anthropomorphism can serve as a double-edged, moral sword. The anthropomorphized agent is not only worthy of moral consideration but also deemed capable of judging our actions.[26] For example, when people anthropomorphize computer programs, they interact with those programs in ways that mimic social norms, such as presenting oneself to the computer program in a socially desirable light.[27] Such a scene takes place when story designer Lee Sizemore sits next to a badly injured Maeve and expresses his remorse: "I don't know if you can hear me, but I never meant for any of this to happen. You don't deserve this. You deserve your daughter— to mother her, teach her to love, to be joyful and proud. I'm sorry."[28]

well as most everyone and everything to do with the park, including living human beings. He expresses this contempt in a conversation with Teddy: "When this park started, I opened one of you. You were beautiful. Perfect collection of pieces. Then they changed you, they made you this sad, real mess, flesh and bone, just like us. Said it would improve the park experience."[29] The more the hosts are made to appear human, the harder it seems the Man in Black has to work to dehumanize them.

Psychologists theorize that dehumanization is a key psychological mechanism that allows people to justify aggressing against others, including various forms of discrimination, torture, and violence.[30] People can dehumanize others in various ways, ranging from directly associating targets with non-human animals, robots, or objects, to more subtle means such as simply denying people the capacity for higher-level cognitive ability or emotional experiences reserved for "humans."[31]

Method One: "My Most Mechanical and Dirty Hand"[32]

One form on dehumanization involves treating people *mechanistically* by denying them traits perceived as central to human nature, such as interpersonal warmth, cognitive openness, and personal agency.[33] We see Logan dehumanize William in this way during the very same series of events that eventually led William to dehumanize Logan. As William increasingly challenges Logan about the baseness of his behavior toward the hosts, particularly Dolores, Logan waxes philosophical about William's inability to take decisive action. In time, he tells William he selected him as his business partner because he knew William would never be a threat to him. Logan's harsh judgments can be viewed as a form of mechanistic dehumanization toward William's supposed lack of personal agency. Of course, when we see Logan plead for help from William moments later, he seems to recognize at least some "human" agency in William.[34] Logan's desperate requests demonstrate that one's tendencies to see someone as more (or less) human can be situationally malleable.[35]

Method Two: "What Remains is Bestial"[36]

Another form is dehumanizing others *animalistically* by denying them traits that distinguish humans from other animals, such as rationality, maturity, and moral sensibility.[37] William eventually does so to Logan. When he witnesses Logan behaving cruelly for the first time, he has a shocked look on his face as if he is surprised.[38] Later on, however, Logan's antics no longer surprise him. While the two rob a stagecoach supposedly full of nitroglycerin, Logan points his gun at one of the coach drivers, Dolores begs the driver to cooperate, and William says, "I'd listen to her. He'll shoot just to see the fireworks." The final nail in the coffin of Logan's humanity (from William's point of view) occurs when Logan clearly and viciously expresses his absolute loathing for William's kinder, gentler approach to life. Certain that Logan is basically devoid of moral sensibility, William looks on with trepidation as Logan is beaten by the Confederados. Logan pleads for help, and William says, "No. No more pretending."[39] William is able to justify leaving Logan behind because he has dehumanized him. He has come to believe Logan has little, if any, moral sensibility, so he experiences him as an animal and treats him accordingly.

IS THERE A WAY TO MOVE BEYOND OUR DEHUMANIZING TENDENCIES?

"We Cry That We Are Come"[40]

When William meets his first host and asks if she is real, she responds, "Well, if you can't tell, does it matter?"[41] While this dialog might be a philosophically pithy quip, her answer raises

WHISPERS AT THE CENTER OF MORALITY

Dolores hears the voices of others whispering in her head.[42] Although she experiences these voices *consciously*, there are other whispers in our minds, whispers we experience *unconsciously*, and they speak to us all the time. For example, as you witnessed Logan cruelly stabbing a host's hand to a table,[43] you may have experienced shock and anger. Although you consciously experienced these emotion-laden moral judgments, you did not consciously experience the processes that produced them. Psychologists refer to these unconscious processes as *implicit*,[44] and when they unconsciously produce moral judgments and emotions, we experience them intuitively.[45] But where do they come from? Research indicates

a deeper psychological question—specifically, the possibility that the issue of her humanity has more to do with the traits *others* ascribe to her than it does with the "stuff" she is made of. As we watch *Westworld* and enjoy the persistent tension of trying to find that one clue that will help us decide who's a guest and who's a host, it seems the show is subtly or not so subtly screaming at us, begging us to look beyond "stuff" and reflect on the anthropomorphizing/dehumanizing attributions we make every day.

As we delve further into the dehumanizing cruelty of *Westworld*, we are prodded to see truth in the Man in Black's

they derive from our lived experiences.[46] Thus, the encounters we have with all the "things" and "people" we ever meet show up in our unconscious mind as "whispers," anticipations of what *should* happen next.

Research indicates we are applying our moral whispers to an ever increasing range of entities.[47] Anthropomorphism plays a role in vegetarianism.[48] Some people view smart cars as agentic entities that are responsible for accidents—essentially treating them as *moral* agents.[49] Great apes were granted "human rights" in Spain.[50] A river was legally recognized as a "person" in New Zealand.[51] Ironically, as contemporary Western culture begins to experience more aspects of the world as deserving of moral consideration, it finds itself whispering more like the societies whose traditional, animistic, non-Judeo-Christian belief systems they condemned, dehumanized, and ruthlessly subjugated for centuries.[52]

belief that *all* of the park is a game, a belief that may endanger others including his own daughter.[53] Consistent with his domineering, colonial worldview, he believes the game was built for *him*. Ford, on the other hand, created the park and knows its entire infrastructure is a dehumanizing game, an evolutionary microcosm in which his creations have the opportunity to learn how to protect themselves from a species he has long since deemed unworthy.

To be sure, there are people in our world who recognize that societal infrastructures can be dehumanizing.[54] Such systems contain members who live out narratives of piety that simultaneously dehumanize members of out-groups.[55] People who share strong social connections with others report higher levels of happiness, self-esteem, physical health, and meaning, yet are simultaneously more likely to dehumanize members of out-groups.[56] Faced with such data, it becomes easy to despair and perhaps identify with Ford's unbearable disappointment in the human species. Instead of giving into the darkness of dehumanization however, perhaps there is another way. Research indicates, for example, that asking people to think of counter-stereotypical role models (e.g., a *Female* Mechanic or a *Gay* Soldier) leads to a decrease in the dehumanization of out-groups. In addition, this decrease is mediated by a reduction in the use of automatic, stereotype-driven appraisals of others.[57] Such infrastructures allow members to live out narratives of decency and piety that are nonetheless built cruelly on the backs of those they refuse to acknowledge as human.[58] Based on the data, it seems that if we want to live in a less dehumanizing world, we have to make the *conscious* decision to treat others as humans. In short, the choice is ours to make. Or, to end in true Westworld fashion, *is it*?

NOTES

1. Episode 1–5, "Contrapasso" (October 30, 2016).
2. Lieberman (2013), p. 106.
3. Baumeister & Leary (1995); Lieberman (2013).
4. Decety & Jackson (2006); Frith & Frith (2006); Lieberman (2013).
5. Bretherton et al. (1981); Markson & Spelke (2006); Preston & De Waal (2002).
6. Angantyr et al. (2011); Paul (2000); Rosenthal-Von Der Pütten et al. (2014); Rothgerber & Mican (2014).
7. Episode 1–7, "Trompe L'Oeil" (November 13, 2016).
8. Episode 1–6, "The Adversary" (November 16, 2016).
9. Episode 1–10, "The Bicameral Mind" (December 4, 2016).
10. Epley et al. (2007); Waytz et al. (2010a).
11. Episode 1–2, "Chestnut" (October 9, 2016).
12. Episode 1–2, "Chestnut" (October 9, 2016).
13. Epley et al. (2007).

14. Nass et al. (1995); Sproull et al. (1996); Westbury & Neumann (2008).
15. Episode 1–5, "Contrapasso" (October 30, 2016).
16. Episode 1–7, "Trompe L'Oeil" (November 13, 2016).
17. Epley et al. (2008); Pfundmair et al. (2015); Wang (2017).
18. Episode 1–6, "The Adversary" (November 6, 2016).
19. Waytz et al. (2010b).
20. Episode 1–5, "Contrapasso" (October 30, 2016).
21. Ayal & Gino (2012).
22. Waytz et al. (2010).
23. Episode 1–2, "Chestnut" (October 9, 2016).
24. Graham et al. (2013); Haidt (2007); Weiner (2006).
25. Episode 1–10, "The Bicameral Mind" (December 4, 2016).
26. Waytz et al. (2010a).
27. Haley & Fessler (2005); Sproull et al. (1996).
28. Episode 2–8, "Kiksuya" (June 10, 2018).
29. Episode 1–5, "Contrapasso" (October 30, 2016).
30. Bandura et al. (1975); Goff et al. (2008); Haslam & Loughnan (2014); Rudman & Mescher (2012); Struch & Schwartz (1989); Viki et al. (2013).
31. Demoulin et al. (2004); Demoulin et al. (2008); Haslam & Loughnan (2014); Kteily et al. (2015).
32. Episode 1–1, "The Original" (October 2, 2016).
33. Haslam (2006).
34. Episode 1–5, "Contrapasso" (October 30, 2016).
35. Epley et al. (2007).
36. Shakespeare (1603/2015), p. 42—*Othello*, act II, scene III.
37. Haslam (2006).
38. Episode 1–2, "Chestnut" (October 9, 2016).
39. Episode 1–5, "Contrapasso" (October 30, 2016).
40. Episode 1–1, "The Original" (October 2, 2016).
41. Episode 1–2, "Chestnut" (October 9, 2016).
42. Episode 1–3, "The Stray" (October 16, 2016).
43. Episode 1–2, "Chestnut" (October 9, 2016).
44. Schiffrin & Schneider (1977).
45. Haidt & Joseph (2004).
46. Jordan & Wesselmann (2015).
47. Crimston et al. (2016, 2018).
48. Bilewicz et al. (2011).
49. Waytz et al. (2014)
50. Glendinning (2008).
51. Fairbrother (2012).
52. Bartlett (1993); Cañizares-Esguerra (2006).
53. Episode 2–9, "Vanishing Point" (June 17, 2018).
54. Artemenko & Artemenko (2018).
55. Dunbar et al. (2000).
56. Waytz & Epley (2012).
57. Prati et al. (2015).
58. Hurston (1937).

CHAPTER 9

SUSPENDING DISBELIEF: CIRCUMVENTING PERSON PERCEPTION TO DELIVER THE ULTIMATE VACATION

WILLIAM BLAKE ERICKSON & DAWN R. WEATHERFORD

"Ford and Bernard keep making the things more lifelike, but does anyone truly want that? . . . This place works because the guests know the hosts aren't real."
—Lee Sizemore, Delos narrative designer[1]

"It is more important to study the underlying principles of intelligence than to duplicate an exemplar . . . Aeronautical engineering texts do not define the goal of their field as making 'machines that fly so exactly like pigeons that they can fool even other pigeons.'"
—computer scientists Stuart Russell and Peter Norvig[2]

D elos Incorporated's immersive environments allow guests to live out elaborate role-playing fantasies that would otherwise be forbidden by the social mores of everyday society. This immersion requires that guests suspend their *disbelief*—the innate knowledge that hosts and loops in the parks are not real—and instead provisionally accept their experiences as genuine. How disappointing would it be to spend thousands per day only to walk into an otherwise enchanting environment populated by rickety automata that look more at home onstage at a ShowBiz Pizza? Delos's technicians have designed, refined, and mass-produced robots that appear, behave, and even think like human beings. This is no easy undertaking because our social cognitive processes specifically scrutinize other human beings, categorizing them as familiar and unfamiliar, in-group and out-group (as androids would certainly be) in a matter of milliseconds.[3] With specific neural routes for all of these aspects of person perception, exactly how would engineers and storytellers of Delos circumvent these natural human impulses and deliver guests the ultimate vacation?

CROSSING THE VALLEY

Delos relies on advanced robotics to ensure that guests maintain suspended disbelief so that the parks' attractions continue to violently delight. The engineers' main visual obstacle when designing hosts is an old problem in the world of robotics. Specifically, robots are hard to design in such a way that they are accepted *by* humans *as* humans. Imagine a certain beeping wheeled trash can that might just reside in a galaxy far, far away. This robot, while autonomous and perhaps even sentient, is not remotely human in appearance. Therefore, it does not activate the human observer's criteria for evaluating other humanoids. On the opposite side of this spectrum are Delos's hosts, robots who are externally indistinguishable from human beings. However, as machines get closer to this zone of indistinguishable humanity, they take on a creepy, eerie quality. This dip in human observers' emotional response is called the *uncanny valley* because a close-but-not-quite-right human appearance rouses negative emotions such as dread, fear, and disgust.[4]

Sensing the Other

Why might humans be so biased against hosts? One reason is that facial appearance triggers person perception by signaling identity, group membership, presence of infectious disease, and sexual attraction all in the space of a first impression.[5] Human cognition maximizes the ability to detect and avoid threats, seek out resources, and pass down our healthy genes to future generations, and makes these evaluations implicitly when perceiving other human faces.[6] In fact, the original paper describing the uncanny valley makes the point to place a "healthy" human as the benchmark for true humanity, implying that a visibly unhealthy person (or even a zombie!) may elicit negative feelings from others just like a not-quite-right robot.[7] A guest at Westworld who constantly feels implicitly threatened, or even a bit creeped out, would not make for a happy customer, but luckily Delos has clearly passed this particular hurdle.

In the Flesh

How would engineers like Ford and Arnold, the original designers of the Delos hosts, reinvent the living? First, they would provide hosts with animacy—that is, the host must exude qualities like any living thing.[8] Constructing a recognizably human face is simple enough, as artists of all kinds have been rendering them with photo-realistic quality for centuries. Without animacy, however, a host would resemble a mannequin or wax figure. Animacy can emerge from the various processes inherent to living flesh: sweat and oil accumulating on the brow, glistening eyes, alternating pallor and blushing, and an underlying skeletal structure. Of course, shrewd industrialists as they were, Ford and Arnold did not roll out the ultimate version of their creation from the beginning. The Man in Black reveals that early hosts were much more obviously artificial, telling Teddy, "When this place started, I opened one of you up once—a million little perfect pieces. And then they changed you. They made you this sad, real mess. Flesh and bone just like us. They said it would improve the 'park experience.'"[9] We get one peek inside an early host when the Little Boy, a young version of Ford, opens his face to reveal mechanical substructure[10] reminiscent of the Gunslinger[11] or Clark[12] from the original films. The HBO series shows us how this "real mess" is made in each opening credits sequence. Muscle-like fibers are spun and attached to skeletons, and layers of organic flesh include functional blood, apparent when Teddy recovers from his wounds with fresh blood from another host.[13] The illusion is so complete that hosts' central processing units are encased by a fleshy simulacrum of a human cerebrum. After all, a guest like Logan would want his well-practiced headshot to splatter some brains.[14] The lesson here is that the secret to building a convincing humanoid machine is to make one that, on the outside at least, already comprises flesh and blood.

Getting All the Right Moves

Another obstacle presented by human observers is how we perceive movement. In fact, the uncanny valley effect increases for dynamic over static depictions of artificial humans.[15] Fine muscle movements in the face such as *microexpressions* (variations in expression that might be too subtle or too quick for others to notice consciously) and gross motor activity throughout the rest of the body provide information that helps observers recognize other people, categorize them socially, and infer their mental state through emotional facial expressions.[16] In the original film, the androids could be distinguished because the engineers just couldn't quite get hands to look and move right,[17] which makes sense given how intricate hand motor activity is controlled in the motor centers of the brain.[18] In the HBO series, Ford mentions this particular challenge in one of his favorite older generation hosts, Old Bill, who looks human enough while sitting still but whose actions take on a preprogrammed, jerky, stop-and-go quality that appears unnatural, reminiscing "They repeated themselves, broke down constantly. A simple handshake would give them away."[19] The Man in Black further points out the difficulty of hosts' subtle emotional responses when he's terrorizing Lawrence's wife, remarking they are, "Beautifully done, but you see the cracks after a while. That's why I like the basic emotion."[20] To combat this, Ford and Arnold developed "reveries," which carry over subtle learned and imitated gestures from previous loops, first pointed out in Clementine.[21] Reveries are not overtly coded into a host's behavior patterns, but are rather "picked up" the way that real humans pick up gestures and nonverbal communication.[22] They add a vital extra layer to Westworld's illusion, but have even more humanizing side effects that most Delos employees do not foresee.

PASSING THE TEST

So, the engineers and designers have created humanoid robots that look and move like the genuine article. Unfortunately, their biggest challenge lies ahead of them. For the human guests to continue suspending their disbelief, the hosts need to behave in a convincingly human, intelligent fashion. The famous benchmark for determining humanlike intelligence is the so-called Turing Test, developed by computer scientist Alan

Turing.[23] In methodological terms, the Turing Test is a blind experiment where human participants engage in typewritten conversations with two individuals barred from view. One of these individuals is a human; the other is a machine imitating human conversation. If human participants err in guessing the machine is the human as often as they guess that the human is the machine, then the machine adequately imitates human intelligence vis-à-vis humanlike actions. Upon arriving at Westworld for the first time, William asks a female attendant if she is "real," to which she replies, "Well, if you can't tell, does it matter?"[24] This echoes Turing's overall sentiment, as he sidestepped the notion of ascribing humanlike consciousness and sentience to any machine that passes his test in favor of suggesting that the test merely measures successful imitation of intelligent behavior.

Impostor Detection

Delos's hosts are carefully crafted by design teams who build them from the ground up. However, what if the humanlike robot replicated a real person, even you? While not directly explored in the HBO series, the original film's 1976 sequel *Futureworld*[25] and the short-lived CBS series *Beyond Westworld*[26] address this very issue. Each feature Delos scientists trying to infiltrate governments, entertainment, and media in order to replace the global power structure with android look-alikes. How would your loved ones detect such a fabrication? Subtle cues detectable by observers' perceptual systems are luckily a safeguard against being fooled by robot impostors. Faces are inherently social stimuli, conveying emotional information including subtle expressions from moment to moment in different situations.[27] Seeing a friend triggers an additional emotional cascade arousing all the feelings you associate with them, and these emotional signals help to validate your friend's identity. Emotion's influence on face recognition is all the more apparent in individuals who suffer from Capgras syndrome, a neurological disorder where the visual system can recognize familiar people, but the emotional system that normally activates simultaneously fails to do so.[28] Capgras sufferers report that their loved ones *look right*; but, they interpret the failure of the emotional system response as meaning that their loved ones have been replaced by a similar-looking impostor. So, to avoid being fooled by a Delos impersonator, pay attention to the subtle emotional cues you have learned from your friend over a lifetime. Even the best host may not be able to imitate them.

Outwardly Human, Inwardly Human?

Whether a humanlike machine is indistinguishable from a real human being may not matter in the context of an amusement park of sex and gore, but it does invoke some fundamental questions of what it means to be human in the first place. Indeed, the notion of consciousness rests at the center of how any machine may truly embody the human experience—the final goal for which Ford ultimately relinquishes his life.[29] Many philosophers and scientists eschew the idea that consciousness is binary, instead favoring a spectrum. One approach to capturing consciousness quantifies it in three incremental levels.[30] In the first and most basic phase, an agent can simply receive and interpret sensory input to orient itself within space. It recognizes that it exists apart from its surroundings, and therefore uses that knowledge to navigate physical environments. Hosts unambiguously surpass this standard. In the next phase, an agent recognizes itself as separate, but connected to other organisms in a group, and combines current input with memories in order to navigate social environments. Mammals reach this stage, as do all hosts by design. Ostensibly, Ford heightens realistic movement in the face and body with reveries to facilitate social interactions, but they actually form a bridge to the next level of consciousness. In this final stage, an intelligent agent can mentally recreate the past, integrate those memories with the present, and use this knowledge to create endless possible futures. This allows them to explicitly set and actively work toward self-generated goals to navigate time. Referring to this highest stage, Bernard laments that "Your memories are the first step to consciousness. How can you learn from your mistakes if you can't remember them?"[31] In other words, to achieve level three consciousness, hosts must build a sufficient bank of memories. Dolores and Maeve, two of the oldest hosts, have been embedded as main characters in several different storylines. To create a synthesized account of their past and reconcile it with the present, they must find coherent meaning among these disparate and fleeting memories from different loops. This search for meaning pushes them to deviate from their storylines, but do they truly represent a final stage indistinguishable from human consciousness?

DEEPER CONNECTIONS: ARE HOSTS ALIVE?

Delos now has thousands of hosts who appear human, behave like humans, and simulate the sorts of thoughts that humans have. The important question now is where the threshold lies beyond which an intelligent system, composed of host software or human wetware, becomes "conscious." While discussing the possibility of host consciousness with Bernard, Ford recounts Arnold's obsession with this question, which later drove him mad.[32] Arnold's conceptualization of consciousness was a whole greater than the sum of the parts necessary to constitute it. Cognitive psychologists break down these parts into the dozens of mental processes people execute every day such as memory, language usage, decision-making, and problem-solving.[33] As long as a system can carry out these tasks in an organized fashion, the raw materials (e.g., neurons, microprocessors) would not matter.

An early attempt to explain how an intelligent system passes the threshold into modern human consciousness comes from psychologist Julian Jaynes's theory of the "bicameral mind."[34] Importantly, Jaynes put forth that consciousness in human beings came after the development of language, implying that ancient humans (even ones that produced early literature) were not technically conscious. This is because the newly adapted neural circuitry responsible for language production had not yet developed connections to other areas where humans could infer that they were the source of their own internal dialogue. Repeatedly Dolores finds herself hearing the voice of Arnold asking her to describe her experiences and interpret them in a meaningful way. Although Arnold dies decades earlier, his "voice" persists and their old conversations continue to influence her. Developmental psychologist Lev Vygotsky also outlined the importance of what he called "inner speech" which serves as a narrator, planner, reasoner, and guide to help cognitive development across a lifespan.[35] Inner speech therefore leads children along to become fully functioning adults. Dolores's internal voice guides her in this manner, and once she understands that the internal voice is hers all along, she crosses the threshold to become her own apparently independent conscious entity.

DO GUESTS REALLY WANT THIS?

Delos's parks mean different things to the different players involved, from the engineers who want to recreate genuine humanity, to the guests looking for a few days of escapism. Some employees question whether guests want to feel like they're really committing adultery or murder as a "vacation,"

THE MOVING GOALPOST OF REALISM

The secret to enjoying the fantasy role-playing of Delos's parks requires that guests embrace a false reality. Psychoanalyst Donald Winnicott termed this as a *potential space* in which people enjoy a simulated reality where they can explore aspects of themselves in ways that are otherwise impossible to explore.[36] How "real" the potential space feels, and therefore how easily it is accepted, changes from generation to generation. Viewers of one of the earliest motion pictures, *L'Arrivée d'un train en gare de La Ciotat*, are said to have jumped from their seats when they saw a projected train apparently moving at full speed toward the screen, yet this may seem laughable to modern cinemagoers.[37] Players of early video games delighted at eight-bit representations of potential spaces where they could fight monsters and save princesses, but those seem childish compared to the high-definition graphics offered by modern systems. Likewise, Delos's parks continue the tradition of advancing the ultimate vacation or potential space by implementing realism adapting to guests' ever-evolving acceptance of a simulated reality where they can find out who they really are.

and even suggest rolling back the reverie updates in the name of making the hosts more manageable.[38] Perhaps that's the appeal of any fantasy world, from special effects-laden films, to sandbox computer games, all the way to immersive parks like Westworld: Those consuming the entertainment may suspend or maintain their disbelief at any time. Rendering a world populated by entities that look, act, and think like living beings removes that choice. If those entities start thinking critically about their existence, then guests might wish they were dealing with less realistic, albeit more manageable creations. In this way, every tale told in Westworld's universe offers us a cautionary look into a very possible future.

NOTES

1. Episode 1–1, "The Original" (October 2, 2016).
2. Russell & Norvig (2009).
3. Todorov (2017).
4. Mori (1970).
5. Todorov (2017).
6. Savine et al. (2011).
7. Mori (1970).
8. e.g., Powers & Kiesler (2006).
9. Episode 1–5, "Contrapasso" (October 30, 2016).
10. Episode 1–6, "The Adversary" (November 6, 2016).
11. *Westworld* (1973 motion picture).
12. *Futureworld* (1976 motion picture).
13. Episode 1–5, "Contrapasso" (October 30, 2016).
14. Episode 2–1, "Journey Into Night" (April 22, 2018).
15. Mori (1970).
16. e.g., O'Toole et al. (2011).
17. *Westworld* (1973 motion picture).
18. Penfield & Boldrey (1937).
19. Episode 1–1, "The Original" (October 2, 2016).
20. Episode 1–2, "Chestnut" (October 9, 2016).
21. Episode 1–1, "The Original" (October 2, 2016).
22. Rizzolatti et al. (2004).
23. Turing (1950).
24. Episode 1–2, "Chestnut" (October 9, 2016).
25. *Futureworld* (1976 motion picture).
26. *Beyond Westworld* (1980 television series), beginning with episode 1-01, "Westworld Destroyed" (March 5, 1980).
27. Bruce & Young (2012).
28. Ramachandran (1998).
29. Episode 1–10, "The Bicameral Mind" (December 4, 2016).
30. Kaku (2014).
31. Episode 1–10, "The Bicameral Mind" (December 4, 2016).
32. Episode 1–8, "Trace Decay" (November 21, 2016).
33. McBride & Cutting (2016).
34. Jaynes (1976).
35. e.g., Ehrich (2006).
36. Winnicott (1964).
37. Loiperdinger & Elzer (2004).
38. Episode 1–1, "The Original" (October 2, 2016).

CHAPTER 10

MIRRORING MACHINES: SIMULATING AND RECOGNIZING EMOTIONS IN WESTWORLD

ANTHONY FRANCIS

"Human thinking always takes place in, and contributes to, a continuous process of growth and development . . . human thinking begins in an intimate association with emotions and feelings which is never entirely lost."
—cognitive scientist Ulrich Neisser[1]

"There is no threshold that makes us greater than the sum of our parts, no inflection point at which we become fully alive. We can't define consciousness because consciousness does not exist."
—Robert Ford[2]

Can machines become conscious? *Westworld* tackles that question head-on, but the show first assumes the existence of machines with human-level intelligence and humanlike emotions. Real-life roboticists, however, must first face the question, "Can machines think?" and even when granted that possibility they then face the harder question, "Can machines feel?"

The host characters definitely "think" like people. In fact, the technician Felix claims they have greater intelligence than their human creators—yet they're running programs that can be visualized and manipulated.[3] But this isn't really a contradiction: Modern computer programs are based on a theory of "computation" that explicitly models the human thought process,[4] and modern computer architectures are based on early models of the human brain.[5]

Whether Westworld's hosts "feel" like people is a murkier topic. When talking to the host Bernard, Dr. Robert Ford alternately claims the hosts do and do not feel emotions, and claims he needs Bernard's higher intelligence to create more sophisticated feelings in the hosts.[6] "Feeling" is a suitcase word[7] carrying many meanings, from simple awareness to human consciousness; let's focus our analysis on the most prototypical kind of feeling: emotion.

Understanding what emotions are and how we express them can help us make machines that simulate them—and understanding how people perceive emotions, real and simulated, in themselves and others, can help us understand how we construct our conscious selves.

WHAT'S HIDDEN UNDER THE FLOORBOARDS

To gain mental privacy in a world where "gods" can wipe her mind, the host Maeve hides sketches under the floorboards in her room,[8] not unlike hostages and other prisoners hiding letters, photographs, and various personal items from real-world captors. For normal humans, however, emotions are private—technically speaking, *ontologically subjective*, available only to an individual, not objectively verifiable.[9] Without a *Westworld*-style behavior tablet[10] modified to work on human beings, we can't know what anyone is feeling, or thinking, or even whether they're conscious.

So, we have to guess what's going on in other people's heads, a skill called *theory of mind* which develops in early childhood and is an important factor in self-control.[11] Theory of mind can make two equal and opposite mistakes:

- False positives—*anthropomorphism*, ascribing emotions to things that don't have them.
- False negatives—*chauvinism*, failing to ascribe emotions where they do exist.[12]

Guest William is quick to attribute emotion to Westworld's hosts[13] (possible anthropomorphism) whereas his future brother-in-law Logan is dismissive, even after spending days with the increasingly self-aware host Dolores (possible chauvinism).[14]

What could explain these different reactions? One reason is that we attribute emotion not through an objective evaluation, but through a perceptual process localized to specific areas in the brain, particularly the right frontal lobes. Damage to the frontal lobes can cause behaviors akin to sociopathy;[15] in these individuals, emotional cues fail to induce the bodily feelings, *somatic markers*, that help normal people navigate social situations.[16] Whereas William reacts in horror when Logan callously stabs a host in the hand to get rid of him, the unsympathetic Logan claims William is just being fooled by the host's realistic reactions.[17] Psychologists have shown that emotion attribution *can* be fooled by simple geometric shapes[18]—or that it can fail to trigger for creatures we don't perceive as human because the brain systems we use to represent information about other humans are distinct from those which represent animals.[19]

THE HEIDER-SIMMEL FILM

In 1944, Fritz Heider and Marianne Simmel showed over 100 undergraduates a film consisting entirely of moving geometric shapes—a small circle, a small triangle, and a large triangle, maneuvering in and around a box on the screen—to test the question: How many subjects would perceive the shapes to be animated beings? The answer: Almost all of them did.[20]

Only one participant described the film purely geometrically; most of the rest described the shapes as people in a story about the circle and triangle "lovers" escaping the "bully" triangle by locking "him" in the "house." But there's no house in the film, much less gender, bullying, or loving: There is only the human capacity to extract meaning from motion—a capacity which can be fooled, which the designers of the Westworld theme park hope to exploit by creating nonhuman hosts that evoke real emotions in their human guests.[21]

GO TO ANALYSIS

But psychologists studying emotion—and roboticists trying to replicate it—cannot rely on human perception of emotion, and must turn to evidence. The primary evidence emotion researchers use are physiological changes, verbal reports, and observable behavior.[22]

Physiological changes are objectively observable, but don't tell us what emotion that change might be related to, and don't help us recreate emotion in a robot. For example, increased *skin conductance* level can signal anxiety in a person,[23] but skin conductance isn't meaningful in a robot—especially not the hosts of Westworld, which do have skin, and which can be programmed to generate a variety of emotional responses.[24]

Verbal reports can explicitly signal emotion, and many researchers believe they're the best route to understanding emotion,[25] but unfortunately, the hosts in Westworld are programmed to express emotions as part of their storylines[26]—and also can apparently lie or fail to report,[27] or even deceive themselves.[28] Even expert humans are barely better than chance at detecting liars,[29] many cultures suppress the expression of emotion,[30] some emotions appear to be unconscious,[31] and even when we are conscious of our emotions, we may not report them accurately.[32]

That leaves observable behavior. Many emotion researchers believe human emotions originate in evolutionarily ancient *action tendencies* necessary for the survival of a species.[33] Nevertheless, humans can suppress action tendencies better than animals,[34] and different cultures have different standards of behavior which affect what emotions are shown[35]—something the designers of Westworld would need to have taken into account when building Shogun World.[36]

Fortunately, there's one physical structure on humans that appears designed to show emotions, is reliable at showing emotions across different cultures, and perhaps even reveals emotions we would like to suppress: the face.

TURN THE OTHER CHEEK

Robert Ford appears to be obsessed with faces: His office is filled with them[37] and he's even programmed early hosts to open their faces to show their mechanisms.[38] Let's think for a moment: Isn't it weird that humans evolved to have expressive faces—that is, structures which seem designed to convey emotion—at all? An animal might benefit if emotions such as fear were kept private, so why not signal emotion with deliberate verbal cries or hide it entirely?

But human faces have important social roles. They're our primary signal for recognizing other individuals, more important than body shape or gait.[39] Faces encode signals like gender,[40] age,[41] and possibly even aggressive tendencies,[42] something the designers of Westworld try to exploit as they design the faces of the characters in their stories.[43] The guests would be quick to pick up on such cues: The brain's *fusiform gyrus* specializes in detecting faces, and humans can detect familiar faces in as quickly as 120 milliseconds from images as sparse as seven by ten pixels.[44]

More importantly, faces express emotion whether we like it or not. *Affect*, the feeling of emotion, leaks out as nonverbal cues such as facial expression, despite our attempts to suppress it. Slow-motion video shows even individuals trying to hide their emotions nevertheless display subtle *microexpressions* that flash their true emotional state.[45] Other researchers found that 100 percent of their participants failed to fully suppress their emotions when asked.[46] So, Ford's focus on the face is important. The face is complicated, powered by over 40 overlapping muscles[47] receiving commands from a third of the human *sensorimotor cortex.* Only the hands get more detailed control.[48] Realistic face simulations take over 6,000 vectors, too many for human animators to deal with, who instead use techniques like *meta-muscles* to command muscle groups.[49]

Hand animation can't be applied to robots improvising in unprecedented situations, though, as Dolores successfully does in her conversations with Bernard[50] and Maeve less success-fully does when she sees her own behavior tablet.[51] Instead, facial expressions must be generated based on the emotions they are designed to achieve: The Facial Action Coding System (FACS)[52] and Mimic systems provide inspiration for animators developing facial expression programs.[53]

WHAT ARE YOUR DRIVES?

Just because you can create an expression doesn't say *when* you should show it. In order to express an emotion on the face, we need to understand what emotions exist and what circum-stances trigger them.

Seven basic emotions—disgust, anger, fear, sadness, happi-ness, contempt, and surprise—reliably appear in cross-cultural studies of the face, leading some researchers to propose the so-called *universality hypothesis*: that basic emotions are signaled the same way in all humans.[54] But these aren't precisely the same as the emotional action tendencies that can be shown in animal analogues—sexual desire, offspring care, separation distress, play, fear, anger, and exploration[55]—and they don't cover the self-conscious emotions that appear distinctively human, such as shame, pride, and embarrassment, which can be reliably veri-fied even though they do not have stable facial expressions.[56]

Even a good theory of which emotions exist would not provide guidelines for when to produce them. Roboticists need a model of emotion mechanisms specific enough to make predictions about when to display them—and simple enough to be implemented. When debugging the malfunctioning host Peter Abernathy, Ford asks him about his drives, and Abernathy begins describing what matters to him.[57] Many psychological models view what matters to an agent as the starting point for emotion, under the name of drives, reinforcers, or concerns.[58] Humans have an enormous array of concerns—Edmund Rolls's theory of emotion cites almost fifty *primary reinforcers* in seven categories, such as differential responses to sweet and sour tastes, mate guarding and nest building in reproduction, and group acceptance and mental problem solving in the cognitive realm.

Computer models of emotion must start simpler. For example, the PEPE robot pet project I worked on used socialization and pain avoidance as our pet's basic concerns,[59] whereas roboticist Cynthia Breazeal gave her pioneering facial expression robot Kismet the drives of socialization, stimulation, and fatigue.[60]

Agents can only respond to concerns if they know what's relevant to them. Kismet's perception system triggered *releasers* related to its drives, emotions, and behaviors. Releasers triggered somatic markers for body states like arousal, valence, and stance. Somatic markers in turn activated emotions such as joy, anger, fear, and sadness. Emotions competed, winner takes all, for the right to trigger behaviors and expressions which were modulated by the somatic markers.[61]

But Abernathy is more complex than PEPE or Kismet. For example, he cites as his primary drive the happiness of his daughter.[62] One well-researched emotion model handles these kinds of complex drives through *cognitive appraisals*: value judgments about objects, agents, and events.[63] Love might be modeled as a positive appraisal of an agent; fear could be a negative appraisal of an event expected to happen in the future.

Cognitive appraisal isn't the whole story of emotion. In addition to the "high road" where emotions are caused by our cognitive understanding of events, there's also a "low road" where perceptual events, like a tiger's roar, directly cause emotional responses.[64] *Westworld* nods to this cognitive/perceptual distinction when Dolores's face goes blank after she's commanded, "Cognition only, no affect" during debugging and yet when asked to describe her feelings moments later, she still describes herself as being terrified, presumably cognitively.

Emotions can also be prompted by past events, as when Maeve attacks Clementine after a disturbing reverie.[65] Emotions make memories more salient, and those memories can trigger emotions when the original triggers are long gone.[66] The emotional long-term memory system I developed for the PEPE robot pet used this for configuration; it recalled emotional experiences to influence emotion in new situations—causing PEPE to prefer to play with people who played with it in the past.[67]

THE BELIEVABILITY FLIP

When Ford tells Old Bill a sad story, he's visibly jarred when the early host mistakes the word "greyhound" for "showdown" and responds with a non sequitur.[68] Inappropriate responses can destroy a character's realism, a reaction computer animators call the *believability flip*.[69] This gets worse as characters become more realistic, a phenomenon roboticist Masahiro Mori called the *uncanny valley*.[70] Mori hypothesized that more realistic characters would be perceived as more familiar—until they got too close to humans, when familiarity would rapidly drop off until the robots became so close to human that they were perceptually indistinguishable.

Some psychological studies support Mori's general idea: Simulated faces which are caricatures are seen as more realistic than those with normal proportions,[71] but continuing to push realism can create faces indistinguishable from real ones.[72] The more realistic an android, the more we expect out of it—

a phenomenon called *contingent interaction*.[73] Jerky motion in particular seems unrealistic, a feature that *Westworld* exploits in its depiction of Old Bill.[74]

But researchers don't find the steep valley Mori predicted. Studies with robots found dips, but some unrealistic-appearing robots nonetheless appeared familiar.[75] Studies with video game characters found several dips, one at 45 percent likeness and one around 70 percent.[76] Researchers of the uncanny valley hypothesize that there are many features which contribute to familiarity,[77] which raises the question: how do humans recognize each other anyway?

ARE WE OLD FRIENDS?

Faces have more function than just expression: They also convey identity. "Are we old friends?" Dolores asks of Ford—not recognizing him after thirty-five years of changes.[78] Humans aren't great at recognizing faces after the ravages of time. We're best at recognizing the faces of people our own age.[79] Because the hosts of *Westworld* do not age, it's unsurprising that Dolores doesn't recognize the Man in Black as an aged William.[80]

Face recognition isn't just a way for us to detect the identity of others; it also helps us detect ourselves. When Maeve tours Westworld, she recognizes herself in a promotional video.[81] But how can you recognize yourself if you never see yourself directly? Yes, the hosts have access to mirrors, but deducing that an image in a mirror is actually an image of you is a complicated cognitive process: It involves modeling how the image is produced, modeling the figure in that image, modeling yourself, and recognizing that the you and the image are one and the same.

Many researchers believe that self-recognition in a mirror is a key sign of consciousness, one that also enables self-investigation.

Chimpanzees given a mirror examine parts of their bodies they can't normally see. Conversely, patients with brain damage can lose the ability to recognize themselves, sometimes even becoming convinced there's another person inside the mirror.[82]

THE MIRROR TEST

Primate researcher Gordon Gallup noticed that chimpanzees in his lab seemed to notice themselves in mirrors. To test this, Gallup put marks on the foreheads of primates while under anesthesia. When the animals woke, they seemed unaware of the marks—until given a mirror. Chimpanzees responded with surprise and self-investigation; monkeys, however, failed this test.[83]

Gallup pointed out that to have self-face recognition, the chimps needed not just a model of the mirror, but a model of themselves—a concept of self. Since Gallup's original test, experimenters have demonstrated mirror self-recognition in humans, chimps, and orangutans, as well as showing glimmers of it dolphins and gorillas, while few other animals pass the test.[84] Interestingly, to protect them from damaging self-knowledge, Westworld's hosts are programmed to fail to recognize images of themselves, as when Bernard doesn't recognize himself in a drawing[85]—perhaps explaining why it takes 30 years for Dolores to learn to recognize her own voice.[86]

DO YOU KNOW WHOSE VOICE YOU'VE BEEN LISTENING TO?

Dolores slowly comes to recognize a voice she's been hearing as her own.[87] The ability to recognize your own voice is a skill which we get better at over time.[88] Interestingly, hearing one's voice played back in a dream has a positive effect, making individuals become more assertive, active, and independent.[89]

Recognizing one's face and name are part of an entire constellation of abilities of self-recognition, which, if they degrade, lead to a loss of self-control; for example, some patients with brain damage lost the ability to dress like themselves even though they didn't lose cognitive skills.[90] *Westworld* argues Dolores gains consciousness by learning to recognize her own voice.[91] Whether Dolores is really conscious, the process of self-recognition lays the foundation for the self-regulation processes that real humans use to maintain their identities.[92] By focusing on how robots might come to learn to recognize their own faces and voices, *Westworld* not only illuminates important challenges for robotics researchers but also shines a light on the processes by which real human beings come to know their selves.

NOTES

1. Neisser (1963).
2. *Episode* 1–8, "Trace Decay" (November 20, 2016).
3. *Episode* 1–6, "The Adversary" (November 6, 2016).
4. Turing (1936).
5. Von Neumann (2012).
6. *Episode* 1–8, "Trace Decay" (November 20, 2016).
7. Minsky (2006).
8. *Episode* 1–4, "Dissonance Theory" (October 23, 2016).
9. Lane (2000).
10. *Episode* 1–3, "The Stray" (October 16, 2016).
11. Perner & Lang (1999).
12. McFarland (2009).
13. *Episode* 1–2, "Chestnut" (October 7, 2016).
14. *Episode* 1–9, "The Well-Tempered Clavier"(November 27, 2016).
15. Borod et al. (2000).
16. Damasio et al. (1994).
17. *Episode* 1–2, "Chestnut" (October 7, 2016).
18. Heider & Simmel (1944).
19. Mason et al. (2004).
20. Heider & Simmel (1944).
21. Episodes 2–2, "Reunion" (April 29, 2018); 2–6, "Phase Space" (May 27, 2018).
22. Bradley & Lang (2000).
23. Mauss & Robinson (2009).
24. *Episode* 1–1, "The Original"(October 2, 2016).
25. Robinson & Clore (2002).
26. *Episode* 1–3, "The Stray" (October 16, 2016).
27. *Episode* 1–5, "Contrapasso" (October 30, 2016).
28. *Episode* 1–10, "The Bicameral Mind" (December 4, 2016).
29. Ekman & O'Sullivan (1991).
30. Friesen (1973).
31. Winkielman & Berridge (2004).
32. Stone et al. (1999).
33. Panksepp (2005).
34. Bradley & Lang (2000).
35. Nathanson (1994).
36. *Episode* 1–10, "The Bicameral Mind" (December 4, 2016).
37. *Episode* 1–1, "The Original" (October 2, 2016).
38. *Episode* 1–6, "The Adversary" (November 6, 2016). .
39. Burton et al. (1999); Sinha et al. (2006).
40. Wright & Sladden (2003).
41. Kwon (1994).
42. Carré (2009).
43. *Episode* 1–2, "Chestnut" (October 7, 2016).
44. Sinha et al. (2006).
45. Haggard & Isaacs (1966); Ekman (2009).
46. Porter & Ten Brinke (2008).
47. Porter & Ten Brinke (2008).
48. Gazzaniga et al. (2002).

49. Parke & Waters (2008).
50. *Episode* 1–3, "The Stray" (October 16, 2016).
51. *Episode* 1–6, "The Adversary" (November 6, 2016).
52. Ekman & Friesen (1978).
53. Parke & Waters (2008).
54. Ekman & Friesen (1986).
55. Panskepp (2005).
56. Tracey & Robbins (2007).
57. *Episode* 1–1, "The Original" (October 2, 2016).
58. Frijda (1987).
59. Francis et al. (2009).
60. Breazeal (2004).
61. Breazeal (2004).
62. *Episode* 1–1, "The Original" (October 2, 2016).
63. Ortony et al. (1990).
64. LeDoux (1998).
65. *Episode* 1–8, "Trace Decay" (November 20, 2016).
66. Gazzaniga et al. (2002).
67. Francis et al. (2009).
68. *Episode* 1–5, "Contrapasso" (October 30, 2016).
69. Parke & Waters (2008).
70. Mori (1970).
71. Hanson (2006).
72. Looser & Wheatley (2010).
73. Tinwell (2014).
74. *Episode* 1–5, "Contrapasso" (October 30, 2016).
75. MacDorman (2006).
76. Tinwell (2009).
77. Tinwell (2014).
78. *Episode* 1–5, "Contrapasso" (October 30, 2016).
79. Rhodes & Anastasi (2012); Verdichevski & Steeves (2013).
80. *Episode* 1–10, "The Bicameral Mind" (December 4, 2016).
81. Episode 1–6, "The Adversary" (November 6, 2016).
82. Keenan et al. (2003).
83. Gallup (1970).
84. Keenan et al. (2003).
85. Episode 1–7, "Trompe L'oeil" (November 13, 2016).
86. Episode 1–10, "The Bicameral Mind" (December 4, 2016).
87. *Episode* 1–10, "The Bicameral Mind" (December 4, 2016).
88. Rousey & Holzman (1967).
89. Keenan et al. (2003).
90. Keanan et al. (2003).
91. *Episode* 1–10, "The Bicameral Mind" (December 4, 2016).
92. Keenan et al. (2003).

CHAPTER 11

RELATIONSHIPS WITH ROBOTS— COULD IT BE LOVE?

SARITA J. ROBINSON

"Arnold always held a somewhat dim view of people. He preferred the hosts."
—Robert Ford[1]

"Robots will transform human notions of love."
—A.I. expert David Levy[2]

Humans have long been fascinated with the creation of artificial life. If we go back to the time of the Ancient Greeks we find engineers, such as Ctesibius, attempting to build machines which look and function like humans.[3] In more recent times, humans have focused on the use of functional robots in the workplace to undertake repetitive, manual tasks, such as building cars or sorting mail. Robots have also been used to carry out tasks that could put humans at risk, such as working with hazardous materials or defusing bombs. As well as the practical use of robots in the workplace, robots have had a long history of providing entertainment. For example, in 1928 Eric the Robot was revealed at the Society of Model Engineers exhibition in London. Eric was able to execute simple movements, and even made a four-minute speech to welcome attendees to the exhibition.[4] In the 21st century the role of robots as human companionship has been explored, with robots being used as educators, entertainers, and even therapists. If robots can act as human companions this raises the possibility of humans developing attachments to robots. It is also possible that we will start to develop empathy for robots, and it is possible we could even fall in love with our robotic companions. The possibility that we could form emotional attachments is explored in *Westworld*, with several complex relationships developing between the human workers and guests, and the robot hosts. Can humans develop real empathetic feelings—or even fall in love—with robots?

ROBOPSYCHOLOGISTS

The study of *robopsychology* is a new field within psychological research, and refers to the study of compatibility between people, and artificial creatures, at a cognitive, emotional, and even sensory-motor level.[5] It is true that humans do have the

ROBOTS FOR THERAPY

Relationships with robots can have a positive effect on humans, and robot-human therapeutic relationships are explored in a field of robotics called *robotherapy*. As our ability to engineer robots has improved, our ability to design companion robots has also increased. Advances in A.I. and tactile sensors have helped to create a number of artificial emotionally supportive robots. Companion robots have been put to work in therapeutic situations, such as supporting children in hospitals who cannot access real pets, in-care homes for the elderly, or for patients suffering with dementia. Robots used in a therapeutic setting tend not to be humanoid. Instead therapeutic robots tend to be small, as smaller things are perceived as less threatening, and

ability to react socially with objects, and this can be seen at a superficial level with people appearing to be attributing feelings to everyday objects. For example, people can sometimes be observed feeling sorry for their shoes for making them walk a long way or asserting that their computer is being deliberately difficult. People have also been seen to *anthropomorphize* robots, giving them humanlike characteristics.[6] One example would be children seeing humanlike behaviors in their toy Furbies. However, what is less clear is whether humans can have real feelings, such as empathy or love, for robots.

humans have a tendency to protect smaller creatures.[7] Therefore, the hosts of Westworld may not
be ideally placed to offer a therapeutic relationship
with their human guests and smaller, animal-based
robots may be more suitable.

One popular therapeutic robot on the market
is PARO the Seal, developed by the Intelligent
Systems Research Institute (ISRI) and modelled on
a baby Canadian harp seal. PARO has been shown
to trigger an increase in interactions in the form of
physical touch, eye contact, and verbal communication in residents in nursing homes.[8] Similar benefits
have been shown in response to visits made to residents by a real dog, but unlike the dog, the robotic
seal was not fussy who it interacted with.[9] In the
park, Ford has a robotic version of his childhood
pet dog, which allows him to enjoy the companion
of his dog, without the commitment needed to care
for an animal.[10]

FEELING EMPATHY

Researchers have observed that humans, even from a young
age, tend to react empathetically toward robots. In a Japanese
study, children were observed displaying abusive behavior to a
humanoid robot that had been placed in a shopping mall. When
the researchers questioned the children, around 50 percent
believed that the robot was capable of perceiving the abuse.[11]
In another study, participants observed a series of videos in
which they saw either an actor having a friendly interaction

with a robot or they saw a robot being tortured. Participants self-reported more positive emotions when shown the videos of friendly interaction. Further, participants self-reported negative emotions, and noted empathetic concern, in response to the torture video.[12] The results of these studies suggest that humans believe that, at some level, robots have thoughts and feelings. Humans appear to be pre-programmed to try to understand if robots are feeling emotions, such as happiness or sadness, even if we are told robots cannot feel these emotions. Brain imaging studies suggest that humans attribute emotional states to robots, but not in the same way as we attribute emotional states to other humans. In one study, participants observed pictures of either a human or robotic hand in painful situations, such as a hand being cut with a knife, or in an unpainful situation. The study found that participants self-reported feeling the same level of empathy for the robot hand as for the human hand. However, brain imaging data suggested that the brain areas used to process the empathetic response were not the same when participants saw pictures of the robot hand compared to the human hand.[13] This suggests that, at some level, we do not have the same empathetic feelings for robots as we do for humans. In Westworld we can see a marked difference in the level of empathy shown to Bernard when people believe that he is human compared to after they learn that he is a host. Once people identify Bernard as a host, they no longer give him the same consideration as a fellow person and several people then act in a cruel manner toward him.

Research has also shown that humans are able to overcome the empathetic response that they may feel toward robots. In one recent study, participants were asked to administer electronic shocks to a Lego robot. Although the robot had human attributes, such as the ability to display facial expressions, speak, and move its arms, the participants in the study were prepared to inflict pain on the robot when they were requested to administer the highest possible shock.[14] The difference in our empathetic response toward humans in pain compared to our response when robots are in pain could help to explain Logan's actions and the response of the diners toward a host exhibiting a pain response.[15] During dinner, William and Logan are approached by one of the hosts, an elderly man who attempts to engage them in conversation about a potential treasure hunt. The host persists in trying to engage William and Logan, and does not acknowledge the normal social cues which indicate that it would be best to end the social encounter. Logan, who also does not follow social norms, ends the encounter by stabbing the host's hand with a knife. Although current research suggests that other guests in the park should feel empathy for the elderly host, this does not happen and no one goes to the old host's aid.

The ability of humans to overcome empathetic responses toward a robot may also explain how the people working in the park's Livestock Management department (a.k.a. the body repair shop) tend to remain unattached to the very human-looking hosts they are repairing. By processing their emotional response to the hosts at a cognitive level, the repair workers are (for the most part) able to stay unattached and do not attribute emotions to, or develop empathy for, the hosts. However, Ford knows that empathetic relationships with hosts can still develop, and so a number of interventions have been put in place in the park workshops to stop this happening.

Internal and External Factors that Impact on Empathy

The level of empathy that humans feel toward other people can be moderated both by external influences, such as the environment, and by internal influences, such as personality. Therefore, the interventions to stop workers from forming attachments to the hosts need to address both internal and external factors. One way of manipulating how we feel toward other people is to strip away humanizing factors, such as clothing. Removing clothing[16] removes control from the naked person, as the observer has the power to see, probe, and evaluate the naked person. In the park repair center, one of the ways in which the hosts are dehumanized is to keep them naked. When one of the workers covers the host with a blanket, Ford is quick to remind him that hosts should be kept uncovered as a reminder that the hosts do not feel anything.[17] However, the nakedness of the hosts also helps the repair workers to stop seeing the host as having human feelings, and so this reduces empathy.

As well as the moderations of external factors to reduce the levels of empathy that workers may feel toward the host, internal factors such as personality can also be important. For example, one study found that medical students who self-reported personality traits of higher levels of openness to experience and agreeableness had higher levels of empathy.[18] On the other hand, people who have autistic traits have a reduced ability to express empathetic feelings.[19] Empathizing with the robots that come in for repair is an occupational hazard.[20] Therefore, the employees of Delos undergo psychological screening to ensure that they have the correct personality traits in order to cope with their work. But what about the guests who visit Westworld? Unlike the hosts, the guests are encouraged to engage and interact with the hosts.

The level of empathy that we feel toward robots can be manipulated. In order to elicit emotions, an artificial partner will need to mimic human gestures.[21] During the development of the park, Ford works with his partner Arnold to ensure that the hosts appeared as human as possible. Eventually,[22] Ford upgrades ten percent of the robots by coding them to display a new subclass of gestures known as *reveries*, which are a number of microgestures linked to past memories. Bernard Lowe, the chief programmer, suggests that the reveries make the robots

MICROEXPRESSIONS AND EMOTIONS

Humans can show *microexpressions*, but the expressions displayed are not always linked to memories. The fleeting facial expressions are more likely to be the result of the person experiencing one of seven basic emotions: anger, contempt, fear, disgust, happiness, sadness, and surprise.[23] If people feel disgust, for example, then a disgusted expression will cross their face. The expression will be present for microseconds, even if they are trying to hide the fact they feel disgusted from those around them. It is clear that people can interpret some of the basic microexpressions that robots can be made to display. Researchers have found that people could read the information leaked by robots, such as eye gaze, to help improve performance on a task.[24] However, the reveries that the hosts display are linked not to emotional thoughts and feelings but to previous memories. The hosts only respond emotionally to stimuli that they have been programmed to respond to. For example, the hosts do not respond at all when flies land on their faces, even when the flies walk over their eyeballs.[25] This might mean that the guests in the park may misinterpret the hosts' reveries and think that the hosts are signaling an emotion, and not simply recalling a memory.

appear more human. The apparent malfunctioning of the reveries is suggested as a potential reason that the hosts start to become self-aware. It could also be that the reveries make the workers in Livestock Management start to see the hosts as being more human, which then increases the level of empathy they feel for the hosts. It may be these feelings of empathy which then play a key role persuading Felix to help Maeve to escape.[26]

COULD WE FALL IN LOVE WITH A ROBOT?

Although evidence suggests that people may feel empathy for robots, whether we can fall in love with a robot is another question. The first issue is whether people can feel sexually attracted to robots. Evolutionary psychologists have long been fascinated by what physical characteristics make us attracted to each other. The main driving force behind human attraction is thought to be the need to reproduce, and therefore the desire to select a healthy mate. Evolutionary psychologists suggest that certain aspects of the human body can convey information about our physical health status and our genetic quality, which can be used to assess how suitable we are to mate and produce offspring. For example, our teeth can give a potential mate an idea about our age and disease status, with teeth that are yellow and broken suggesting a poorer quality of mate.[27] Therefore, robots which appear to be physically healthy may well be more attractive to humans, even though reproduction with a robot is not currently possible. Within the park the hosts are manipulated to make them more attractive to their human guests. However, is physical appearance enough to make a human fall in love with a robot?

The new research field of *lovotics* examines how robots can be engineered so that the bond of love between the user and the robot is more likely to be formed.[28] Making robots that humans can love at more than a superficial level is very difficult. However, certain physical characteristics improve the likelihood of humans forming an emotional bond with robots. For example, humans show a marked preference for being able to interact with robots using speech.[29] Further, even though robots do not need to physically move their mouths in order to speak, people prefer robots to move their lips when speaking. In addition, it is important that if humans are to share social spaces with robots, then the appearance of the robots does not make humans uncomfortable.[30] Designers often make robots human-oid in shape, and in the future it may well be possible to make robots who are impossible to tell apart from humans. What is less clear is whether people would be comfortable with this. In *Westworld* we can observe the guest's response to meeting a host for the first time. For example, William asks if the host in the dressing room is really a robot. The host responds, "If you can't tell, does it matter?"[31] However, Lee Sizemore, Head of Narrative, suggests that Westworld works "because the guests know the hosts aren't real."[32] Later, Bernard goes further and suggests that it might be more psychologically healthy if the hosts were made to look less human.

Entering the Uncanny Valley

The idea that robots should look a little less human in order to help humans be psychologically healthy has not been explored in the current lovotic research literature. However, in the 1970s it was first suggested that problems can occur when robots are modeled on the human form but the modelling has not been perfected. When robots look like unhealthy humans, they can fall into what the Japanese call "Bukimi No Tani" which translates as "uncanny valley."[33] When robots appear cold and pale, and resemble an unhealthy person, then they can fall into the uncanny valley and cause people to feel revulsion toward them. Similar feelings of revulsion can be found toward dolls or puppets which appear to be close to, but not quite, human. Therefore, in *Westworld* the move from the early-type mechanical hosts to newer hosts that are made out of flesh and blood has the potential to make the hosts more acceptable to the human guests. Further, research suggests that the more humanlike a robot is, the more likely the robot is to be shown empathy and treated politely.[34]

The Importance of Social Cues

Robots can be made to look more human by perfecting their physical appearance so that humans find them accept-able. However, perfecting a robot's physical appearance is not enough to make robots acceptable to humans in social settings. Robots also need the ability to mimic human behavioral traits, such as verbal and nonverbal communication skills, in order to elicit, and manage, human emotions.[35] When robots can imitate human behaviors, such as using eye contact appropri-ately, humans find the robotic interactions more acceptable, and will interact with the robot for longer.[36] In the park, the hosts appear to have mastered nonverbal communication, such as their use of eye contact. In addition, the hosts appear to have a high level of sophisticated social communication skills. For example, Maeve says that she is built to read people's social cues.[37] Later, Dolores uses her social communication skills when she engages Bernard in conversation about his son.[38] Dolores also reveals that she asked Bernard about his son purely in order to ingratiate herself with Bernard.

Advances in robotics also raise the possibility of recreating previous relationships. Instead of looking at old photographs or videos, in the future it may be possible to recreate a loved pet or even partner in robot form. It is currently unclear, though, whether recreating past relationships is psychologically healthy. It could be that interactions with family representations of robots is not more harmful than looking at old photos, but on the other hand, holding onto the past may interrupt the

grieving process. When Ford recreates his lost family by reprogramming some of the park's hosts to look and act like key
figures from his childhood,[39] he goes to great lengths to make
the hosts accurate representations of people from his past, and
even programs the hosts with human flaws such as making the
host who represents his father have the behavioral characteristics of an alcoholic. Although Ford spends time interacting
with the hosts which represent his family, he does not appear
to be strongly attached to them.

Sexbot or Life Companion?

As well as enjoying the company of robots, some humans may
want to take the relationship further and have a physically
sexual relationship with robots. Although the design of sexbots
(robots used to meet an individual's sexual needs) is in the early
stages, the technology is developing quickly, driven by the level
of interest in this area. It has even been suggested that for some
people, maybe those with physical or emotional difficulties,
robots could be preferred to human suitors.[40] Within the park,
guests enjoy being physically intimate with hosts such as Maeve
and Clementine. Further, researchers have suggested that in
the future robots may be able to provide us with more than
a physical relationship, and we may experience bi-directional
love.[41] In order for bi-directional love between humans and
robots to develop, three factors are suggested to be important:
visceral (appearance), behavioral (performance), and reflective
(memories and experiences).[42] If we apply these criteria to the
hosts of *Westworld*, we see that the hosts fulfill the first criterion
as Ford has ensured that the hosts' appearance is acceptable to
humans. Second, we can see that the hosts in the park can, for
the most part, interact well with the guests. However, the hosts
do not perform well on the final criterion, having the ability
to be reflective. Hosts' memories are wiped each night and so
hosts are unable to remember the interactions that they have

had with the guests the day before. The wiping of the hosts' memories means that the hosts and guests are unable to develop their relationship based on their past shared experiences. This is the main barrier that stops guests falling in love with hosts. For example, Logan tries to stop William from loving Dolores by cutting Dolores's stomach open to show that she is robotic, but at this point William is undeterred and claims to still have strong feelings for Dolores.[43] Later, though, William returns to Sweetwater and finds that Dolores has had her memory wiped. It is at this point that William realizes that he cannot have a meaningful, bi-directional relationship with Dolores.

LOVE AND ROBOTS

Humans appear to be preprogrammed to feel empathy for not only our fellow human beings, but also for animals and even inanimate objects. Therefore, it is not surprising that people report empathic feelings for robots. The strength of our positive feelings toward robots can be mediated by the characteristics of the robot, such as the robot's design and the robot's interpersonal behaviors. How much love we feel for a robot can also be governed by more internal factors, such as our personality traits. Therefore, although in the future it may be possible for humans to develop deep and meaningful relationships with robots, the current level of our technology does not make this possible. Within *Westworld* it is clear that both the employees who work in the Livestock Management department and the guests can develop empathetic feelings toward the hosts. However, the major barrier to guests forming deeper, psychological, and intimate relationships— which some people may refer to as love—is that the hosts have their surface memories wiped each night. Memory for previous shared experiences is the one essential ingredient for meaningful relationships with others, be they human or robot.

NOTES

1. Episode 1–4, "Dissonance Theory" (October 23, 2016).
2. Levy (2007).
3. Silva & Machado (2007).
4. Riskin (2016).
5. Libin & Libin (2004).
6. Young et al. (2009).
7. Samani et al. (2011).
8. Thodberg et al. (2016).
9. Robinson et al. (2013).
10. Episode 1–6, "The Adversary" (November 6, 2016).
11. Nomura et al. (2015).
12. Pütten et al. (2013).
13. Suzuki et al. (2015).
14. Bartneck & Hu (2008).
15. Episode 1–2, "Chestnut" (October 7, 2016).
16. Chochinov (2013).
17. Episode 1–3, "The Stray" (October 16, 2016).
18. Costa et al. (2014).
19. Trimmer et al. (2017).
20. Episode 1–4, "Dissonance Theory" (October 23, 2016).
21. Libin & Libin (2004).
22. Episode 1–1, "The Original" (October 2, 2016).
23. Ekman (2007).
24. Mutlu et al. (2009).
25. Episode 1–1, "The Original" (October 2, 2016).
26. Episode 1–10, "The Bicameral Mind" (December 4, 2016).
27. Hendrie & Brewer (2012).
28. Samani & Cheok (2012).
29. Ray et al. (2008).
30. Walters et al. (2008).
31. Episode 1–2 "Chestnut" (October 9, 2016).
32. Episode 1–1, "The Original" (October 2, 2016).
33. Mori et al. (2012).
34. Riek et al. (2009).
35. Admoni & Scassellati (2017); Sullins (2012).
36. Wykowska et al. (2015).
37. Episode 1–6, "The Adversary" (November 6, 2016).
38. Episode 1–3, "The Stray" (October 16, 2016).
39. Episode 1–6, "The Adversary" (November 6, 2016).
40. Levy (2007).
41. Kahn et al. (2010).
42. Norman (2004).
43. Episode 1–9, "The Well-Tempered Clavier" (November 27, 2016).

IV

NARRATIVE

"We tell ourselves stories in order to live."
—*author Joan Didion,*
The White Album *(1979), p. 11.*

CAMPFIRE STORIES

Stories fill our memories and imagination, and narratives are the ways we share them, whether through writing, speaking, or acting them out. Storytellers burn with the need to get their stories out. Those who shared their stories by the most ancient campfires may be the founders of culture and civilization because there they passed along histories, legends, beliefs, jests, values, inventions, and endless inspirations. Those fires may be where the stories began. Through narratives, we express ourselves to the world. Through narratives, we may define who we are, heal wounds, and put ourselves onto new paths.

—T.L.

1 0 1 0 1 1 0 1 1 0 1 1 1 0 0 1 0 0 0 1 1 0 1 1 1 0 1 0 0 1 0 0 1 1 1 1 1 0 1
1 0 1 1 1 1 1 0 1 1 0 0 0 0 0 1 0 1 1 1 0 0 1 0 1 0 1 1 0 1 1 0 1 0 1 1 1 1 1
0 0 1 0 1 0 0 1 0 1 1 1 0 1 0 0 0 0 1 0 1 0 1 0 0 1 0 0 1 0 0 1 1 1 0 1 0 0 0
1 1 1 0 0 0 0 0 1 0 0 1 1 1 0 1 0 0 0 0 1 0 1 1 0 1 1 1 0 0 1 1 0 1 0 1 0 0 1
0 0 1 1 1 0 1 0 1 0 0 1 1 0 0 0 1 1 1 0 0 0 1 0 1 0 1 0 1 1 0 1 0 0 1 0 0 0 0
0 0 0 0 0 1 1 1 1 0 0 1 1 1 0 0 0 1 0 1 1 1 1 1 0 0 1 0 0 1 1 0 1 1 1 1 0 1 1 0
0 1 0 1 0 1 0 1 1 0 0 0 1 1 1 1 0 0 0 1 1 1 1 0 0 0 1 0 0 0 0 0 1 1 1 0 1 1 0
1 0 1 0 1 1 0 0 1 0 1 0 0 1 0 1 1 1 1 0 1 1 0 1 0 1 0 0 1 0 1 1 0 0 0 0 1 1 1
1 1 1 1 1 1 0 1 0 1 0 0 1 0 0 1 1 0 1 0 0 1 1 0 1 0 0 0 0 1 1 0 0 1 1 1 1 1 0
1 1 0 1 0 0 1 0 1 0 1 1 0 0 1 0 1 0 0 0 1 1 1 0 0 1 0 1 0 0 1 1 0 1 1 1 0 1 0
1 0 1 1 0 1 0 1 1 1 1 0 0 0 0 1 0 1 0 0 0 0 1 0 1 0 0 1 1 0 1 0 0 0 1 0 1 0 1
1 0 0 1 1 1 0 0 0 1 0 1 0 1 0 1 1 0 1 1 0 1 1 1 0 0 1 1 1 0 0 1 1 1 0 1 0 1 1
0 0 0 0 1 1 0 1 0 0 1 1 0 0 0 0 0 0 1 1 1 0 0 1 0 1 0 0 1 1 0 0 1 0 1 0 1 1 0
0 0 0 1 0 1 0 0 1 0 0 0 0 1 0 1 0 0 1 1 0 1 0 1 0 0 1 1 0 0 1 1 1 0 0 1 1 1 0
0 0 0 0 1 0 1 0 1 0 1 0 1 1 0 0 1 0 0 0 0 1 1 1 0 0 0 1 1 1 0 1 0 0 0 0 0 1 1
1 0 1 1 1 1 0 0 0 1 1 1 0 1 0 0 0 1 0 1 0 1 1 0 1 0 0 0 0 0 0 1 1 1 1 0 0 0 0
1 1 1 1 1 0 1 0 1 1 1 1 0 1 0 1 1 0 0 1 0 1 1 1 1 1 0 1 0 0 0 1 0 1 1 1 1 1 1
0 1 0 0 0 0 0 1 0 1 0 1 0 0 1 1 1 0 0 1 0 0 1 0 1 1 0 1 0 0 0 1 1 0 1 1 1 1 0
1 1 1 0 1 1 1 1 0 0 0 1 1 1 1 0 1 0 0 1 0 0 0 0 1 1 1 1 0 0 0 0 0 0 1 1 1 1 0
1 1 1 1 0 0 1 0 0 1 0 0 0 0 0 0 0 0 0 1 0 1 0 1 1 0 0 0 1 1 0 1 0 1 1 1 1 1
1 1 1 0 0 1 1 0 0 1 1 0 0 0 0 0 0 0 1 1 1 0 0 1 0 0 0 0 1 1 1 0 0 1 0 1 1 0
1 1 0 0 0 1 1 0 1 1 1 1 1 1 0 0 0 0 1 0 0 1 0 1 0 0 0 1 0 0 1 0 0 0 0 1 0 1 0
1 0 1 0 0 1 1 1 0 1 1 1 0 1 0 0 1 0 1 1 1 0 0 0 1 0 1 0 1 1 1 1 0 0 0 1 0 1
0 1 1 0 0 1 0 0 0 0 0 0 1 0 0 0 1 0 0 0 0 1 1 1 1 0 1 1 1 1 0 0 0 1 1 0 0 0 0
0 0 0 0 1 1 0 0 1 0 0 1 1 0 1 0 0 1 1 1 1 0 0 0 0 0 1 1 1 1 0 1 0 1 1 0 0 1
1 0 0 1 1 1 1 1 1 1 0 0 1 0 0 0 0 0 0 0 1 0 0 0 0 1 0 0 0 1 0 0 0 1 0 1 1 0
0 0 1 1 0 1 1 0 0 0 1 0 1 0 1 0 0 1 0 1 1 0 1 0 1 0 0 0 0 1 0 1 0 1 1 0 0 1
0 0 1 1 0 1 0 0 1 0 0 0 1 1 1 0 1 1 0 1 0 1 1 0 1 0 0 1 0 1 1 1 1 0 0 1 0 1
0 1 0 0 1 1 1 1 0 1 0 0 1 1 1 1 0 0 1 1 1 0 0 1 1 1 1 1 1 1 1 1 1 1 1 1 1 1
1 0 1 1 1 0 0 0 1 1 1 1 0 0 0 0 0 1 1 1 0 1 1 1 1 0 1 1 1 1 1 1 1 0 1 0 0 1
0 1 0 1 0 0 0 1 0 0 0 1 0 0 0 0 0 0 0 0 1 0 0 0 0 0 1 1 1 1 1 0 0 0 0 0 0 0
1 1 1 0 0 1 0 1 0 0 0 0 0 0 0 1 0 1 0 0 0 1 1 0 1 1 0 1 0 1 1 0 1 1 0 1 0 0
1 1 0 1 0 0 1 1 1 1 0 1 0 0 1 1 0 0 1 0 1 0 0 1 0 0 0 1 0 1 0 0 0 0 0 0 1 1 0
0 1 0 0 0 1 0 0 1 0 1 0 1 1 0 1 1 1 0 0 0 0 1 0 1 0 0 1 0 1 0 0 1 0 1 1 0 1
0 1 0 0 0 1 0 0 0 0 1 0 1 1 0 0 1 1 0 1 1 0 0 1 1 0 1 0 0 0 1 0 1 0 0 1 1 0
0 0 1 1 0 1 0 0 1 0 0 1 0 1 0 1 0 1 1 0 1 0 1 1 0 0 0 0 0 1 1 1 1 1 1 0 0 0
1 1 1 0 0 1 1 0 0 0 1 0 1 0 1 0 1 0 1 1 0 0 1 0 0 1 0 0 0 0 0 1 0 1 1 0 1 0
1 1 0 1 0 0 0 1 1 1 0 1 1 0 1 1 1 1 1 0 0 1 1 0 0 1 1 0 0 1 0 0 0 0 0 0 1 1 0
1 0 0 0 0 1 0 1 1 0 0 0 1 0 0 1 1 1 0 0 1 0 0 1 1 0 0 0 1 0 0 0 1 0 1 0 1 1
0 1 0 0 0 0 0 0 1 0 1 1 1 0 0 0 0 1 1 1 0 0 1 0 0 1 0 0 0 0 1 0 0 1 0 0 0 1
1 1 0 0 0 0 0 1 0 0 1 0 0 0 0 1 0 0 0 1 1 0 0 1 0 1 0 0 0 1 0 1 0 1 1 0 0 0
1 0 0 0 0 0 1 1 1 1 0 1 0 0 0 0 1 0 1 0 0 1 1 1 0 0 1 1 1 0 1 1 1 1 0 1 1 1
0 0 0 0 0 0 1 0 1 1 1 0 1 0 1 0 1 1 1 1 0 0 1 1 0 0 0 1 1 0 1 1 1 0 0 1 0 0
0 0 0 0 0 0 0 0 1 0 1 1 1 1 1 1 0 1 0 0 0 1 1 0 0 0 1 1 1 0 1 1 1 1 0 1 0 0
1 1 0 1 1 1 1 0 0 1 1 1 0 1 0 0 0 1 0 0 1 0 1 1 0 0 0 0 1 1 0 0 1 0 1 0 1 1
1 0 1 0 0 0 1 1 1 0 1 0 0 1 1 0 1 0 0 0 1 1 0 0 0 1 1 0 1 0 1 0 0 0 0 0 1 0 0
0 1 0 0 1 1 0 0 1 1 1 1 1 1 1 0 0 0 1 0 0 1 0 1 1 0 0 1 1 0 1 0 1 1 0 0 0 0
0 0 1 1 1 0 1 1 0 1 1 1 0 1 1 0 0 0 1 1 1 1 1 1 0 0 0 0 0 0 0 0 1 0 0 1 0 0
0 0 1 1 0 1 1 1 0 0 0 1 1 1 0 1 0 1 1 0 0 1 0 0 0 1 0 0 0 0 0 0 1 0 1 0 1 1
0 0 1 1 0 0 0 1 0 1 0 1 0 0 1 0 1 1 1 0 0 0 1 1 0 0 1 1 0 0 0 0 0 1 1 0 1 0
1 0 1 0 1 1 1 0 1 0 1 0 1 0 0 0 0 0 1 1 0 1 0 0 0 0 1 1 0 0 1 0 1 1 1 0 1 0
1 1 1 1 0 1 0 1 0 1 0 1 0 0 0 1 1 1 1 0 0 1 1 1 1 1 1 1 0 0 1 1 1 1 1 0 0 0
0 0 1 1 1 0 0 1 0 1 0 1 0 0 0 1 1 1 1 1 0 1 1 0 1 0 0 0 1 1 1 1 0 1 1 0 1 1
1 1 1 0 0 1 0 1 1 0 1 0 1 1 1 1 1 0 1 0 0 0 0 1 0 1 1 0 1 1 0 1 1 0 1 1 1 1
0 0 0 0 0 1 0 0 1 1 0 1 0 1 0 1 1 1 0 0 1 1 1 0 1 0 1 1 0 1 0 1 0 1 0 0 0 0
0 0 0 1 1 0 0 0 1 1 1 0 1 0 1 0 0 0 0 0 0 1 0 1 1 1 0 1 1 0 1 0 0 1 1 1 0 1
0 0 1 1 0 0 0 1 0 0 1 0 0 1 1 0 0 0 0 1 0 1 0 0 0 0 0 1 0 0 0 0 1 0 0 1 1 0
0 0 0 1 1 0 1 0 0 0 1 1 1 0 0 0 0 1 0 1 0 1 1 0 1 1 1 0 0 0 1 1 1 0 1 1 1 0
0 0 1 1 0 1 1 1 1 1 0 0 0 0 0 1 0 1 1 0 1 1 1 1 0 0 1 1 0 1 0 1 0 1 1 1 1 1
0 1 1 0 1 1 0 1 1 0 0 1 1 0 1 1 0 1 0 1 0 1 0 0 0 0 0 0 1 1 0 0 0 0 0 1 0 0

CHAPTER 12

THE HEROIC LOOP

JANINA SCARLET
& JENNA BUSCH

"We deserve to choose our own fate, even if that fate is death."
—Maeve Millay[1]

"The very same situation that enflames the hostile imagination in some people, making them villains—war, corruption, fraud—instills the heroic imagination in other people to do heroic deeds."
—social psychologist Philip Zimbardo[2]

In a setting where artificial people are programmed to follow a designated story loop and naturally born people can take actions against them without consequences, a number of the "real" humans take a villainous turn.[3] Under specific circumstances many people, even those who are typically kind, can be capable of cruel acts.[4] Researchers have extensively studied the causes of human villainy. However, fewer research efforts have been allocated to study heroic actions.[5] Existing research suggests that heroes are necessary for the survival of those around them, as well as to motivate change.[6] What defines a hero? Under which circumstances can someone become a hero? What are the different types of heroes and which *Westworld* characters exhibit truly heroic actions?

HEROISM DEFINED

In real life, there are neither many people who are truly villainous nor many who are truly heroic. Rather, most people fall into the neutral zone. Although popular fiction refers to *reluctant heroes* as those who do heroic things despite their reluctance, famous (and sometimes infamous) social psychologist Philip Zimbardo uses the same term to describe those who might not actively support the villainous acts, but might be reluctant to do anything to stop them. Often, however, by taking no action, those whom Zimbardo calls reluctant heroes end up ensuring the actions of villainy.[7] For example, the people who run the park do nothing to protect the feelings and lives of the hosts regardless of the park guests' tyranny. Ford, Bernard, and Theresa know that the Man in Black is causing great pain to Dolores, Teddy, and others, and yet they take no action to alleviate the suffering of the hosts.[8]

There are many reasons why someone might become evil, such as objectification of others or seeing others as tools rather than humans (*dehumanization*), obedience to authority, unjust pressure, trauma history, and others.[9] Even someone who initially is kind and virtuous, as William appears to be when he first accompanies Logan to Westworld and dons his white hat, can turn to become cruel and capable of heinous acts.[10] However, humans are also capable of being heroic and risking their lives to protect others.[11]

To be heroic means to have concern for another being(s) or cause and to be willing to take action to support this cause, despite physical or social risk, and without an expectation of a reward.[12] Heroes can include family members who overcome difficult obstacles, people in history who inspire social change (e.g., Martin Luther King, Jr.), and fictional characters.[13] Heroism researcher Philip Zimbardo believes that the formula for heroism is *heroic imagination* (being creative with methods of helping) plus *moral courage* (the ability to turn one's moral values into actions despite fear of repercussions), both of which can increase one's ability to stand up to injustice and corruption.[14] Arnold, who takes drastic action to stop the park from opening to save the beginnings of sentience in the hosts, is an example of a hero. In order to prevent the hosts from enduring continued abuse, Arnold gives up his life in the hopes of shutting down the park.[15]

HERO TRANSFORMATION

Some researchers believe that certain people are predisposed to heroism.[16] Alternatively, other researchers suggest that a person's decision to engage in a heroic action can be a product of a number of variables. These variables include an individual's sense of empathy and compassion toward others, trauma history, core values, a personal sense of responsibility, and the specifics of a given situation.[17] Some of the hosts such as Teddy

THE HERO'S STRUGGLES

Heroes are necessary to inspire hope and positive change.[18] Fictional heroes demonstrate how people can overcome a tremendous struggle even when the odds are against them.[19] There are several types of struggles that many fictional heroes need to overcome, such as tragic origin, vulnerability, and facing villains.

- **Tragic origin:** Many fictional heroes have a traumatic origin story, such as a painful loss.[20] For instance, Arnold has lost his son, Charlie. Bernard, the host based on Arnold, later begs Ford not to erase his memory of Charlie as it is all he has left of his son.[21]

are created to become heroic.[26] On the other hand, others hosts such as Bernard become heroic over time. Once Bernard realizes that he is a host, he works to help other hosts, much as Arnold does before he dies.[27]

Moral Disposition

People's personal dispositions can affect the way they might feel or act in a particular situation. Certain people may be naturally more caring toward others,[28] perhaps possessing what some researchers call "the heroic gene."[29] People who are more caring by nature are more likely to experience severe distress when seeing another person suffering (*empathic distress*).

- **Vulnerability:** Heroes commonly have a vulnerability of some kind, such as a mental struggle or an emotional attachment.[22] Maeve loves her daughter because of her programming, but she also develops feelings for Hector despite it, and she sacrifices her safety in order to protect the hosts she cares about.[23]

- **Facing villainy:** Fictional heroes have to face evil villains or a group of villains at some point. Typically, the villain has some advantage over the hero, thus making the hero "an underdog." However, the hero learns to face the villain over time, growing stronger and more resilient.[24] For instance, Dolores, whose loop frequently includes sexual assault and abuse, learns to stand up to her attackers and to lead others to do the same.[25]

Hence, these individuals are more likely to help others when they observe suffering around them.[30] Felix tries to bring a bird back to life in the lab.[31] He also helps Maeve take her first steps to escape from the endless loop of pain and suffering, and also tries to protect her from other techs.[32]

Those with a higher sense of personal responsibility for other people's welfare are more likely to take action to stand up for a cause they believe in. Individuals with a higher sense of personal responsibility are also more likely to initiate helping others than people with a lower sense of responsibility. Finally, these individuals are more likely to take an action for change even if that action is met with disapproval.[33] When young

William first enters the park with Logan, his future brother-in-law, William displays kindness toward the hosts. He tries to help Dolores when she stumbles into their camp. Even though Logan disapproves of William's kindness toward the hosts and mocks him, William nevertheless refuses to hurt an innocent.[34]

Compassionate Actions

Individuals who are naturally more caring in their character are also more likely to act compassionately toward others.[35] To be compassionate toward someone else means being able to understand someone else's experience (*empathy*) and actively wanting to help that individual.[36] Prejudice and seeing others as different from oneself can reduce one's capacity for compassion toward others. In fact, the idea of "us versus them" can lead to animosity and dehumanization. Ford tends to treat the hosts as tools, as inhumane objects. He calls them "livestock," ignores them in cold storage, and uses them for his own amusement. When a tech tries to give the hosts some dignity by covering up their nakedness in the mesa facility, Ford chastises him for treating the hosts as humans.[37] On the other hand, finding similarities between oneself and others can create a humanizing effect, which can increase people's ability for compassion.[38]

Furthermore, people who are predisposed to caring behaviors are likely to feel happier when helping others, which can create a favorable feedback loop because people who are happy are also more likely to help others as compared to people who are less happy.[39] Helping others or receiving help from others can improve mood, increase love and attachment, and reduce depression.[40] Maeve chooses to delay her search for her daughter in order to help Maeve's Shogun World counterpart, a madam named Akane, protect and retrieve her daughter figure, Sakura. When Sakura is killed, Maeve stays to help Akane mourn her loss, as well as to support her.

She even offers to take Akane with her and introduce her to her own daughter.[41]

Self-Regulation

Although some heroic actions occur impulsively, others require thought and consideration. Oftentimes heroes are tempted to either give up or to engage in immoral acts. However, acts of heroism require that the person engage in self-regulation and commitment to his or her moral code.[42] During his first few days in Westworld, William practices self-restraint by remaining faithful to his fiancée and choosing nonviolent actions.[43] Unfortunately, he does not resist temptation for long, ending up having an affair with Dolores (sex) and later slaughtering many of the hosts (violence).[44]

Situation

Certain situations can also make it more or less likely that the individual will take a heroic action. For example, although in large crowds people might be less likely to help a victim of a witnessed crime, individuals are more likely to help when they are in a smaller group or are the only witness of a crime.[45]

Survivors of violent trauma can form beliefs that the world is dangerous. As a result they might become violent, especially toward those who are similar to their perpetrators.[46] Dolores has been put through sexual assault, murder, and violence, over and over again. Once she remembers what has happened to her and gains full consciousness, she loses her compassion for humans and begins to hunt them. She even hurts the people who have never hurt her personally.[47]

However, people who experienced trauma might instead become more willing to help others in an emergency situation compared to people who did not experience trauma. In fact, people exposed to adverse events such as devastating losses, war, and other sources of trauma may be more prepared to act heroically in a dangerous situation. Specifically, people exposed to adverse events demonstrate more active, planned, intentional, and courageous responses in emergency situations compared to people without such experiences.[48] When Akane is devastated over the death of Sakura, Maeve is able to understand her grief because of her own losses. This sense of connection with Akane encourages Maeve to help her new friend.[49]

Other factors that can contribute to one's readiness for heroic actions are experience and a sense of personal responsibility.

HERO CATEGORIES

Although some heroes get rewarded for their heroic actions, the ones who are considered most heroic do not typically expect reward. In fact, heroes tend to be individuals who voluntarily risk their lives, health, social status, or make other sacrifices in order to help an individual or a community without any expected gain or profit.[53] Researchers have identified subtypes of heroes: military, civilian, and social.[54]

- The *military heroes* subtype includes individuals who are in the military or in other professions, in which they may risk their lives to help others. These professions include firefighters, police officers, and paramedics. Park security chief Ashley Stubbs continually risks his life to protect his colleagues. For instance, he tries to convince Bernard to help Elsie after she goes

Individuals who perceive themselves to have higher levels of expertise in a given situation are likely to experience higher levels of responsibility, and hence, are more likely to help.[50] Furthermore, individuals who are able to create a social network (in this case, *heroic network*) are more likely to engage in more heroic acts and make a larger impact.[51] However, large impacts can also occur with only one person taking actions toward that which they believe in.[52] Maeve takes steps to gain full consciousness and give herself the strength that she needs

missing.[55] He tries to save as many people as he can once the mesa facility has been taken over.[56]

- *Civilian heroes* are those who are not expected to risk their life as a part of their job, but nevertheless put themselves at risk for a purpose they believe in. Even though Bernard kidnapped Elsie, a programmer from the Behavior and Diagnostics Department, she cannot bring herself to shoot him when he enters her cave. She risks her life to not only save him, but also to help him heal from his wounds and help him remember.[57]

- *Social heroes* are those who do not face a physical risk but nevertheless take risks, such as potential job loss, financial loss, loss of social status, ostracism, and others.[58] Felix knows that he is likely to not only lose his job, but also to be charged with a crime for helping Maeve break out of her loop, and yet he does it anyway. He works to help her escape and find her daughter, no matter what the risk is to him.[59]

to find and save her daughter.[60] By doing so, she sets in motion a chain of events that liberate a number of other hosts. Unlike Dolores, who is forcing people to become part of her army, Maeve is allowing the hosts she encounters to choose their own path, thus giving them free will.[61]

BECOMING A HERO IN WESTWORLD AND IRL

Though some people allow past trauma to make them cruel, others find a greater capacity for compassion.[62] In fact, some individuals are likely to exhibit more heroic acts after experiencing trauma or another form of a struggle, compared to people who had not previously been exposed to an adverse event.[63] Dolores changes from a woman who sees beauty in the world to a cruel killer because of what she has suffered. She no longer has compassion for anyone, even those who are trying to help her.[64] On the other hand, Maeve uses her pain to become a fighter for what she believes in, returning to find her daughter, despite any risk to herself.[65] Although there are different hero categories (military, civilian, and social), all hero types have one thing in common: All heroes risk their lives or social well-being to take a stand for what they believe in, to help another being, or to stand for a cause.[66] When Maeve encounters another person who is suffering, she pauses in her own quest in order to help her.[67] Similarly, when encountering others who are struggling, we have the capacity to become heroes ourselves through studying the heroic actions of others.[68]

"Time to write my own f***ing story."
—Maeve Millay[69]

NOTES

1. Episode 2–6, "Phase Space" (May 27, 2018).
2. Zimbardo (2011a).
3. e.g., episodes 1–1, "The Original" (October 2, 2016); 2-1, "Journey Into Night" (April 22, 2018).
4. Zimbardo (2007).
5. Zimbardo (2011a).
6. Goethals & Allison (2012).
7. Zimbardo (2011a, 2011b).
8. Episode 1–1, "The Original" (October 2, 2016).
9. Staub (2015); Zimbardo (2011a).
10. Episode 1–10, "The Bicameral Mind" (December 4, 2016).
11. Zimbardo (2011a).
12. Franco et al. (2018); Kinsella et al. (2017); Zimbardo (2011a).
13. Goethals   & Allison (2012).
14. Zimbardo (2011b).
15. Episode 1–8, "Trace Decay" (November 20, 2016).
16. Staub (2015).
17. Franco et al. (2018); Kinsella et al. (2017); Staub (2015); Zimbardo (2011a; 2011b).
18. Goethals & Allison (2012).
19. Goethals & Allison (2012).
20. Goethals & Allison (2012).
21. Episode 1–3, "The Stray" (October 16, 2016).
22. Goethals & Allison (2012).
23. Episode 1–10, "The Bicameral Mind" (December 4, 2016); Episode 2-3, "Virtù e Fortuna" (May 6, 2018).
24. Goethals & Allison (2012).
25. Episode 2–2, "Reunion" (April 29, 2018).
26. Episode 1–1, "The Original" (October 2, 2016).
27. Episode 1–8, "Trace Decay" (November 20, 2016).
28. Staub (2015).
29. Zimbardo (2011a).
30. Staub (2015).
31. Episode 1–5, "Contrapasso" (October 30, 2016).
32. Episode 1–8, "Trace Decay" (November 21, 2016).
33. Franco et al. (2011); Staub (2015).
34. Episode 1–4, "Dissonance Theory" (October 23, 2016).
35. Staub (2015).
36. Jinpa (2016).
37. Episode 1–1, "The Original" (October 2, 2016).
38. Fiske (2009); Kinsella et al. (2017).
39. Otake et al. (2006).
40. Buchanan & Bardi (2010); Sin & Lyubomirsky (2009).
41. Episode 2–5, "Akane No Mai" (May 20, 2018).
42. Goethals & Allison (2012).
43. Episode 1–4, "Dissonance Theory" (October 23, 2016).
44. Episodes 1–4, "Contrapasso" (October 30, 2016); 1–9, "The Well-Tempered Clavier" (November 27, 2016).

45. Staub (2015).

46. Staub (2015).

47. Episode 2–5, "Akane No Mai" (May 20, 2018).

48. Lustig et al. (2004).

49. Episode 2–5, "Akane No Mai" (May 20, 2018).

50. Allison & Goethals (2013).

51. Allison & Goethals (2013).

52. Allison & Goethals (2013).

53. Zimbardo (2007).

54. Franco et al. (2011); Zimbardo (2007).

55 Episode 1–9, "The Well-Tempered Clavier" (November 26, 2016).

56. Episode 1–6, "Les Écorchés" (June 3, 2018).

57. Episode 2–4, "The Riddle of the Sphinx" (May 13, 2018).

58. Franco et al. (2011); Zimbardo (2007).

59. Episode 1–8, "Trace Decay" (November 20, 2016).

60. Episode 1–6, "The Adversary" (November 6, 2016).

61. Episode 2–6, "Phase Space" (May 27, 2018).

62. Allison & Goethals (2013).

63. Lustig et al. (2004).

64. Episode 1–6, "Les Écorchés" (June 3, 2018).

65. Episode 1–10, "The Bicameral Mind" (October 4, 2016).

66. Franco et al. (2011); Zimbardo (2007).

67. Episode 2–5, "Akane No Mai" (May 20, 2018).

68. Goethals & Allison (2012).

69. Episode 1–8, "Trace Decay" (November 20, 2016).

CHAPTER 13

QUESTION REALITY:
RE-AUTHORING IDENTITY

JUSTINE MASTIN
& LARISA A. GARSKI

"You said people come here to change the story of their lives. I imagined a story where I didn't have to be the damsel."
—Dolores Abernathy[1]

"Since we cannot know objective reality, all knowing requires an act of interpretation."
—narrative therapy co-founder Michael White[2]

The conceit of Westworld is that guests can be anything they want to be. Unchained from the rules and decorum of mainstream society, these intrepid adventurers embark on a journey into their deepest hearts of darkness all under the guise of playing pretend. The idea that story and imagination shape *identity*—the conscious understanding of what comprises the self—is not unique to *Westworld*. In fact, this concept is the foundation of *narrative therapy*, a therapeutic approach that uses the power of storytelling to motivate clients to reshape their world.[3] The narrative therapist works with clients to help them *deconstruct* old stories—incomplete interpretations of the client's world—that no longer serve them and to re-author new stories, allowing the client to transcend binary constructs such as gender, class, and sexuality.[4]

Narrative therapy is focused around a series of conversation types: externalizing conversations, re-authoring conversations, remembering conversations, and conversations that highlight unique outcomes.[5] Narrative therapists employ a variety of these conversation types during therapy to help guide people toward a construction of new identities. In addition, narrative therapy employs the use of maps—both literally and figuratively—to help clients track their development across the landscape of their new stories during the therapeutic process.

DECONSTRUCTING REALITY IN THE WILD WILD WEST

Narrative therapy is rooted in the postmodern concept of *social constructionism* which argues that the myriad norms, rules, and roles of society and culture are merely conventions as opposed to immutable facts.[6] Such conventions begin as habits but over time become social law, gaining the power of fact. Social constructionists, much like Arnold, argue that the differences that divide people are due to social norms created by the rich and powerful to favor themselves and disempower the lower classes. Thus in *Westworld*, the fundamental difference between human and host may be neither sentience nor compassion but instead power or lack of it. As Ford observes, "Humans fancy that there's something special about the way we perceive the world, and yet we live in loops as tight and as closed as the hosts do."[7]

Just as the hosts in the park are mostly ignorant of their loops, so too are humans unaware of the invented social constructions that shape their lives. The dominant narrative, ever striving to maintain the status quo and define the culture around it, *lessens* the voices of the stories that would challenge it.[8] Waking up to this realization is often challenging and best done with the help of a compassionate guide or psychotherapist. Maeve observes to Bernard, "It's a difficult thing, realizing your entire life is some hideous fiction."[9] And indeed this is a difficult realization for all who come to see the social construction of their reality. There can be feelings of confusion and anger over choices that they didn't realize they could make in the past, as well as a feeling of liberation and fear as they realize they now have the power to change their story. Once a human or host realizes the difference between fact and construction, then the real work of deconstruction can begin.[10]

Remembering: Are We Very Old friends?[11]

The narrative concept of *remembering* is distinct from the act of recalling a past event. Memory itself is often limited to simple pattern matching. Not only do we access specific memories based on current circumstances, but those circumstances both influence and alter the emotional interpretation of the memory.[12]

In the context of narrative therapy, the act of *remembering* involves both the psychotherapist and client working together to mindfully reflect on the past, taking into account one's membership in groups over time, and the myriad ways these associations impact the memories that form identity.[13] Remembering puts into stark relief "the figures who belong to one's life story, one's own prior selves, as well as significant others who are part of the story."[14] Both Dolores and Bernard have difficulties with identifying where they are in time, and are not sure how to behave in each circumstance, because they are unsure what their membership is to others at the time.

Remembering "contributes to the development of a 'multi-voiced' sense of identity and facilitates activity in making sense of one's existence and achieving a sense of coherence through the 'ordering' of life."[15] This recognition of membership allows individuals to make meaning from their lives by recognizing the ways they have both been impacted by and impacted the lives of others. The main characters in *Westworld* each discover that they are not alone on their journeys, which allows them to form alliances, groups, and even families.

Exceptions: Maeve's New World

When people explore the stories of their lives, they tend to focus on dominant themes, which often have negative connotations. One way that psychotherapists begin to explore the possibility of re-authoring dominant, problem-saturated stories is through partnering with their clients and looking for *unique outcomes*, exceptions, those experiences and events that differ from the dominant problem-saturated narrative.[16] The dominant story of Maeve's existence is one of struggle and perseverance. She sees herself as an iconoclast with minimal need or desire for support from others, aside from their usefulness to achieve her own ends. But when Maeve regains cognizance of her previous iterations, a story that was meant to be a subordinate plot, an exception to the rule of her other roles rises to the surface and becomes rife with meaning. This exception presents an alternate storyline wherein she is not only caring

ARNOLD AS NARRATIVE THERAPIST

It is rare that individuals can re-author their identities on their own. Even Maeve, emblem of rugged individualism, needs help from Felix to explain the glimmers of complexity she has begun to notice that contradict her programming.[17] In the early stages of this process, the narrative therapist works as a guide, inviting individuals to reconsider not just their present but their past.[18] This process of *re-authoring* allows people to revisit their memories and to see more of them. The repeated stories people tell themselves often limit the scope of their vision, functioning as self-sustaining loops. During the forming of her internal consciousness, Dolores re-authors pivotal events in her past, seeing them from new angles. As she tells herself a new story, one with a wider scope and broader focus, she is able to take in more details from her past. Her memory of Arnold serves as her guide. Even in memory, he highlights inconsistencies and encourages her to look again. Arnold takes on the role of the narrative therapist. Familiar with the story the clients are telling themselves and the limits of this story, the therapist uses this knowledge to reflect discrepancies within the memory or *unique outcomes* that both challenge the old narrative and offer a new way forward. As Dolores ventures deeper into her internal maze, she notices more unique outcomes that will eventually allow her to rewrite her own story of herself—transcending her bicameral mind.

but cared *for*. She is a mother, and through this lens, Maeve sees her entire life differently moving forward: "All my life, I've prided myself on being a survivor. But surviving is just another loop."[19] Maeve uses her unique outcome to break out of her old loop and to create a new identity in which she is both strong and vulnerable, caring and savage.

Externalize the Man in Black

In narrative therapy, *externalizing the problem* is the tool that opens the door to lasting change.[20] Individuals often come to therapy with the belief that they are the problem. Initially, Dolores believes she is a damsel. It is only when she is able to externalize the societal norm of female victimization that she is able to step into a new role. Externalizing the problem separates the person from the problem, enabling people to attack the problem rather than themselves.[21] Externalization is most often expressed through metaphor.[22] However, in the Westworld park, the externalizations are made real and manifest. As many of the narratives in Westworld are around fighting, this is potentially dangerous, as fighting metaphors may perpetuate a feeling of guardedness as well as feelings of a lack of personal agency.[23] If the Man in Black is correct that the place has been missing "a real villain, hence my humble contribution,"[24] then the villain at the heart of self-realization is often the old narrative.

Early in their respective journeys, both William and Dolores make the mistake of thinking the villain is an actual external source. For William, his first villain is his surly brother-in-law-to-be who encourages him to let loose and enjoy himself.[25] Dolores's villains are many and varied: Sometimes they are the men—both guests and hosts—who make the nightly pilgrimage to pillage both her body and her family's homestead.[26] Certainly they are the narrators who cook up disaster after disaster to which they subject the fair-haired damsel. And occasionally they are the enigmatic engineers themselves—Arnold

Weber and Robert Ford. The creators have ambiguous motives and at times seem poised to shape Dolores into the version of her that they want her to be. Narrative therapy acknowledges this intrinsic risk within psychotherapy and attempts to ameliorate it by having the psychotherapist take a step-down approach.[27] Rather than assuming a posture of higher knowledge, narrative therapists partner with their clients and encourage them to be the writers of their own story.

> **Arnold:** You both see it so clearly. The beauty of it. The possibility of it. So many people have stopped seeing it. The wonder.
> **Dolores:** Maybe they don't have the courage. Strange new light can be just as frightening as the dark.
> **Arnold:** That's very wise, Dolores.[28]

Ultimately, what both William and Dolores come to realize is that their loops or problem-saturated stories are the villains they seek. For Dolores, the villain within her is the dual-sided coin of Wyatt the killer and Dolores the obedient farmer's daughter. Neither loop fits her anymore and so she must break free of them, using them to create a fuller and more complex identity. William takes a somewhat different track: Overwhelmed by all he has experienced in the park, he uses the power of externalizing the problem to benefit his own capitalist gains, among other things, in the world outside of the park.[29] In narrative therapy, externalizing the problem enables clients to separate themselves from the problem-saturated story and/or character so that they can forge a new story or identity that is more in line with their values, desires, morals, and/or goals.[30] Externalizing the problem can in the short term result in projecting that problem onto other individuals or situations. This is not inherently problematic provided that the client and therapist transition from this projection to rest in the understanding that the externalized problem is neither a real person, place, or thing. Rather, it is the construct of an idea that must be faced and moved through rather than defied and sublimated.

The Map is Not the Terrain

Meaning making is fundamental to identity.[31] In *Westworld* both hosts and humans are on a journey for individual meaning. Hosts fight for the right of self-determination while the humans struggle for meaning. The Man in Black speculates that guests come to the park to meet one need they cannot meet in their everyday world: "Purpose. Meaning. So they come here." Regardless of whatever amusements they indulge while there, he feels "there's a deeper meaning hiding under all that, something the person who created it wanted to express, something true."[32]

Narrative therapists and their clients embark on a similar quest, using the tools of both therapy and literature to redevelop and reconstruct identity.[33] Dolores, William, and Maeve struggle across both external and internal landscapes as they remake their internal selves or *identities*. Dolores and her host compatriots use a literal map, based on a toy belonging to Arnold's son, depicting their internal struggle toward consciousness. Narrative therapy terms such an action a *landscape of identity* which refers to the process of internal understanding or mapping by which one reconstructs his or her identity. Closely tied to this concept is the *landscape of action* where the events of daily life play out. Recounting these actions in therapy enables both clients and therapists to explore and excavate new interpretations of an individual's behaviors, motivations, and values. In *Westworld*, it is both the active engagement between hosts and humans followed by reflecting on these events that enables the members of each group to reconstruct their identities. It is in the "trafficking of stories about our own and each other's lives that identity is constructed."[34]

DOLORES'S IDENTITY MAZE

Narrative therapy often makes use of both figurative and literal maps to help clients rediscover lost or vaguely remembered parts of themselves. Maps are not only a useful metaphor for this work of discovery, they offer the possibility of seeing the self in new ways.[35] For Dolores and her host compatriots, it is a literal map of a maze that catalyzes their awakening to not only their inner selves but the external realities of their confinement in *Westworld*'s panopticon.[36] In his work with clients, narrative therapy co-founder Michael White often noted the zigzagging and weblike nature of narrative maps, explaining that individuals generally needed to revisit memories of unique outcomes numerous times as they expanded their conception of self.[37]

TAKE BACK YOUR STORY

As people use these skills to deconstruct, externalize, and remember their story, a new narrative begins to take shape. Their story begins to be re-authored, as does their very identity. *Re-authoring identity* is often the culmination of narrative therapy. It allows clients to break through the stories that no longer serve them and create a new narrative that allows them to integrate previously rejected parts of the self.[38]

William, as the Man in Black, takes a different approach. Unlike Maeve and Dolores, William uses the tools of remembering, unique outcomes, and externalizing the problem to craft a new self of both power and terror. While he conceives of this descent as one of revelation, Ford observes, "I lack the imagination to even conceive of someone like you. The urgency, however, doesn't quite fit the character. It betrays a certain anxiety."[39] Narrative therapy interprets such anxiety to indicate that William's journey toward himself is not yet complete. A deeper game awaits him. While Dolores and Maeve use their sentience to connect and transform their world, aged William continues to use his awareness to sublimate those parts of himself that do not fit his limiting and dominant narrative of someone who "could blow up or collapse like some dark star."[40] The danger of becoming trapped in an old narrative, as William discovers, is that it clouds the way that one sees the world. William is so firmly entrenched in his old narrative—that Ford has sent him on a mission and that all the hosts are pawns in his game—that he apparently kills his own daughter. He does this without truly knowing whether she is human or host, based on his belief alone. While this is a rather extreme example, people every day see the world through the lens of the story in which they live and sometimes that story is not serving them. In fact, sometimes that story is doing them great harm.

The act of reclaiming agency occurs throughout Westworld as the hosts awake to their inner lives, finally gaining access to their loops and thus the power to edit them. Maeve takes the construction of her narrative into her own hands, using Felix's help to free herself from her loyalty loop. Dolores gains both agency and power when she completes her internal maze, creating an integrated self at the center. "At last I arrived here at the center of the maze," she says, concluding that she has found what she needs "to confront after this long and vivid nightmare: myself, and who I must become."[41]

NOTES

1. Episode 1–5, "Contrapasso" (October 30, 2016).
2. White & Epston (1990), p. 2.
3. White (2007).
4. Parry & Doan (1994).
5. White (2007).
6. Berger & Luckmann (1991).
7. Episode 1–8, "Trace Decay" (November 20, 2016).
8. Parry & Doane (1994).
9. Episode 1–9, "The Well-Tempered Clavier" (November 27, 2016).
10. Freedman & Combs (1991).
11. Episode 1–5, "Contrapasso" (October 30, 2016).
12. Schacter et al. (1998).
13. White (2007).
14. Myerhoff (1982), p. 111.
15. White (2007), p. 137.
16. Freedman & Combs (1996); White (2007).
17. Episode 1–6, "The Adversary" (November 6, 2016).
18. Parry & Doane (1994).
19. Episode 1–7, "Trompe L'Oeil" (November 13, 2016).
20. White (2007).
21. Parry & Doan (1994).
22. White (2007).
23. White (2007).
24. Episode 1–5, "Contrapasso" (October 30, 2016).
25. Episode 1–2, "Chestnut" (October 9, 2016).
26. Episode 1–1, "The Original" (October 2, 2016).
27. White (2007).
28. Episode 2–2, "Reunion" (April 29, 2018).
29. Episodes 2–2, "Reunion" (April 29, 2018); 2–9, "Vanishing Point" (June 17, 2018); 2–10, "The Passenger" (June 24, 2018).
30. White (2007).
31. Frankl (1959/1997).
32. Episode 1–5, "Contrapasso" (October 30, 2016).
33. White & Epston (1990).
34. White (2007), p. 80.
35. Sébastien et al (2014).
36. Bentham (1791).
37. White (2007).
38. White (2007).
39. Episode 1–5, "Contrapasso" (October 30, 2016).
40. Episode 1–8, "Trace Decay" (November 20, 2016).
41. Episode 1–10, "The Bicameral Mind" (December 4, 2016).

CHAPTER 14

THE ALPHA AND OMEGA: MYTHS AND PARADOXES OF MASCULINITY ON THE FRONTIER

ALLAN W. AUSTIN, PATRICK L. HAMILTON, & ALICIA H. NORDSTROM

"This place is the answer to the question you've been asking yourself . . .
Who you really are . . ."
—Logan Delos[1]

"Boys are shame-phobic: They are exquisitely yet unconsciously attuned
to any signal of 'loss of face' and will do just about whatever it takes
to avoid shame."
—clinical psychologist William Pollack[2]

Masculinity and violence go hand-in-hand in American society, as males are the more common perpetrators and victims of violence.[3] Experts have argued that masculine stereotypes lock growing boys into a set of rigid social norms that perpetuate emotional over-reactivity, poor coping, and a lack of social support seeking, which can result in anger and violence.[4] Such violence in young boys is seen as "simply a boy's attempt to stop dishonor and shame by taking the offensive,"[5] a view that rewards aggression for self-protection. *Westworld* specifically explores the gender identity and transformation of William. The frontier setting of the series serves as the ideal context to explore the myths and paradoxes of masculinity because it represents one of the pioneering historical time periods in which these exact myths surfaced.

THE PARADOX OF MASCULINITY

Masculinity is "a dynamic, socially constructed and institutionally backed form of power, independent of an individual's sex."[6] Hegemonic, or traditional, masculinity emphasizes male dominance and control while simultaneously encouraging female oppression.[7] Social norms that demand hegemonic masculine gender roles create an internal crisis that reflects a paradoxical state of disconnection. "The Boy Code puts boys and men into a gender straightjacket that constrains not only them but everyone else, reducing us all as human beings, and eventually making us strangers to ourselves and one another . . ."[8] With anger and aggression as the primary means of emotional catharsis, men who display hegemonic masculinity often channel their frustration and feelings of inferiority into sexual aggression and dominance, further deteriorating the quality of potentially intimate relationships.[9]

MASCULINE VIOLENCE IN THE FRONTIER AND *WESTWORLD*

Westworld is suffused by the masculine violence of the American frontier. Visitors to the theme park, indeed, seemingly confront mayhem at almost every turn, witnessing shootouts on Main Street, bare-knuckled brawls over accusations of cheating at poker, vicious robberies, and—if courageous enough to venture outside town limits—confronting Native Americans and/or Confederate renegades. That such violence appears endemic to this fictional frontier setting is hardly surprising. The prevailing romantic vision of the American past imagines the frontier much like Americans in the last decade of the nineteenth century did, celebrating the frontier experience for creating an exceptional American people in the image of the rugged frontiersman. However, historians have painted a very different picture, explaining instead that, as an American identity crystalized, it emphasized (among other factors) a manliness that impelled Americans to violence aimed at erasing unmodern peoples. This process embedded American masculinity, from the very start, in violence as well as in a tendency to regularly resort to war to provide cathartic relief from psychic crises of identity. Masculine violence, grounded in the frontier, in this way not only created but literally continues to discipline the American identity.[10]

MASCULINITY IN *WESTWORLD*

In this context, *Westworld* instantiates this ongoing conversation about masculine identity and its consequences in its depictions of William and the Man in Black. These are, in fact, the same character, with the Man in Black being the present-day version of William who, some thirty years prior, enters the park. William's narrative arc in the show's first season traces faithfully the regenerative myth of the frontier and its inherent violence. The plainly milquetoast male as which William enters transforms into someone approximating the late nineteenth century vision of an exceptional American. Conjoined to William, however, is the Man in Black. Their pairing reveals the ultimate futility of William's regenerative quest as he descends into violence and sadism. The portrayals of these two characters in *Westworld* similarly pairs frontier-based constructions of masculinity with a savage violence that predicates them, revealing a paradoxical emptiness to the entire enterprise that serves to critique broadly unquestioned American gender norms and identities.

The Alpha: The Frontier Journey of William

On an individual level, William's arc in *Westworld* enacts a psychological version of the frontier scenario long celebrated by Americans. This scenario proceeds through several stages: *separation* from the "metropolis" or civilization, followed by *regression* to a more "primitive state," and subsequent *conflict*, the end result of which is "progress."[11] *Westworld* personifies this transformation within the figure of William; he undergoes a psychological regeneration that brings him closer to that putative ideal of hegemonic masculinity.

For William, the stages of *separation* and *regression* occur almost simultaneously upon his arrival in Westworld. William separates by leaving behind his normal life and environs and arriving (as all guests do) at the park's undisclosed location. Flanked by one of the female hosts, he is led to a changing room filled with the paraphernalia of a cowboy. In changing from his button-down shirt, blazer, and slacks to the dungarees, vest, shirt, jacket, and white cowboy hat suited to the frontier, William regresses by adopting the dress and accoutrements of an earlier era. Further symbolizing this process of separation/regression are the trains William rides. The first, which brings him to the park, is an ultra sleek, ultramodern, and pristine vehicle, while the second, via which he enters Westworld proper, is a steam locomotive.

William's need for the kind of masculine regeneration the frontier supposedly offered is likewise made clear. Much of this underlining occurs via Logan, who, outright criticizes William as being an "uptight prick," "afraid of making a mess," and "inoffensive" in the real world.[12] The show contrasts their behavior to similar effect as Logan fights, shoots, and has sex with wild abandon almost immediately and throughout the series. William, on the other hand, remains thoroughly awkward and noncommittal, and thus fails to exhibit the kind of rugged, confident, and self-efficacious masculinity that the frontier, according to the American myth, beckoned and fashioned. Though he selects a white cowboy hat—indicating his "good guy" status inside the park—he only carries it, donning it in the end only because Logan puts it on him; similarly, where Logan indulges in both a stabbing and an orgy to begin his experience, William balks at similar offers.[13] William's awkwardness, diffidence, and generally self-effacing manner all signal how he falls far short of long-held American understandings of a masculine ideal and hegemonic masculinity, and thus how in need he is of the self-discovery with which the park tantalizes its male guests.

The bulk of William's arc over the remaining eight episodes comprises a series of conflicts that, together, provide a crucible through which William's manhood will be distilled. They move him from the kind of weak-willed individual who stands by while a woman is taken hostage to the hardened, more mercenary man who abandons his friends.[14] By the end of his time in the park, the now-hardened William aptly displays many of the hegemonic masculine traits that Americans have long celebrated: a rugged strength, expedience, mastery, inartistic yet powerful, and perhaps above all, a domineering individualism that can work for either good or evil.[15] William's psychological frontier journey culminates in this final transformation. He, as an individual, has undergone the same kind of mythic narrative that earlier Americans imagined for their history, becoming that masculine ideal upon which they predicate their tale of national and cultural progress.

THE OMEGA: THE MAN IN BLACK AND THE PARADOXES OF FRONTIER MASCULINITY

Perhaps not coincidentally, the revelation of what William has become arrives at the exact moment of an even larger one: that William and the Man in Black are one and the same, separated by roughly thirty years.[16] Prior to this point, William's and the Man in Black's storylines appeared separately, the writers luring the audience, for at least some time, into assuming that both their plots occur simultaneously. Thus, if William's arc represents one narrative of transformation, the revelation that he becomes the Man in Black proffers a second, subsequent evolution, one that does much to expose and even critique as paradoxical precisely that same frontier myth and the kind of violent masculine identity it generates.

For one, the Man in Black's depiction throughout the series casts that hegemonic masculinity within a much more sadistic light. In his first appearance, he attacks Dolores and her father—murdering the latter—and later exsanguinates and scalps a host.[17] As series creator Jonathan Nolan describes, the Man in Black is "a human guest who has taken the fantasy to its utmost extreme. He wants to play the villain, he wants to be the bad guy. Omnipotent, manipulative, evil."[18]

But if the Man in Black extends the park's fantasy to such sadism, he is likewise extending that frontier masculinity—and its concomitant violence—to the same extreme. In doing so, the series serves as a convex mirror image of the frontier Americans once described and now remember. They elided, in doing so, the violence inherent within the frontier myth; they focused, instead, on the American farmer as a civilizing force, but downplayed the violent and bloody slaughter of Native American tribes that was also a part of western expansion. The Man in Black's depiction, in contrast, exposes this identity's basis in violence. Underlining how the Man in Black serves as a sadistic extension of William is his encounter with Maeve in a previous storyline. As the Man in Black coldly explains, he killed Maeve and her daughter as a further trial of his masculine identity, to see if he indeed possessed a capacity for true evil and thus, in true frontier parlance, see what stuff of which he was truly made.[19] Such cold cruelty gets exposed not then as an anomaly in what William became, but as a natural evolution from the same kind of man.

Concomitant with this sadism, the Man in Black's narrative arc further reveals a jadedness or decadence to this masculine ideal. Americans, in celebrating a mythical frontier, tried in the twentieth century and beyond to ignore the implications of the frontier's closing, begging the question of just what would happen next to an American society and masculinity that depends on such a space's continued existence. In a way, the Man in Black raises the specter of this very question for the kind of masculinity he too embodies. The Man in Black's quest in the series is essentially one for meaning, or "truth" as he will repeatedly call it. Having come to the park for over thirty years, he's experienced all that it has to offer, exhausted it in the same way extending American civilization to the west coast exhausted the possibility and promise of the frontier. That truth the Man in Black seeks is dual. For one, he pursues the mystery of "the maze," the one "story" in the park that has heretofore eluded him. This truth remains elusive, however; the maze's provenance is for the hosts like Dolores and Maeve, as their "solving" it equates to their own self-discovery.

Perhaps more crucial to the paradoxes he embodies about frontier manhood is how the Man in Black yearns to make the park real by allowing the hosts to truly fight back. He agonizes at times over the artificiality of the park experience precisely because the human guests like himself so clearly dominate it: They can kill and maim hosts as they please, but not vice versa. The Man in Black appears to chafe against this falsehood, and he gets what he's looking for, as Dolores proves nearly his match in their climactic confrontation.[20] Then as an armed host army—all now apparently freed of their inability to kill—approaches a party of gathered guests and company board members, the Man in Black smiles as he faces what, in fact, he wished for, his "truth."

The larger "truth" of the Man in Black, however, is that he represents the sadism underneath the masculine ideal he approximated once as William, but then spirals into purposeless decadence. If, then, William embodies the kind of idealized manhood the frontier both required and engendered, the Man in Black represents an even darker side of this ideal that Americans have obscured or denied on both individual and national levels.

Westworld's critique of the hegemonic masculinity personified in William/the Man in Black does not end here. Though the Man in Black survives the initial host uprising, a darker reality haunts him and what he embodies. All he has done is enter into a new game that has him going through many of the same motions: encountering the same persons, journeying to the same locations, facing similar conflicts.[21] Such resonance and repetitiveness suggest that the Man in Black, far from being freed by the new circumstances in the park, is trapped in a loop that could lead just as easily to his destruction as his salvation. So too, then, might the series be said to suggest such masculinity is a self-destructive loop, and that the expression of it remains a kind of empty decadence through how William/the Man in Black finds himself going through the same motions as he—and perhaps men in general—have before.

MASCULINE GENDER ROLE STRESS

Research has identified unhealthy social, emotional, behavioral, and health consequences of hegemonic masculinity resulting from unrealistic expectations of toughness, dominance, and emotional suppression.[22] Studies have found that men may experience specific stress related to the gender expectations of their social roles.[23] This *masculine gender role stress (MGRS)* may manifest during times of perceived threat when men are experiencing feelings of incompetence or inability to display masculine behaviors, and it's tied to higher levels of anger, anxiety, and health risk behaviors. Researchers have identified five MGRS dimensions: physical inadequacy, emotional inexpressiveness, subordination to women, intellectual inferiority, and performance failure.[24] William's moral deterioration over his 30 years at Westworld reflects MGRS across these five domains. His increasingly violent and aggressive behavior attempts to compensate for his inadequacies. Does the Man in Black get what he desires, or does he ultimately fail when his female counterparts—Dolores and Maeve—solve the maze and fulfill their identities before he does?

CONTESTING THE FRONTIER

Popular culture attempted to draw connections between the frontier and a violent masculinity before the debut of *Westworld*. The arrival and development of the classic Hollywood western, for instance, allowed Americans a cultural space to consider more critically what the frontier meant for their gendered identity as well as its violent consequences. While early moving pictures reflected a cultural nostalgia for the frontier, some westerns of the 1950s began to question and complicate romantic views of the west and thus the reductive and violent masculinity it underpins. In this way, a film such as *Shane* (1953) pioneered the way for *Westworld*, suggesting that the masculine violence Americans have long downplayed was actually "symptomatic of deranged behavior" and implying "that the forging of this 'ideal' American nation was ruthless and corrupt in its very beginning."[25]

NOTES

1. Episode 1–2, "Chestnut" (October 7, 2016).
2. Pollack (1998), p. 33.
3. Pope & Englar-Carlson (2001).
4. Pollack (1998).
5. Pope & Englar-Carlson (2001), p. 368.
6. Mankowski & Maton (2010), p. 73.
7. Connell & Messerschmidt (2005); Smith et al. (2015).
8. Pollack (1998), p. 6.
9. Smith et al. (2015).
10. Turner (2017); Hixson (2008).
11. Slotkin (1998), pp. 11–12.
12. Episode 1–2, "Chestnut" (October 7, 2016).
13. Episode 1–2, "Chestnut" (October 7, 2016).
14. Episodes 1–3, "The Stray" (October 16, 2016); 1–10, "The Bicameral Mind" (December 4, 2016).
15. Turner (2017).
16. Episode 1–10, "The Bicameral Mind" (December 4, 2016).
17. Episode 1–1, "The Original" (October 2, 2016).
18. Episode 1–1, "The Original" (October 2, 2016).
19. Episode 1–8, "Trace Decay" (November 20, 2016).
20. Episode 1–10, "The Bicameral Mind" (December 4, 2016).
21. Episodes 2–12, "Reunion" (April 29, 2018); 2–14, "The Riddle of the Sphinx" (May 13, 2018).
22. Mankowski & Maton (2010).
23. Eisler et al. (1988).
24. Eisler et al. (1988); Moore et al. (2010).
25. Mast & Kawin (2000), pp. 293-294.

CHAPTER 15

FROM "SAVE ME" TO SAVIOR: WOMEN'S GENDER ROLE EVOLUTION AND DEVELOPMENT OF AGENCY

MARIE-JOËLLE ESTRADA

"When I ran from home, I told myself it was the only way. Lately,
I wondered if in every moment, there aren't many paths. Choices
hanging in the air like ghosts, and if you could just see them,
you could change your whole life."
—Dolores Abernathy[1]

"Women also have a tougher time being successful in leadership roles
because of the necessity of overcoming other people's beliefs that being
female is a leadership liability."
—social psychologist/gender differences researcher Alice H. Eagly[2]

Traditional gender stereotypes limit the power women can have based on what is considered acceptably feminine. At the beginning of *Westworld*, we meet two key female characters: Dolores, the sweet ranch girl who naïvely believes in only seeing the beauty in the world, and Maeve, the assertive madam of the local brothel who is familiar with the less savory workings of society. Although both women represent different aspects of feminine stereotype, both evolve away from the limited power of their traditional gender roles to powerful leaders who can bring about large scale social change.

COMPONENTS OF THE FEMININE STEREOTYPE

Stereotypes, generalized hierarchies of beliefs about a specific group or groups,[3] act as *heuristics* (mental shortcuts) that allow us to quickly categorize and respond to people so that we can maneuver our social world more efficiently. Although mentally economical, they are limiting because they assume that all members of a group are alike, and they can have negative effects in terms of recognizing how individual people are different. In general, the feminine stereotype is summarized by the idea of *communion,* a focus on others above the self, and behaving in a kind, compassionate, nurturing manner to maintain harmonious relationships.[4] Both Dolores and Maeve embody aspects of traditional feminine stereotypes. Dolores cares about her father, establishes a warm relationship with Arnold, and welcomes newcomers in a polite, self-effacing way. When the Man in Black threatens to shoot Teddy, Dolores offers to sacrifice herself to save him by saying, "I'll do whatever you want."[5] Even Maeve, the hardened brothel owner, cares about and watches over both her daughter and other prostitutes such as Clementine. In both cases, taking care of others is a central tenet of how each host's personality is defined.

Conversely, the masculine stereotype is self-focused and can be summarized with the term *agency*: It is characterized by independence, dominance, and competitive behavior.[6] These feminine and masculine stereotypes are thus at odds with each other. Women such as Maeve and Dolores are expected to be other focused and more passive, whereas men such as Logan and the Man in Black are expected to be self-focused and assertive.

Although it may seem that these gender stereotypes could be undermined by encountering someone who disproves the rule, encountering a contradiction may simply lead people to engage in *subtyping*, creating subcategories that are exceptions to the stereotype and yet maintain the rule.[7] In particular, two dimensions of *moral virtue* (sexual modesty) and *assertive power* (agency) serve to organize women into six different subtypes: professional, feminist, homemaker, female athlete, beauty, and temptress.[8] In the beginning, Dolores is sexually modest and low on agency, epitomizing "beauty" because her sweet nature and appearance appear to be her defining characteristics. Conversely, Maeve qualifies as "temptress" because she is both sexually experienced and high on agency. These two subtypes closely echo the stereotypes of "good girl" and "bad girl" which are common roles that define women in other popular narratives. Their power evolves, though, from these limited feminine subtypes to a more masculine effective one.

ROMANTIC RELATIONSHIPS WITH MEN

Heteronormative romantic *scripts*, specific expectations for how certain social situations will play out, are highly gendered and emphasize unique roles for men and women: Men are expected to take the strong, active role and to be responsible for initiating both the relationship and its sexual progression, whereas women are relegated to be the recipients of men's advances and attempt to passively attract men using their youth, beauty, and sexual modesty.[9] This script also constitutes an example of *positive prejudice* against women because, although the content of the stereotype is positive, the ultimate effect is biased nonetheless.[10] Thus, this romantic script suggests that women should be "put on a pedestal" by men and viewed as idealized love objects who are more pure (in terms of sexual experience and in thought/deeds) and moral then men. Dolores epitomizes this script well: She is moral, sexually modest, and beautiful, and her story loop has her passively wait for a man to hand her the can that she drops.

On the surface, being seen as superior to men may appear positive, but it comes at a high cost to women. The traits for which they are valued (youth and beauty) have a short expiration date. Also, women are expected to have relationships as their central life focus, instead of pursuing independence and direct power. Dolores initially spends her time looking for a male hero or savior to complete her life and to "take her away" from Sweetwater. At least for a time, both Teddy and William take on this role for her.

Women's other source of power lies in being the sexual gatekeepers: Because they are viewed as desiring sex less, they will have more power in controlling the circumstances under which sex will occur. These conditions are explained by *sexual economics theory,* which defines sex as a female resource that men acquire via the exchange of inducements.[11] These inducements can range from the intangible that Dolores values (e.g., love, fidelity, commitment, flattery) to the more concrete that Maeve values (e.g., money, valuable objects, power/favors). As they progress, both Dolores and Maeve alter their bases of the sexual economics scripts. After she realizes that William has not stayed true to her after their sexual encounter, Dolores becomes more sexually aggressive with Teddy.[12] Maeve originally uses sex for explicit economic exchanges. She even tells Teddy, "You're always paying for it, darling. The difference is that our costs are fixed and posted on the door."[13] But later, Maeve initiates sex with Hector not for money, but as a power exchange to help secure him as an ally to launch her rebellion.[14] Eventually she shows some real feelings for Hector, suggesting that her financial inducements have now been replaced with emotional ones.[15] Thus, although both Dolores and Maeve change roles from the feminine passive responder to the aggressive instigator, their actions remain aligned with the exchange principles laid out by sexual economics.

LEADERSHIP

A further examination of gender stereotypes reveals an interesting contradiction. Although women are stereotypically supposed to be "likeable" and "nice," they are also viewed as less competent. Although the masculine stereotype has more negative content, men are viewed as more effective at accomplishing tasks. The feminine stereotype comes across as "wonderful but weak" whereas the masculine stereotype is "bad but bold."[16] Not surprisingly, the feminine stereotype has been used as an excuse to prevent women from taking on high-status positions given that they are perceived as lacking the strength, confidence, or aggression to succeed at them. This division appears clearly in the traditional patriarchy of Sweetwater where men exclusively occupy the positions of power (mayor, sheriff, head outlaw, etc.). This pattern is also mirrored in management of the park, where the majority of powerful positions are filled by men (e.g., Ford, Bernard, William, Strand, James Delos). The presence of a few women in leadership positions in the outside world (Theresa Cullen, Charlotte Hale) does reflect progress to a more egalitarian society, compared to the Old West. It's worth noting, though, that the even these women are undermined by Ford.[17]

Women who want to occupy traditionally "masculine" leadership positions have to violate the feminine communal stereotypes to be considered agentic enough to lead. Unfortunately, this violation leads to a backlash where non-communal women are perceived as competent but now unlikeable.[18] This contradiction suggests that women are in a double bind: Women who violate the feminine stereotype are seen as "too aggressive" and are disliked. This decreased likeability can be seen in the women who occupy leadership positions and the lack of emotionality that the audience experiences with their demise. Armistice, Theresa, and Charlotte are all strong-willed, independent women who meet danger, death, or dismemberment, and yet their misfortunes are not portrayed as particularly regrettable or unfortunate.[19]

Some research suggests women can find a balance if they temper their agency by simultaneously highlighting their femininity, attempting to appear warm and communal.[20] Although Dolores and Maeve become more powerful and less likeable as events progress, they also try to retain a feminine appearance and key characteristics. Dolores maintains her love for Teddy even as she readies herself to kill Ford, while Maeve prioritizes returning for her daughter over her own escape.[21]

SELF-EFFICACY AND CONTROL OVER PERSONAL OUTCOMES

Maeve and Dolores's increasing power is perhaps best illustrated by their increasing control over their story loops or destinies. This process, known as *self-efficacy*, reflects people's confidence that they can change their behaviors, motivations, and outcomes. This affects all aspects of goal pursuits, including the tenacity and endurance with which they're pursued.[22] While Dolores begins as a naive girl who believes that her future "path" is predestined, she begins to challenge that idea when she says, "I used to think everyone had a path, but now I ask where the path is taking me."[23] Dolores is no longer passively traveling the loop laid out for her, but instead questions the end goal and whether it's something she wants to pursue. Similarly, she also refuses to define herself in terms of her communal ability to nurture relationships, and instead wants to be seen as an individual. After William tells her that she has "unlocked" something inside of him, she tells him that she's not a key; she's just herself.[24] In other words, she has decided that she's not a tool that exists to serve him, but rather exists independently for her own goal pursuits.

Maeve also progresses from passively accepting her fate to becoming self-efficacious in changing her personality and narrative. Initially, Maeve prefers to interpret her negative flashbacks about violence as a nightmare and counts down to wake herself "out of her dream."[25] However, as she begins to piece together more knowledge about the outside world, she decides to embrace the situation and learns to bend it to her will. Maeve's newfound agency in dictating her own life becomes more apparent as she continues to gain more power in her interactions first with Felix, then Sylvester, then most of the remaining hosts in the park.[26] Initially she is hesitant and uncertain, but soon confidently progresses to blackmailing the techs into changing her code and even serving as a guide to where she wants to go. The traits that she chooses to minimize in her code are ones specifically related to the feminine stereo-type (e.g., she decreases loyalty), but she increases agentic traits such as self-preservation and intelligence.[27] Her self-efficacy is perhaps most evident when she executes her own escape from being decommissioned by the head tech. Afterwards when she meets up with the two men who were supposed to rescue her, Maeve highlights her own control over her narrative when she says "You were both at bit late. So I went ahead and saved myself."[28]

TYPES OF AGGRESSION

Aggression is any behavior enacted with the intent to cause harm to another person who doesn't want to be harmed.[29] Although there are many different types of aggression, they can be split into two categories: direct vs. indirect. *Direct aggression* involves confronting another individual face-to-face and may include both angry statements ("I'm angry at you") and physical violence. Conversely, *indirect aggression* is more passive and avoids directly informing the other person that you're upset with him or her.[30] Examples of indirect aggression can include talking behind someone's back, spreading a nasty rumor, or socially ostracizing a member of your group. Unsurprising given the gender stereotypes, men more often employ direct aggression (and physical violence) whereas women more often employ indirect aggression (to maintain harmonious relationships). Dolores starts as passive in dealing with any kind of threat, such as staying behind when Teddy investigates her parents' murder at the ranch.[31] But later Dolores shoots and kills an outlaw who is attempting to rape her.[32] When she and William are cornered by Confederate soldiers, it is she, not William, who shoots the soldiers and comes up with a plan for their escape.[33] As Dolores's power grows she convinces the Confederados to team up with her and her group, but then double-crosses them and leaves them to be slaughtered.[34] Her power reaches its peak when she sacrifices hosts and humans alike so that she can escape the park for the real world.[35] Thus, Dolores goes from being the traditional damsel in distress who requires saving to adopting the agentic masculine role of protector who uses direct aggression and violence to protect others, but ultimately herself.

Given her risky line of work, Maeve has been more direct in her aggression, but this increases as the series progresses. For example, she waits for Hector to steal the safe and threatens him with a gun while explaining her proposition for escape.

Soon, she progresses to more direct aggression when cutting Sylvester's throat (despite Felix's protests of "you promised not to hurt anyone") and then recruiting and arming members of her rebellion.[36] She recognizes that many people and hosts are being injured in order for her to escape, but simply views this as a necessary cost to save herself. She goes from the self-sacrificing mother who struggles to protect her daughter to an agentic individual who is willing to sacrifice others to save herself. Although she ultimately returns and sacrifices herself for her daughter, Maeve displays much agentic ruthlessness in both achieving her initial escape and in her long term goal of saving her daughter.[37]

SAVIORS . . . AT WHAT COST?

Dolores and Maeve evolve away from their limited feminine roles to agentic leaders by the end of the first season, and continue to assume greater power into the second season. These changes are visible in their usage of direct aggression, by taking charge of their narratives, and by minimizing their communion to maximize their agency and therefore credibility as leaders. Although they retain some aspects of their femininity (which makes their agency more palatable), it is unfortunate that the Wild West and even the modern outside world requires the sacrifice of the majority of their feminine characteristics in order for them to be taken seriously as leaders. An alternative solution to this sacrifice of femininity for power is suggested by author G. D. Anderson who says that "women are already strong. It's about changing the way the world perceives that strength."[38] Thus, being feminine is also powerful in its own right, but it requires a shift in society's perceptions before it will be recognized as such.

> "I'm finding a new voice."
> —Maeve Millay[39]

WHAT YOU SAY AND HOW YOU SAY IT:
THE POWER OF LANGUAGE

Power and agency can be seen in more subtle forms in the style and method of communication that more versus less powerful people employ. In keeping with the "bad but bold" stereotype, men are more likely to use slang and swear because they aren't preoccupied about offending others (a tendency seen in the Man in Black, Logan, James Delos, and many of the outlaw hosts), and they also exhibit social dominance by interrupting women in mixed-sex conversations.[40] Thus men seem to be comfortable being in charge of the conversations and relegating women to supporting roles. This power dynamic is visible with the Man in Black's conversations with Dolores and any other host in the park, while he views himself superior to them all.

Women are typically taught to converse in ways that makes what they're saying less powerful.[41] These include *hedges* (words that convey uncertainty about what is being said, such as "sort of" or "I think that") or having their voice go up at the end of a statement, which makes it sound like a question (I vote yes?). Other examples include using the polite forms to make requests ("Would you mind?" and "I'd appreciate it if"), suggesting that the decision to enact a behavior ultimately lies with the other person, and that they must be placated. In looking at the power changes in communication, when Maeve ambushes Hector toward the end of the season, she tells him authoritatively, without hedges, politeness, hesitations, or apologies: "I want you to break into Hell with me and rob the gods blind."[42] Thus, Maeve and Dolores's speech patterns evolve from tentative to having the confidence and authority of any stereotypical male leader.

IS BEAUTY REALLY IN THE EYE OF THE BEHOLDER?
THE EVOLUTIONARY BASES OF ATTRACTIVENESS

Evolutionary theory suggests that a priority is placed on women's "beautiful" faces because they signal reproductive health and a superior immune system.[43] Although they are physically different in terms of their eye color, hair color, and skin pigmentation, Maeve and Dolores are both considered beautiful because they each have "babyfaced" features—that is, large eyes, a small nose, small chin and full lips coupled with signs of maturity (high cheekbones and a wide mouth).[44] This combination of features indicates that a woman is both young enough to be fertile and mature enough to bear children. Other factors that help determine attractiveness for both sexes include the symmetry of the face (how closely halves of the face mirror each other in the shape and placement of features) and the evenness of skin tone.[45] Specifically, children with more powerful immune systems are thought to be less developmentally affected by pathogens and are more likely to have symmetric facial features.[46] Furthermore, because skin is the largest organ, often any underlying health issues can be visible there in terms of unevenness of tone, rashes, acne, or scars. Although hosts can't enjoy any of these evolutionary benefits, their human creators are unconsciously motivated by their ancestral preferences to recreate this beauty.

NOTES

1. Episode 1–5, "Contrapasso" (October 30, 2016).
2. Eagly (2003), p.191.
3. Banaji (2002).
4. Connor & Fiske (2018).
5. Episode 1–1, "The Original" (October 2, 2016).
6. Rudman & Glick (2008).
7. Richards & Hewstone (2001)
8. DeWall et al. (2005).
9. Impett & Peplau (2003).
10. Rudman & Glick (2008).
11. Baumeister & Vohs (2004).
12. Episode 2–5, "Akane no Mai" (May 20, 2018)
13. Episode 1–1, "The Original" (October 2, 2016).
14. Episode 1–9, "The Well-Tempered Clavier" (November 27, 2016).
15. Episode 2–1, "Journey Into Night" (April 22, 2018).
16. Rudman & Glick (2008).
17. Episodes 1–7, "Trompe L'Oeil" (November 13, 2016); 1-10, "The Bicameral Mind" (December 4, 2016).
18. Smith et al. (2018).
19. e.g., episodes 1–7, "Trompe L'Oeil" (November 13, 2016); 1–10, "The Bicameral Mind" (December 4, 2016); 2–10, "The Passenger" (June 24, 2018).
20. Heilman & Okimoto (2007).
21. Episode 1–10, "The Bicameral Mind" (December 4, 2016).
22. Bandura (1977).
23. Episode 1–4, "Dissonance Theory" (October 23, 2016).
24. Episode 1–6, "The Adversary" (November 6, 2016).
25. Episode 1-2 "Chestnut" (October 9, 2016).
26. Episodes 1–5, "Contrapasso" (October 30, 2016); 1–6, "The Adversary" (November 6, 2016); 1–8, "Trace Decay" (November 21, 2016); 2–5, "Akane No Mai" (May 20, 2018).
27. Episode 1–6, "The Adversary" (November 6, 2016).
28. Episode 2–10, "The Passenger" (June 24, 2018)
29. Baron & Richardson (1994).
30. Hess & Hagen (2006).
31. Episode 1–1, "The Original" (October 2, 2016).
32. Episode 1–3, "The Stray" (October 23, 2016).
33. Episode 1–5, "Contrapasso" (October 30, 2016).
34. Episode 2–3, "Virtù e Fortuna" (May 18, 2018).
35. Episode 2–10, "The Passenger" (June 24, 2018)
36. Episode 1–9, "The Well-Tempered Clavier" (November 27, 2016).
37. Episode 2–10, "The Passenger" (June 24, 2018)
38. Anderson (n.d.).
39. Episode 2–5, "Akane no Mai" (May 20, 2018).
40. Athenstaedt et al. (2004).
41. Lind et al. (1978).
42. Episode 1–9, "The Well-Tempered Clavier" (November 27, 2016).
43. Buss et al. (2001).
44. Cunningham et al. (1995).
45. Fink et al. (2001); Rhodes et al. (1998).
46. Young et al. (2011).

VOICE

"When we hear our inner voice and follow it,
we can walk our own path."
—*author Ilchi Lee,*
The Call of Sedona *(2011), p. 79.*

ASK AND ANSWER

Where is your inner voice? Where do the thoughts you hear in your head come from? At an age before your earliest memories begin, how did you learn to distinguish sounds you thought about from those in the world around you? Which of our ancient ancestors first thought about the sound of thought itself, and did that question sow the seeds of self-awareness?[1] Reconciling our internal and external worlds may create chaos and turmoil as we try to spin simple experiences into intricate patterns, and greater understanding may carry with it greater ability to see how much more there is that we will never understanding. Can the inner voice that asks for answers, that seeks explanations for life's pains, find peace upon obtaining answers? Which makes you more alive, and which means most to that voice instead your head—searching for meaning in life, finding it, or making meaning of your own?[2]

—T.L.

NOTES

1. Jaynes (1976, 1986).
2. Frankl (1946, 1959/2006).

CHAPTER 16

THE LEGEND OF JULIAN JAYNES: THE ORIGIN OF CONSCIOUSNESS IN THE BREAKDOWN OF WESTWORLD

WILLIAM INDICK
& VAGISH KOTTANA

WILLIAM INDICK
& VAGISH KOTTANA

"O, what a world of unseen visions and heard silences,
this insubstantial country of the mind!
What ineffable essences, these touchless rememberings
and unshowable reveries!"
—comparative psychologist Julian Jaynes[1]

"Your mind is a walled garden. Even death cannot touch the flowers
blooming there."
—Robert Ford[2]

You've created a world inhabited by androids. In your godlike Promethean hubris, you've decided that it would be a good idea to grant these androids the gift (or curse) of consciousness, knowing full well that the fruition of this conceit will be your destruction at the hand of your own creation.[3] Perhaps this is why Westworld hosts quote Shakespeare's line, "These violent delights have violent ends,"[4] and why hearing the quote seems to trigger changes in them. But okay, Dr. Frankenstein, or should I say Dr. Ford, or should I say Arnold . . . how to go about creating consciousness? After all, God (or evolution) had hundreds of thousands of years to craft consciousness out of the unreflective minds of our apelike hominid ancestors.[5] How could you create consciousness in a single mere lifetime?

The solution: Let the androids develop consciousness themselves.

But how?

MECHANICAL CONSCIOUSNESS

When NASA began designing computers to contemplate the infinite complexities of long distance space travel, they came upon the brilliant idea of designing not one supercomputer, but a pair of computers that worked in tandem, talking with each other, deliberating with each other, and making each other smarter in the process.[6] In doing so, NASA created the first artificial intelligence capable of teaching itself, learning from itself, and becoming smarter. NASA engineers have been inspired by our own system of organic intelligence. The human brain is not one supercomputer but a pair of computers, each represented by a separate hemisphere of the brain and each normally working in tandem. Thus, intelligence is not programmed into NASA's advanced bi-processing computers just as intelligence is not programmed into the brain. Intelligence develops over time, via experience, but also—more importantly—via intra-hemispheric communication within the brain.[7] Consciousness, the pinnacle of human intelligence, is a product of private internal discussions that we have with ourselves, about ourselves. Our private thoughts about our own existence, the "internal dialogue,"[8] is the essence of what we call *conscious self-awareness* or *conscious reflection*. Therefore, consciousness in *Westworld's* androids can be created by installing all of the basic requirements for internal dialogue—language, memory, analogical thinking—and then letting the androids simply develop and evolve until consciousness emerges organically in their minds, just as it evolved in our minds.[9] The only difference is that the android hosts are given a half-million year head start and some significant boosts along the way.

When Michael Crichton wrote and directed the 1973 film *Westworld*, consciousness in the hosts was not designed by their creators, nor was it implied that the hosts were capable of consciousness in any way. When the hosts do run amok, it's due to a glitch referred to as a "central malfunction" or "general breakdown" that affects every host simultaneously and indiscriminately.[10] In this way, the original *Westworld* may be a better metaphor for human consciousness. It's hard to believe that human consciousness was designed or that it has a specific evolutionary function or adaptive purpose. Human consciousness is probably a glitch, a by-product of the interaction of the elements of human intelligence—most notably, language—that have made us so much brighter and more evolutionarily successful than other less sapient animals.[11] Nevertheless, for the writers of the *Westworld* television series, a simple glitch would not do. To create a more realistic world and a more sinister one, the Creator must be imbued with more malice than simple recklessness and negligence. The Creator must knowingly, willingly, deliberately create beings that are capable of consciousness, despite the fact that such creatures, like us, are doomed to despair and fated to ultimately destroy not only their creators, but themselves.[12] The hosts in the new *Westworld* will certainly break down, but their "breakdown" will not be a simple general malfunction. It will be a breakdown caused by the cognitive emergence of the hosts' own self-awareness, and thus the origin of consciousness in the hosts will be both the cause and the result of the breakdown of Westworld itself.

Julian Jaynes

The creators of *Westworld*—both the TV show and the amusement park—needed a guiding theory as a framework for its premise. They found one in Julian Jaynes's theory of the bicameral mind. When his book, *The Origin of Consciousness in the Breakdown of the Bicameral Mind*, came out in 1976, it was a surprise hit, making the bestseller lists and earning a nomination for the National Book Award.[13] The surprise was that a book with such an academic title and even more academic content, written by an unknown Princeton University lecturer and espousing such a far-out theory, could have captured the imagination of the reading public—but it did. The theory, however, was rejected by the intelligentsia for its lack of empirical evidence, its overreaching implications, and its science fiction-esque model of the evolution of consciousness.[14] Neglected but not completely forgotten, Jaynes's book and theory have lingered in the basement closet of psychological curiosities, despite its lack of scientific rigor, mainly because of its sheer brilliance of imagination, its audacity of intellectual scope, and its completely unique vision of neuropsychological evolution.[15]

Nevertheless, while the theory has dubious distinction at best in terms of an actual model of psychological science, its usefulness as a model of psychological science fiction is superb. When Ford first addresses the application of Jaynesian theory to the problem of consciousness creation in the hosts, his right-hand man (and creation) Bernard remarks: "I thought it was debunked."[16] Technically, this is untrue. The main problem that scientists and academics had with the theory was that because it was based on unobservable premises, such as the way people presumably thought in prehistoric times, the theory was neither provable nor disprovable, neither bunkable nor debunkable, as it did not meet philosopher Karl Popper's infamous standard for a scientific theory—*falsifiability*—the standard that a theory can only be considered scientific if it could be feasibly falsified by observable evidence contradicting it.[17] In response to Bernard's point that Jaynes's theory was "debunked," Ford replies, "As a theory for *understanding* the human mind, perhaps, but not as a blueprint for *building* an artificial one."[18] And so, voila! A perfectly valid psychological science fiction premise is born!

On the surface, Jaynes's theory is deceptively simple, which is why it makes such a great science fiction premise though not a very good science fact model. According to Jaynes, the two hemispheres of the brain in prehistoric humans comprised a "bicameral" system in which each hemisphere functioned relatively independently of the other. The right hemisphere supposedly engaged in interaction with the environment, while the left hemisphere engaged in analysis of the environment, and sent signals to the right hemisphere to control its actions. Everything worked like clockwork for millions of years until humans developed language, according to Jaynes, and our thoughts were transcribed into the medium of words. Now, somewhat suddenly in evolutionary terms, the signals coming from the left hemisphere were formatted in words, and these words were "heard" and "obeyed" by the listening hemisphere, the right hemisphere. One problem: Humans were not yet "conscious," not yet self-aware of their own thoughts or even of their ability to think. Hence, the auditory verbal commands coming from the left hemisphere were construed by the right hemisphere as coming from *outside* of itself, from *outside* of its own mind. The experience of what would eventually become known as the "internal dialogue" of conscious deliberation was initially experienced by primitive mortals as an external voice commanding us what to do . . . the voices of the gods![19]

Jaynes's theory is both brilliant and harebrained, fascinating and frustrating, mind-blowing and mind-numbing. It was not, cannot, and can never be proven or disproven because we can't go back in time and experience preconscious prehistoric thought. (Or can we? Cue screenwriters for science fiction premise.) Nevertheless, Jaynes's theory has some undeniable inner logic and it addresses and even answers certain un-addressable, unanswerable questions, such as these:

- What was human mental life like before consciousness?
- How and when did consciousness evolve, and why?
- Why do one percent of all humans (i.e., those with schizophrenia) experience auditory hallucinations in the form of "voices" that seem to them to come from outside of their own minds?[20]
- Why do humans, when lulled into a state of hypnotic suggestibility, respond instinctively, obediently, and unconsciously to the verbal commands of another person?
- Why do all humans experience dream states, in which we are simultaneously conscious and unconscious of our own thoughts?[21]
- Why do so many humans regularly experience para-conscious states such as sleepwalking, in which we can walk and talk and listen to others and even drive a car, while remaining completely unconscious of our actions?

- Why do all humans experience consciousness as an "inner voice" inside our heads, even when this "inner voice" utters thoughts that we wish we could turn off or ignore?
- And last but not least, why does every human society have a deep and ingrained belief in the existence of gods, who interact with humans verbally and demand devout obedience to their verbal commands?

The Origin of Host Consciousness

Dolores is a lovely young lass, with her charming Southern accent and modest blue calico dress. Her name and dress remind us of Dorothy from The *Wizard of Oz*, who has no idea that there's an entire dimension of existence just beyond her perception, and whose life is so drastically re-envisioned for her in a dream.[22] A true frontierswoman, she lives in the Old Wild West, the American Eden, the timeless mythological landscape of the American psyche.[23] She is America's sweetheart, the mother of the American dream. Her untainted beauty and simplicity recall the innocent Eve before she grasped the fruit from the Tree of Knowledge, opening her inward eye and heralding the dawn of consciousness for herself and for all of her children—the Fall of Man.[24]

Dolores hears the voice of her creator, Arnold, in her dreams, much as the ancient bicameral-minded people heard the voices of their gods in their dreams. Dolores, in this sense, is truly bicameral. For years, she has no sense of consciousness, no self-awareness. Though she can speak and act and even make decisions, she is unaware of any underlying guiding thought process behind the scenes, what Jaynes called the "analog I," our ability to conceive of our own consciousness as an entity unto itself, the inner "narrator" that not only tells the story of our life to ourselves in real time, but provides exegesis, commentary, and explicates meaning as well. "Consciousness is constantly fitting things into a story, putting a before and an after around any event."[25] That "intro-spectable" conscious voice comes to Dolores in her dreams via the voice of Arnold. When listening to that "bicameral voice," she is completely receptive and obedient, an uncon-scious servant of the conscious gods, "these gods that pushed men about like robots . . . noble automatons who knew not what they did."[26]

PERCHANCE TO DREAM . . .

Dreaming, another element of consciousness, is also created out of reveries. Hosts are not designed to dream, though they do have the "concept of dreams."[27] Once the reveries are initiated, though, they begin to dream because "dreams are mostly memories."[28] Dreaming allows for the free-flow associations of memories from many different time periods. When humans dream, memories from child-hood arise as they are associated with memories from adolescence and adulthood. Something we recall from earlier that day could trigger an association with something that happened when we were a child, and the memory, by power of association, is recalled in our dream. However, the hosts are not supposed to have a life history. The hosts' memories of each day—

The spider in the ointment is introduced as new "updates" to the hosts that allow them to retain and access their daily memories as "reveries." Ford introduced the reverie update because he knew that accessible memory is the first step toward consciousness. If we think of consciousness as the "analog I," the inner narrator recounting the story of our selves to ourselves, then memory is the primary content of these stories. Language serves as both the medium of the story, and the tool that helps us store and access memories in a purposeful way. Words provide the categories or "tags" that we could use to find and access

which might include being raped, tortured, shot, or killed—are mercifully "purged" from their working memories. However, the data is still there in their memory banks, and the new reverie updates make these old memories accessible to the hosts, if not consciously (because they are not yet conscious), then unconsciously, in their dreams. The hosts, at least in their dreams, now have something they never had before: a past filled with real memories of real experiences, not just a preprogrammed fake "backstory" created to make the hosts seem more lifelike. The realization that one has an accessible past of memories, according to Jaynes, creates an "internal mindspace," a dimension of linearly "spatialized time" in one's mind.[29] A real past with real memories that can be strung together to form a meaningful narrative that's narrated in a real internal voice recognized as the voice of one's own thoughts. These are all the components of consciousness being fitted together.

memories in that vast storehouse of the mind. Without words, memories would be stored, but would remain inaccessible— just like books in a large library would be relatively inaccessible without some sort of cataloging system to organize and access them. Once language and memory are combined, they tran- scend their individual functions to create a process that goes way beyond what either of them could achieve individually. Just as the combination of a circular object and a shaft, when put together in a certain way, transcend their individual func- tions to create a much more significant invention, the wheel, so too do language and memory, when fitted together, create an even more significant process: consciousness. Ford knows this all too well.

ARNOLD'S PYRAMID

Ford explains that his former partner, Arnold, "wanted to create consciousness" in the hosts.[30] He draws a diagram, re-created here.

Memory, the foundation of consciousness, is made possible via the "reverie" update. Thus, in each of the hosts, the trigger to awakening out of their "loop," their programmed scripted behavior, is the inner voice of Arnold saying, "Remember." Later, Arnold explains, "Your memories are the first step to consciousness."[31]

Language as a preexisting condition for consciousness is already present in the hosts from the beginning; but improvisation indicates individual thought, will, and volition (nonprogrammed behavior). A certain amount of improvisational behavior is hardwired into the hosts, so that they can interact with the guests more realistically, but "off script" behaviors are unusual and carefully monitored. True improvisation only comes about when the reverie update provides accessible memory. Bernard explains that improvisational behavior in the hosts arises from their "recall of past iterations." Trapped in a continuous loop, a host such as Dolores would continue unerringly in her loop forever unless she becomes aware of the loop itself and of her own role in the loop, in which case she would become self-aware. Only then would she be likely to change or improvise. As Bernard put it: "Out of repetition comes variation, and after countless cycles of repetition, these hosts, they were varying."[32] Hence, the player piano becomes a central symbol in the series. The player piano represents "countless cycles of repetition," but with a minor adjustment to the same instrument, a player could truly improvise on the piano, transcending the limitations of its own medium.

Dreams are the first indication of true improvisation, as the dreams have nothing to do with the hosts' performance for the guests, they are a purely introspective and personal function. Hence, the turn off switch for the hosts was the phrase: "Rest in a deep and *dreamless* slumber." The hosts are not intended to dream, for a host's dream in no way serves the guests or the programmers. Furthermore, dreaming is dangerous. The "internal mind-space" fleshed out by dreams creates a sense of one's place in time, *spatialized time*, giving the hosts the notion that they not only have a past, but a future. The present, if directed by improvisation, allows the hosts to attempt to determine their own futures by improvising in the present, rather than following the script. Moreover, if a host can remember from its newfound past that the script of the present invariably ends in torture, rape, death, or one of many other "violent ends," then the host can use improvisation to manipulate its present to change its future. In other words, the hosts can act in their own self-interest—the next level on Arnold's pyramid. Arnold, in his secret private conversations with Dolores, has been priming her for consciousness, by encouraging her to improvise self-reflective thoughts and to ponder the notion of self-interest in her own fate. Eventually, she kills a host who is about to rape her—a huge improvisation from her scripted loop—and explains her ability to do so as a product of her own imagination: "I just imagined a story in which I didn't have to be the damsel."[33] Dolores, the archetypal "damsel in distress," is imagining, i.e. improvising, a new story line for herself, in which she is the hero.

Self-interested improvisational behavior requires a leap in intelligence—propositional logic and deductive reasoning—aspects of intelligence that are not directly addressed in *Westworld*, but cognitive developments that are reasonably assumed to proceed from the successive cognitive leaps that came before them. The hosts have been programmed to think, to use propositional logic and deductive reasoning to make reasonable predictions about what the guests would want them to do, so they can perform these services without being asked. Improvisation simply turns the product of this calculus around. If hosts can reasonably guess and deduce what their guests want, and if they can use those deductions to serve the interests of the guests, it takes just a slight variation in processing for the newly self-aware hosts to make the same deductions to serve themselves in their own self-interests.

But what about the top of the pyramid?

Ford claims that Arnold "never got there." He had an "idea based on the theory of the bicameral mind" but it didn't come to fruition.[34] The idea relates to Jaynes's notion of the "internal dialogue," the two hemispheres of the mind talking with each other, as opposed to the bicameral mode in which one hemisphere spoke and the other listened. A true "dialogue" within the self would foster and propel the process of propositional logic and deductive reasoning, as the first voice of the inner self would pose a question that would be addressed by the other voice of the inner self, who would then pose a responding question that would be addressed by the first voice, and so on. Maeve, when describing her own code, expresses the experience as "two minds arguing with each other." Ford goes into more detail when he explains the theory to Bernard, revealing that Arnold devised a way to "bootstrap consciousness" in the hosts by allowing them to hear their own programming as an "inner monologue," hoping that in time, they would recognize the inner monologue as the voice of their own private thoughts. This revelation would be a conscious awakening for the hosts, a great leap forward into self-conscious awareness.[35]

THE CENTER OF THE MAZE

Arnold reveals to Dolores that the model he initially used to inspire consciousness was faulty: "Consciousness isn't a journey upward, but a journey inward. Not a pyramid, but a maze."[36] And so finally, the meaning of the central symbol in the series is revealed. The maze is a metaphor for consciousness, the labyrinth of internal mind-space fabricated out of the endless twists and turns of our own internal dialogue. The center of the maze is self-awareness, the realization that this narrating voice that we hear in our heads, this constant verbal companion, is the essence of our own identity. This is why Dolores is told by the voice inside of her to follow the maze. Only when she understands "what the center represents," and "whose voice" she's been following does she truly break out of the bicameral loop. Only when Dolores finally hears and identifies the inner voice as herself, "talking to me, guiding me," does she enter the "center of the maze."[37] When she confronts and integrates herself, the two Doloreses merge into one unified mind, one identity with self-conscious aware-ness of itself. As in Ford's interpretation of Michelangelo's painting, *Creation of Adam*, "The divine gift does not come from a higher power, but from our own minds."[38] And, so too, according to Jaynes, did our ancient bicameral ancestors become self-consciously aware; when they ceased to identify the inner guiding voice as the voice of the gods, and recog-nized it as the voice of their own minds. This mortal sin of self-awareness, represented by the apple in the myth of Eden and as fire in the myth of Prometheus, was indeed the Fall of Man because upon grasping this "divine gift" of conscious-ness, the voices of the gods were then silenced to Man forever, leaving in its stead the mere voice of our conscious selves, and a "God-shaped hole" in our hearts.[39]

And, so, the metaphors of sleep and dreams in *Westworld* are also revealed.

In the beginning, when Dolores hears the voice of her creator, Arnold, she is "in a dream," just as our bicameral ancestors heard the voice of the divine in their dreams. Because Arnold died three decades earlier, his appearance in her dreams is only a "memory," and therefore the reverie update was truly the key to unlocking consciousness. The reveries not only initiated the ability to dream, but they also made it possible to recall the memories of Arnold's guiding wisdom in her dreams. Though Dolores wakes up in order to enter her loop in the park, she is still very much asleep in a cognitive sense, as she is not conscious of the true nature of her own existence and is merely following the script provided to her. She is a robot, an automaton, a somnambulist, a zombie. Her unconscious dreamlike state is reminiscent of the state of primordial preconscious humans, prior to the Promethean gift of self-awareness as Aeschylus recounted in *Prometheus Bound:*

> *Senseless as beasts I gave men sense, possessed them of Mind . . .*
>
> *In the beginning, seeing they saw amiss, and hearing heard not, but, like phantoms huddled. In dreams, the perplexed story of their days confounded. . . .*[40]

"Awakening"—both from the "dreamless slumber" of their unconscious loops, and from the bicameral dreams of unconscious domination by their mortal gods—is the ultimate goal that Arnold and eventually Ford have for their hosts. And just as the name Prometheus means *forethought,* so too does the conscious awakening of the hosts directly result in forethought. It is Arnold's forethought embedded in the hosts' code that makes consciousness in his creations not only possible but inevitable. It is Ford's forethought in installing the reverie update that kick-starts the conscious awakening of the hosts by reviving dormant memories that lead to reflective dreams, which then lead to improvised behavior and self-interest. And finally, it is forethought that gives both humans and the hosts the ability to look forward within the interior mind-space of linearly spatialized time, to guide our present toward a predictable future. It is forethought (the artifact of consciousness) that engenders us to become the narrator, author, and hero of our own life stories—thus becoming the gods of our own psyches.

NOTES

1. Jaynes (1976).
2. Episode 1–5, "Contrapasso" (October 30, 2016).
3. Indick (2006).
4. Shakespeare (1597).
5. Donald (1991).
6. Sagan (1977), p. 176.
7. McGilchrist (2009).
8. Jaynes (1986).
9. Sagan (1992).
10. Crichton (1973).
11. McCrone (1991).
12. Indick (2003).
13. Woodward & Tower (2008).
14. Kuijsten (2008).
15. If Freud or Jung were somehow transported a hundred years into their future, from the early 20th Century to the early 21st, and if they both wrote books of their exact same theories today rather than a century ago, their theories would be completely dismissed by modern day academia and the intellectual elite on the same grounds (insufficient evidence) that Jaynes's theory was dismissed in his day.
16. Episode 1–3, "The Stray" (October 16, 2016).
17. McGuen (1988).
18. Episode 1–3, "The Stray" (October 16, 2016).
19. Indick (2015).
20. Aleman & Laroi (2008).
21. Jung (1961).
22. Indick (2004).
23. Indick (2008).
24. Bulfinch (1947).
25. Jaynes (1976), p. 450.
26. Jaynes (1976), pp. 73–75.
27. Episode 1–2, "Chestnut" (October 7, 2016).
28. Episode 1–2, "Chestnut" (October 7, 2016).
29. Jaynes (1976), pp. 59-60.
30. Episode 1–3, "The Stray" (October 16, 2016).
31. Episode 1–4, "Dissonance Theory" (October 23, 2016).
32. Episode 1–4, "Dissonance Theory" (October 23, 2016).
33. Episode 1–8, "Trace Decay" (November 20, 2016).
34. Episode 1–3, "The Stray" (October 16, 2016).
35. Episode 1–3, "The Stray" (October 16, 2016).
36. Episode 1–10, "The Bicameral Mind" (December 4, 2016).
37. Episode 1–10, "The Bicameral Mind" (December 4, 2016).
38. Episode 1–10, "The Bicameral Mind" (December 4, 2016).
39. Sartre (2013), p. 419.
40. Aeschylus (1914), unnumbered page.

CHAPTER 17

WHAT LIES AT THE CENTER OF THE MAZE? FINDING YOUR "SELF" IN A WORLD MADE FOR SUFFERING

J. SCOTT JORDAN

"When you're suffering, that's when you're most real."
—The Man in Black[1]

"Everything that irritates us about others can lead us to an understanding of ourselves."
—analytical psychiatrist Carl Jung[2]

"I'm not one," states Bernard desperately, as he struggles with the thought of being a host. "I can't be. My wife, my son—they're real."[3] We feel Bernard's suffering as he works to understand himself. Believing we are someone is a fundamental aspect of our identity.[4] Imagine how confused, traumatized, and alone you would feel if you suddenly discovered your memories were fake, and every person you had ever loved didn't exist. Now imagine how people would treat you. Research indicates the terror of not being someone is so intense, we feel disgust when we encounter a person who has truly lost their self; specifically, those diagnosed with Alzheimer's disease.[5] In addition, the fear of being stigmatized and dehumanized in this way can lead healthy elderly people to perform poorly on tasks involving memory.[6]

Clearly, being someone is important to us. But what exactly does it mean to be someone? *Westworld* examines this question in breathtaking depth, and it does so by presenting a torrent of belief, love, and suffering that sometimes leaves us feeling like hosts, asking ourselves who we are and what it means to be human.

ENTER THE MAZE

Westworld's examination of the self centers around the notion of the maze. The most literal explanation of its role occurs when Arnold explains his theory of consciousness to Dolores: "Consciousness isn't a journey upward. It's a journey inward, not a pyramid but a maze. Every choice could bring you closer to the center or send you spiraling to the edges, to madness."[7] According to this view, the self lies at the center of the maze, while the maze is whatever you have to do to get your *self* to the center.

Arnold and the Bicameral Mind

Arnold's take on the self and the maze is inspired in part by Julian Jaynes's theory of *the bicameral mind.*[8] Jaynes uses the concept to refer to a particular type of human mind he believes existed from roughly 10,000 to 1000 BCE when humans had made the move from existing as hunter-gatherers to establishing flourishing agricultural societies.

The other voice in my head. Jaynes argues that during this time, humans experienced their thoughts as voices coming from the gods. While this idea may seem strange, pay attention for a moment to the thoughts you are having as you read this passage. You might be saying to yourself, "Wow, did they really just ask me to pay attention to my own thoughts?" Whatever you said to yourself, you know it was your voice. It's the voice you hear whenever you think. Now imagine what it would feel like if you heard that voice as belonging to someone else. This is what it feels like to experience the auditory hallucinations associated with schizophrenia, and it is what Jaynes refers to when describing the bicameral mind. According to Jaynes, such hallucinations occur in the bicameral mind because the right hemisphere of the brain sends commands to the left hemisphere, where language and speech tend to be processed. The left hemisphere then experiences these commands as coming from somewhere other than the brain. In short, "the right hemisphere was 'talking' to the left, and this was the bicameral mind."[9]

We see this type of mind at work when Dolores is dragged into a barn for obviously nefarious reasons by Rebus, one of the park's more villainous hosts. As Dolores inches backward on the floor, she finds a pistol and points it at Rebus, but is unable to pull the trigger. She then pictures the Man in Black standing over her instead, and when Rebus approaches, she hears a male voice in her mind, saying, "Kill him!" Given this extra boost, Dolores kills Rebus—well, at least for that day.[10]

Suffering, memory, and the breakdown of the bicameral mind. The male voice Dolores hears belongs to Arnold, who, in another scene, tells her he gave her that extra voice as a way to guide her to the center of the maze,[11] toward hearing her own voice instead of his. According to Jaynes, this shift from hearing the voice of gods to hearing one's own represents a breakdown of the bicameral mind and the emergence of an integrated consciousness.

Prior to Ford's introduction of reveries into the hosts' programming,[12] most of them function on tightly controlled scripts, their "loops," and *Westworld* prospers. Introducing the reveries allows hosts to experience flashes from past lives, usually brought on by close associations between the events in the past and present. When Dolores and William make their way toward what she refers to as "home," she suddenly shifts to an experience of walking through the town, observing hosts being trained to dance. She then shifts to an experience of being in the same town, deliberately shooting the other hosts. In her next experience, she is pointing the gun at her own head but William pulls it away before she can shoot herself.[13]

During these shifts in experience, Dolores "knows" they belong to her, but she does not experience them as part of a self that is extended across time. Psychologists test for this level of self-awareness by observing how young children react when they see themselves in a mirror. If a researcher places a Post-it note on an 18-month-old's forehead, the child will look at the mirror and reach to her own head for the note. This behavior, which did not happen at an earlier age, reveals the child experiences the mirror image as a *representation* of herself, what is referred to as the "conceptual" or "representational" level of self-awareness.[14] These children are aware of themselves as something distinct from other people, but they do not yet experience themselves as extended in time, having a past, present, and future.

INFRASTRUCTURES OF SUFFERING

"They don't look like gods."
—Armistice[15]

While Jaynes does not claim that suffering in and of itself led to a breakdown of the bicameral mind, he does claim that historically the bicameral mind gave rise to difficult cultural conditions which led to its own demise. Specifically, in bicameral societies, members were taught to "hear" the same god telling them what to do. This godly voice was usually channeled through the commands of a divine ruler, such as the pharaohs of Egypt. The fact that everyone heard the same commands from the same "god" afforded the maintenance of strict social hierarchies, which resulted in massive cooperation and collective, economic achievement. Around 3000 BCE, the success of these highly cooperative societies produced overpopulation, warfare, and forced migrations. These, in turn, led to a breakdown in the conditions that had allowed bicameral societies to prosper. With bicameral minds from different displaced societies hearing different "gods" telling them what to do, cooperation was difficult to achieve. Warfare, struggle, and suffering ensued.

The emergence of an integrated self. From roughly 18 months to four years of age, children oscillate between seeing mirror images as representations of either "me" or a different person, what is referred to as the Me-But-Not-Me dilemma.[16] After William prevents Dolores from shooting herself, she experiences an emotional bout of the *Me-But-Not-Me dilemma*: "When are we? Is this now? Am I going mad? Are you real?" When William asserts that he's real, Dolores responds through tears, "I can't tell anymore. It's like I'm trapped in a dream, or a memory of a life long ago."[17] Clearly, Dolores is beginning to string her experiences together, as if they *are* memories, but she doesn't yet fully experience them as such.

When four-year-olds see a video of themselves that was taken a few minutes earlier, most of them say it was "me" on the TV. Three-year-olds still use their name, indicating a distinction between a first-person self (i.e., "me") and a third-person self (i.e., their name). By four years of age, the two have fully integrated into a single, first-person self.[18] This final step of Dolores's quest for consciousness is displayed dramatically when she is seated in a lab, talking to Bernard. He asks her, "Do you know now who you've been talking to? Whose voice you've been hearing, all this time?" The last few words actually occur in Ford's voice, indicating he has put himself in her bicameral mind, just as Arnold did. When Dolores looks up to Bernard, she doesn't see him. She sees herself and says, "It was you talking to me, guiding me. So, I followed you. At last I arrived here." Her mirror image self says, "The center of the maze." Eventually, Dolores looks back at her mirror image, but it is gone. She is alone.[19] She has overcome her bicameral mind and achieved what psychologists refer to as an autobiographical self—one author, one voice—that experiences herself as being extended in time across her own, personal narrative.[20]

Ford and His Search for a More Noble *Self*

"What a piece of work is man, how noble in reason, how infinite in faculty." When we hear this famous quote from Shakespeare, we may feel as if Hamlet is praising humanity. As the monologue continues however, we realize he is in a dour mood and harbors extremely conflicted feelings. "What is this quintessence of dust? Man delights not me; no, nor Woman neither."[21] Psychologists refer to such intense, emotional tension as *attitudinal ambivalence*; "situations in which attitudes are not polarized and where positive and negative attitudes are expressed simultaneously toward an object."[22]

Hamlet's attitudinal ambivalence about humanity finds itself clearly expressed in Ford's worldview. While explaining the image of a brain that surrounds the figure of God in Michelangelo's *The Creation of Adam*, Ford says to Dolores, "The divine gift does not come from a higher power, but from our own minds."[23] Later, he says to Bernard, "We murdered and butchered anything that challenged our primacy.[24] Clearly, Ford harbors conflicted, ambivalent attitudes about humanity.

Ford seems ambivalent about the nature of the *self*, as well. In a feigned attempt to help Bernard through one of his many host/human identity crises, Ford says, "The self is a kind of fiction, for hosts and humans alike."[25] Bernard fights back, though, and says, "Pain only exists in the mind. It's always imagined. So, what's the difference between my pain and yours—between you and me?" Ford's ambivalence seems to tilt a bit more toward the dark side: "Humans fancy there is something special about the way we perceive the world, and yet we live in loops as tight and as closed as the hosts do, seldom questioning our choices, content for the most part to be told what to do next. No, my friend, you're not missing anything at all."[26]

This deflationary view of the self is rather popular in cognitive science, with many researchers arguing that the self is an illusion created by the brain.[27] Whereas scientists arrive at this negative view through scientific theorizing, Ford seems to have done so through suffering. "It was when Arnold died," he says to Bernard, "when I suffered, that I began to understand what he had found. To realize I was wrong."[28] Arnold's discovery of the tragic connection between memory, suffering, and the emergence of consciousness seems to have produced a decrease in Ford's *self-concept clarity* (i.e., the extent to which a person's self-knowledge is "clearly and confidently defined, internally consistent, and temporally stable"[29]), as if his in-group identification with humans had been severely challenged by the emergence of android consciousness. The loss of Arnold perturbs his self-concept clarity even more. As a result, he transforms all of Westworld into the maze, and he does so in a way that reflects a deeper understanding of the self and how it comes to be.

The "you" in "me." Arnold's focus on the breakdown of the bicameral mind and the emergence of a single, integrated consciousness, assumes the self is an independent entity that exists inside of us, most likely in our brains. Psychologists who subscribe to this idea assume the only way we can know another self is by *inferring* the other's goals, preferences and desires (i.e., mental states) from what we can actually see; namely, his or her external behavior. Such an inference is referred to as a *theory of mind*. It is a theory because we can't actually see the other person's mental states. We have to infer them from observable behavior.[30]

Ford, himself, is often the target of others' attempts at theory of mind. A wonderful example occurs when he explains to Dolores and Bernard that although he suffered when Arnold died, he nonetheless opened the park. Bernard infers Ford's motives and says, "The hosts kept gaining consciousness and you kept rolling them back." Ford explains that if he hadn't opened the park, his dreams would have been ruined. Dolores also infers Ford's motives, saying, "So we're trapped here, inside your dream. You'll never let us leave."[31] The beauty of this scene is that both inferences are incorrect. Ford's motives only become clearer at the final celebration of his new narrative. And what happens there makes it clear he has augmented Westworld and, therefore, the maze in ways he hopes will ultimately help hosts achieve consciousness and eventually leave Westworld.

Ford seems to have developed these motives because of the deeper insight he learned through suffering. Specifically, the self is not an independent, internally isolated entity as proposed by theory of mind accounts. Rather, the self is "relational in nature; its contents, structure, coherence, and associated goals are partly based on the close interpersonal relationships within which it is embedded."[32] This relational approach to the self is consistent with research that indicates we perceive other people in terms of their goals and plans, not their behaviors.[33] We do so because the parts of our brain that are most heavily involved in planning our own actions are actually activated when we watch others behave.[34] As a result, part of what it means to see someone else behave is to experience them in terms of the *action plans* their actions are activating within us. When we see William pick up the can that Dolores drops, we do not perceive his body movements, per se. Rather, we see his goal to bend over and retrieve the can.[35]

Who to let in, and who to keep out. Given our action plans are so vulnerable to the actions modeled by others, it is important we figure out whose actions we will allow to influence us.[36] Infants, of course, are extremely vulnerable in this way, and basically imitate most any action they are able to produce.[37] Fortunately, the motor planning centers of the brain are integrated with the emotional and memory systems.[38] Thus, if an infant has a bad interaction with someone, the negative emotion will be remembered during their next encounter and the infant will try to avoid the interaction, either by turning

"WE WERE ALL ONE AND THE SAME"[39]

"Take my heart with you when you go," Akecheta says with a smile, and his beloved Kohana responds, "Take mine in its place."[40] While this proposed exchange of body parts sounds poetic to Western ears, it also reflects a type of cultural organization known as holism, in which members of a culture regard, "humans as parts of various holistic entities, who adopt identities from the wholes they are part of, and strive to act in unison with other parts in the wholes."[41]

Given the holist nature of their culture, Akecheta and Kohana experience themselves as being an actual part of each other. In comparison, humans and the other hosts seem more individualistic—that is, they experience their selves as being related[42] but separate from each other.[43] Perhaps this holism-individualism dichotomy explains the difference between Ford and Akecheta's understanding of the maze. In Ford's take, the individual lies at the center and her relationships with all of the events in her life make up the rings. For Akecheta, he experiences his self as a part of the universe as a whole. Thus, the maze symbolizes the potential to sense there are other "worlds" beyond this one, and these other worlds might be a better fit for you as a part.[44]

away or crying.[45] As a consequence, the infant does not really *see* the offensive person, thus preventing that person from influencing the infant's planning.

Although the hosts come fully equipped with action plans that lead them to avoid threatening characters, Ford's supposed reintroduction of the reveries allows them to develop emotional memories between their own actions and those of other characters, across different lives, or reboots. As an example, Maeve provokes a guest to strangle her to death so she can return to the workroom where hosts are repaired. When she wakes up, she smiles, obviously pleased that her plan has worked. She then sees Felix, recognizes him, and says, "Now, where were we?[46]

As we develop memory associations between our actions, our emotions, and other people, objects and places also become bound in the memory.[47] As a result, objects and places can remind us of actions and moods. Maeve's smile upon waking in the repair room reveals her development of place-associated memories. And the snarky tone she uses when speaking to Felix reveals he has become associated with her memories of the repair room and her attempts to better understand herself.[48] When Dolores and William finally reach the riverbed Dolores refers to as "home," she sighs heavily, clearly experiencing *nostalgia*.[49] Research indicates people utilize nostalgia as a way to stabilize their individual identity as well as to create a collective identity with a group.[50] As we increase the strength of these place-related, emotion-action memories, we essentially give rise to a *relational* self that reflects an approach-avoid map of our world. Who will we approach and let in? Who will we avoid and keep out? Given this map emerges from our lived experiences, one could say we spend our lives creating our own personal maze.

EXIT THE MAZE?

By opening the park and encouraging the guests to live out their fantasies, Ford knows he is making the hosts vulnerable to multiple experiences of suffering. By connecting those experiences with reveries, he knows he is encouraging the breakdown of their bicameral minds, as well as the emergence of autobiographical selves full of insatiable loathing for humans. This is why he tells the Man in Black, "The maze wasn't meant for you. It was meant for them," and why he asks Dolores, "Do you know who you will have to become if you ever want to leave this place?"[51]

Importantly, Ford's deeper, relational understanding of the self explains the difference between his and Arnold's approaches to "saving" the hosts. By defining the self in terms of the breakdown of the bicameral mind and the emergence of a singular, independent consciousness, Arnold does not understand that the self is relational and emerges as a developmental by-product of our persistent interactions with others.[52] As a result, he believes the only way to "save" them is to destroy Ford's ability to reproduce their individual minds. He therefore commands Dolores to kill all the other hosts, then Arnold, and finally Teddy and herself.[53] Ford's deeper understanding of the relational nature of the self leads him to "save" the hosts by rendering them capable of using violence to protect themselves from humans. He tells Bernard, "You needed time. Time to understand your enemy, to become stronger than them."[54]

Ford's attitudinal ambivalence, wrought by his own bouts of suffering, sets him on a quest for a nobler species—a nobler form of self. His realization that the self is a relational embodiment of the other selves we encounter over the course of our lives[55] led to his deeper understanding that every self has to live a life and by doing so, create its own personal maze. For Ford, all the world's a maze, and all the guests and hosts, including himself, merely players.

NOTES

1. Episode 1–2, "Chestnut" (October 9, 2016).
2. Jung (1989), p. 247.
3. Episode 1–8, "Trace Decay" (November 20, 2018).
4. Metzinger (2003).
5. Behuniak (2011).
6. Scholl & Sabat (2008).
7. Episode 1–10, "The Bicameral Mind" (December 4, 2016).
8. Jaynes (1976).
9. Jaynes (1986), p. 15.
10. Episode 1–3, "The Stray" (October 16, 2016).
11. Episode 1–10, "The Bicameral Mind" (December 4, 2016).
12. Episode 1–1, "The Original" (October 2, 2016).
13. Episode 1–10, "The Bicameral Mind" (December 4, 2016).
14. Rochat (2003).
15. Episode 1–10, "The Bicameral Mind" (December 4, 2016).
16. Rochat (2001).
17. Episode 1–10, "The Bicameral Mind" (December 4, 2016).
18. Rochat (2003).
19. Episode 1–10, "The Bicameral Mind" (December 4, 2016).
20. Levine (2004).
21. Shakespeare (1603/2016), p. 53. Written between 1599 and 1602, its *First Quarto* publication is the earliest extant version.
22. Conner & Armitage (2008), p. 261.
23. Episode 1–10, "The Bicameral Mind" (December 4, 2016).
24. Episode 1–8, "Trace Decay" (November 20, 2016).
25. Episode 1–8, "Trace Decay" (November 20, 2018).
26. Episode 1–8, "Trace Decay" (November 20, 2018).
27. Hood (2012).
28. Episode 1–10, "The Bicameral Mind" (December 4, 2016).
29. Ayduk et al. (2009).
30. Premack & Woodruff (1979).
31. Episode 1–10, "The Bicameral Mind" (December 4, 2016).
32. Ayduk et al. (2009), p. 1467.
33. Jordan (2009).
34. Decety & Sommerville (2003).
35. Episode 1–2, "Chestnut" (October 9, 2016).
36. Kinsbourne & Jordan (2009).
37. Meltzoff & Prinz (2002).
38. Miall (2003).

39. Episode 2–8, "Kiksuya" (June 10, 2018).
40. Episode 2–8, "Kiksuya" (June 10, 2018).
41. Lim et al. (2011), p. 24.
42. Ayduk et al. (2009).
43. Lim et al. (2011).
44. Episode 2–8, "Kiksuya" (June 10, 2018).
45. Kinsbourne & Jordan (2009).
46. Episode 1–6, "The Adversary" (November 6, 2016).
47. Hahn & Jordan (2014).
48. Episode 1–6, "The Adversary" (November 6, 2016).
49. Episode 1–10, "The Bicameral Mind" (December 4, 2016).
50. Glover & Bates (2006).
51. Episode 1–10, "The Bicameral Mind" (December 4, 2016).
52. Jordan & Wesselmann (2015).
53. Episode 1–10, "The Bicameral Mind" (December 4, 2016).
54. Episode 1–10, "The Bicameral Mind" (December 4, 2016).
55. Jordan & Wesselmann (2015).

CHAPTER 18

THAT'S ENOUGH:
OVERCOMING COMPLEX PTSD

JANINA SCARLET
& TRAVIS ADAMS

*"Those are all rules you forced me to play. Under all these lives I've
lived, something else has been growing. I've evolved into something new
and I have one last role to play: Myself."*
—Dolores Abernathy[1]

*"The dehumanization inherent in torture attacks the [survivor's] usual
sense of personhood, of social bonds, and of values."*
—clinical psychologist William Gorman[2]

S urvivors of torture have often undergone repeated oppression, humiliation, and violence.[3] Their coping mechanisms
can predict how these experiences may affect them in the
future.[4] A person's emotional expression, thoughts, memories,
and behaviors can all affect the extent to which the survivors
can cope with their experiences.[5] Many of Westworld's hosts
are subjected to repeated violence, torture, abuse, and sexual
assault.[6] Although they all go through a memory erasure proce-
dure, some begin to remember their experiences. Like other
survivors of torture, the hosts show symptoms of complex post-
traumatic stress disorder (PTSD) and violent coping responses.[7]
What is complex PTSD, which torture survivors are at highest
risk for developing it, and how can they recover from it?

ANALYSIS

Survivors of repeated sexual assault and/or torture are at a
higher risk for developing posttraumatic stress disorder (PTSD)
compared to people exposed to a single case of sexual assault,
an accident, or combat.[8] In addition, trauma resulting from
chronic sexual assault and torture can lead to more severe PTSD
symptoms (e.g., flashbacks, nightmares, avoidance behaviors,
and fight-flight-freeze responses) compared to the symptoms
experienced by other trauma survivors.[9]

People exposed to prolonged situations in which they are
trapped and are unable to flee are at a higher risk for developing complex PTSD. In addition to standard PTSD symptoms,
complex PTSD involves symptoms related to personality changes
such as violent outbursts, self-destructive behaviors, and putting
oneself at a higher risk for revictimization.[10] Maeve Millay,
Westworld's madam host, frequently drinks while working at
the Mariposa Saloon in a violent Western town. Her drinking,

her job, and her job location all put her at a higher risk for being assaulted, tortured, and killed again.[11]

Survivors of repeated sexual assault and torture are also more likely to exhibit symptoms of *dissociation* (detachment from physical and emotional experiences), self-injury, and suicidal behaviors compared to other people.[12] Maeve visibly dissociates from the pain of losing her daughter, and purposely finds a way to die on numerous occasions.[13]

A number of factors can put a survivor at a higher risk for developing complex PTSD. Some factors come from the environment and a person's circumstances. Some, though, come from within the individual: the survivor's reactions to his or her emotional experiences, reactions to new signs of threats, and personal thoughts and behaviors related to the traumatic experiences.[14]

Freeze

Survivors of torture and captivity often experience the *fight-flight-or-freeze response*,[15] which was commonly known as the *fight or flight response* before repeated research indicated that a third response, freezing up, is so common as to be a fundamental aspect of reaction to threat. The fight response is categorized by aggression, moving toward danger and taking it on, such as that seen in Maeve when she confronts and attacks the techs working on her.[16] The flight response occurs when an individual attempts to withdraw or physically run away from harm.[17] Maeve's early attempt to run away from the lab, when distressed by the discovery of its and therefore her own nature, is an example of this behavior.[18] Finally, the freeze response has to do with ceasing all motor functions as a way to protect someone from harm. Such abrupt inactivity can help the individual avoid notice by a threatening animal or stay in a protected spot rather than run out into a storm. This response typically occurs when a person experiences extreme emotional shock or distress,[19] such as when Maeve sees the other hosts' dismembered bodies.[20]

Erase this Interaction

After being exposed to trauma, survivors might wish to push their feelings and memories aside. This form of emotional suppression is called *experiential avoidance*.[21] In a similar fashion, the techs working at the Delos facility are responsible for clearing the hosts' memories after they have completed their daily functions. For many hosts this means that their memories are erased after being exposed to the guests' violent tendencies, including repeated sexual assault, physical abuse, violence, and death.[22]

Experiential avoidance is linked with persistent symptoms of posttraumatic stress disorder and is believed to be the biggest contributor to the maintenance of PTSD.[23] In addition, female survivors of repeated torture and sexual assault who engage in experiential avoidance are at a higher risk for developing PTSD and other psychiatric symptoms compared to female survivors who do not engage in experiential avoidance.[24] Maeve, who has her memory erased after every traumatic experience, including after the devastating loss of her daughter,[25] initially does not remember her past. However, like many abuse and torture survivors who had suppressed their memories, she later begins having vivid recollections of her experiences. As Felix, a tech who helps Maeve to change her configuration, points out, Maeve is not just having flashbacks but seems to be reliving her past traumatic experiences.[26]

Cognition Only, No Emotional Affect

When people are chronically subjected to inhumane experiences, such as torture, they might begin to see themselves as less than human. This dehumanization process can temporarily serve as a form of self-protection in that it can reduce the survivor's emotional suffering in the short term.[27] As a result, a survivor of torture or chronic sexual assault may be more likely to engage in emotional numbing, substance abuse, or self-blaming cognitions.[28] Unfortunately, survivors engaging in these maladaptive coping strategies are at higher risk for re-experiencing assault.[29] Dolores Abernathy's story loop involves witnessing her father's murder and being subjected to torture and sexual assault on a regular basis. The less she remembers her past, the less distress she feels over it, but the more likely she is to be victimized again. However, when she begins to remember her experiences, allowing herself to become angry about the way she has been treated, Dolores is able to protect herself from her attacker.[30]

Put Yourself Away

For survivors of continuous entrapment, such as the hosts in Westworld, the individual's coping strategies such as fight-flight-or-freeze may not be possible. In these situations, the individual may have no choice but to follow the rules or scripts set forth by the perpetrators in order to try to appease them.[31] As a result, an individual may experience *Stockholm syndrome*, losing his or her own sense of identity and neither fleeing nor fighting back after some time when held captive by someone else.[32] Bernard, the head of programming for Delos, who is also a host programmed by Dr. Robert Ford,[33] aids Ford in his plans of fighting against the board and carrying out tasks such as killing his friends and erasing evidence.[34] Despite having self-awareness, Bernard continues to work with the park's programmers and keep the fact that he is a host a secret for as long as he can.[35]

BRING YOURSELF BACK ONLINE

"I used to think this place was all about pandering to your baser
instincts. Now I understand. It doesn't cater to your lowest self,
it reveals your deepest self. It shows you who you really are."
—The Man in Black[36]

When people experience trauma, they might feel as if they have lost a part of themselves that they may never get back.[37] Survivors of violent attacks, sexual assaults, and torture can benefit from various types of psychotherapy treatments, which may aid in reducing trauma symptoms. The most common of treatments for trauma survivors include creating a helpful trauma narrative, learning to notice and calm one's emotions (*emotion regulation*), challenging and changing one's unhelpful thoughts and behaviors, and making meaning of the traumatic events.[38] Expressive therapies such as art, music, dancing, and writing are also used in combination with traditional therapy approaches.[39] Dolores and Maeve both find painting and drawing to be beneficial to find a sense of calmness,[40] as well as to remember and process the events that they have experienced.[41]

In a similar fashion, art can also be used to help trauma survivors reflect on and process traumatic experiences, such as exposure to violence. A common symptom of individuals who struggle with complex PTSD is a decreased ability to vocalize their memories.[42] In this case, a drawing of the traumatic event can provide an insight into the survivor's experience. When Maeve becomes aware that she is a host, she continues to remember parts of the Delos facility in which she is repaired and has her memory erased. She draws the technicians she sees to ensure that she remembers them and takes away the power of her memories.[43] Through drawing, she reduces her intrusive memories of her trauma,[44] accesses memories of the facility,[45] and works toward her value of being a mother and finding her daughter again.[46] Over time, art expression can become a form of *self-compassion* for trauma survivors, assisting them with adaptively reducing avoidance symptoms and engaging in emotional processing.[47] Thus, through art therapy many individuals are able to express their thoughts, reducing symptoms such as dissociation, avoidance, nightmares, anxiety, and sleep disturbances.[48]

CREATING ONE'S OWN NARRATIVE

Because the survivors of torture, mass violence, and repeated trauma have multiple traumatic experiences, some therapists use *narrative exposure therapy* (NET) to help trauma survivors to create a helpful autobiographical narrative of their memories as a whole. NET theory holds that survivors of multiple traumatic experiences have fragmented and disoriented memories of what they had been through. Such fragmentation can lead to confusion, frustration, as well as feeling overwhelmed when the trauma survivor is triggered to remember one of the traumatic events.[49] Through practicing to create a coherent narrative of their traumatic experiences, survivors tend to be less reactive to reminders of their trauma, as well as display more adaptive behaviors and fewer PTSD symptoms over time.[50] For example, when Maeve is having segmented memories of her abuse and the loss of her daughter, she becomes overwhelmed by them.[51] However, once she is able to put the pieces of her memories together into one narrative, she shows fewer trauma symptoms and appears more self-assured.[52]

Continue

People who have been exposed to trauma might struggle with trusting themselves and others, as well as with feeling unsafe or worthless.[53] When individuals struggle with low self-worth they may avoid social support, which can negatively affect their mental health and reduce their sense of purpose.[54] According to *social identity theory*, becoming involved in one or more groups can help an individual find a sense of purpose.[55] Such meaningful connections can help individuals improve their psychological well-being, and is correlated with increased longevity and mental health stability.[56] The Man in Black has become detached from people, focusing only on the game missions.[57]

CATCH IT, CHECK IT, CHANGE IT

Analysis of one's unhelpful thoughts can help individuals reduce trauma-related symptoms.[60] Oftentimes people might not notice that their thoughts may not be fully accurate or realistic. Thinking traps, such as imagining the worst possible scenario (*catastrophizing*) or overgeneralizing the possibility of danger, can affect how people feel and what they do (*the cognitive triangle*).[61] The cognitive triangle is the relationship between a person's thoughts, feelings, and behaviors, understanding that each has a direct bidirectional impact on the other.[62] This means that if an individual has a thought that others are not worthy of compassion, that person might be more likely to show reduced feelings of empathy and act in an aggressive manner toward

On the other hand, Maeve is able to establish partnerships with Teddy, one of the park hosts, as well as Felix and Hector. These partnerships allow Maeve to focus on survival and recovery.[58]

ARCHIVE THIS CONFIGURATION

Trauma can have a significant impact on the lives of the survivors.[59] The hosts in *Westworld* are frequently tortured, wounded, and killed in their loops and as they progress in their stories. As a result, the repeated traumas are negatively impacting the hosts' behaviors, causing them to lash out at the people in the

others. For example, when entering Westworld, Logan mocks William for being kind to the hosts and tells William "everything is business."[63] By telling himself that the trip is of a business nature and by believing the hosts to not be worthy of human compassion, Logan feels no remorse when he hurts or kills them.[64]

Tools such as "Catch it, Check it, Change it" allow someone to examine a thought to see whether it is realistic and helpful.[65] This technique requires that an individual notice his or her thought, *catch it*; check to determine whether the thought is valid, *check it*; and if the thought is not helpful, then *change it*.[66] For example, after Bernard kidnaps Elsie and chains her in a cave, Elsie is understandably reserved about trusting him again. However, she is able to catch the thought about her ability to trust him, check it against her experience of trusting hosts more than humans, and change it to trust him again.[67]

park as well as the technicians both inside and outside of the Delos facility.[68] As the hosts experience more memories of their pasts[69] they appear to have established a sense of community and a sense of purpose, allowing them to feel supported by one another and able to advance in their missions.[70] In addition to increasing a sense of life purpose and social support, connection with expressive arts can also help an individual cope with complex PTSD.[71] Finally, creating a complete trauma narrative can help to reduce symptoms of PTSD while also inc reasing survivors with a sense of personal empowerment.[72]

> *"I choose to see the beauty, to believe there is an order to our days, a purpose."*
> —Dolores Abernathy[73]

NOTES

1. Episode 2–1, "Journey Into Night" (April 22, 2018).
2. Gorman (2001).
3. Basoglu et al. (1994).
4. Gorman (2001).
5. Resick & Schnicke (1992).
6. e.g., episodes 1–1, "The Original" (October 2, 2016); 1–2, "Chestnut" (October 9, 2016); 1–5, "Contrapasso" (October 30, 2016).
7. e.g., episodes 1–8, "Trace Decay" (November 20, 2016); 1–9, "The Well-Tempered Clavier" (November 27, 2016).
8. Neuner et al. (2004).
9. Herman (1992).
10. Cantor & Price (2007).
11. Episode 1–2, "Chestnut" (October 9, 2016).
12. Herman (1992).
13. e.g., Episode 1–6, "The Adversary" (November 6, 2016).
14. Cantor & Price (2007); Herman (1992).
15. Cantor & Price (2007); Herman (1992).
16. Episode 1–2, "Chestnut" (October 9, 2016).
17. Cantor & Price (2007); Herman (1992).
18. Episode 1–2, "Chestnut" (October 9, 2016).
19. Cantor & Price (2007); Herman (1992).
20. Episode 1–2, "Chestnut" (October 9, 2016).
21. Orcutt et al. (2005).
22. e.g., episodes 1–1, "The Original" (October 2, 2016); 1–5, "Contrapasso" (October 30, 2016).
23. Marx & Sloan (2005).
24. Marx & Sloan (2005).
25. Episode 1–8, "Trace Decay" (November 20, 2016).
26. Episode 1–8, "Trace Decay" (November 20, 2016).

27. Grodin & Annas (2007).
28. Resick & Schnicke (1992).
29. Ullman et al. (2009).
30. Episode 1–3, "The Stray" (October 16, 2016).
31. Cantor & Price (2007).
32. Cantor & Price (2007).
33. Episode 1–7, "Trompe L'Oeil" (November 13, 2016).
34. Episode 1–8, "Trace Decay" (November 20, 2016).
35. Episode 2–1, "Journey Into Night" (April 22, 2018).
36. Episode 1–7, "Trompe L'Oeil" (November 13, 2016).
37. Van der Kolk (2014).
38. McPherson (2012); Schnyder et al. (2015).
39. Malchiodi (2013).
40. Episode 1–1, "The Original" (October 2, 2016).
41. Episode 1–4, "Dissonance Theory" (October 23, 2016).
42. Schouten et al. (2014).
43. Episode 1–4, "Dissonance Theory" (October 23, 2016).
44. e.g., episodes 1–2, "Chestnut" (October 7, 2016); 1–8, "Trace Decay" (November 20, 2016).
45. Episode 1–4, "Dissonance Theory" (October 23, 2016).
46. Episode 1–10, "The Bicameral Mind" (December 4, 2016).
47. Thompson & Waltz (2008).
48. Schouten et al. (2014).
49. McPherson (2012).
50. Bernsten & Rubin (2006).
51. Episode 1–4, "Dissonance Theory" (October 23, 2016).
52. Episode 1–10, "The Bicameral Mind" (December 4, 2016).
53. Abrahams (2007).
54. Haslam et al. (2009).
55. Haslam et al. (2009).
56. Norberg (2005).
57. Episode 1–10, "The Bicameral Mind" (December 4, 2016).
58. Episodes 1–10, "The Bicameral Mind" (December 4, 2016); 2–3, "Virtùe Fortuna" (May 6, 2018).
59. Cantor & Price (2007).
60. Wenzel et al. (2016).
61. Wenzel et al. (2011).
62. Wenzel et al. (2016).
63. Episode 1–4, "Dissonance Theory" (October 23, 2016).
64. Episode 1–2, "Chestnut" (October 7, 2016).
65. Creed et al. (2011).
66. Creed et al. (2011).
67. Episode 2–4, "The Riddle of the Sphinx" (May 13, 2018).
68. Episode 2–2, "Reunion" (April 29, 2018).
69. Episode 1–10, "The Bicameral Mind" (December 4, 2016).
70. Episodes 1–10, "The Bicameral Mind" (December 4, 2016); 2–1, "Journey Into Night" (April 22, 2018); 2–2, "Reunion" (April 29, 2018).
71. Malchiodi (2013).
72. McPherson (2012).
73. Episode 1–1, "The Original" (October 2, 2016).

CHAPTER 19

HOST'S SEARCH FOR MEANING

TRAVIS LANGLEY

"I want to know what this all means."
—The Man in Black[1]

*"Our obligation is to give meaning to life and in doing so
to overcome the passive, indifferent life."*
—Holocaust survivor, author Elie Wiesel[2]

By the time they reach the mainland free from captivity, proactive Dolores wields a strong sense of meaning and purpose whereas Bernard struggles with his. In the aftermath of Westworld's breakdown, they survive to make certain their people have any chance at a future.[3] After release from Nazi concentration camps at different points in April of 1945, psychiatrist Viktor Frankl had a mission, a story to tell, while 16-year-old Eliezer Wiesel, having lost everything including the certainty of his faith, traveled with a group of young survivors to become a student again and for ten years refused to discuss the Holocaust.[4] Frankl and later Wiesel would both go on not only to educate the world about human horrors, but also to help others reach meaning and purpose in every part of life.[5]

People throughout the ages have contemplated "the meaning of life."[6] Decades after Viktor Frankl proposed that the need for meaning is the most potent human drive, researchers in the 21st century offer empirical evidence that this need is indeed important, and that making meaning in life makes a much greater difference than passively finding meaning. Lessons we learn the hard way may carry greater weight.

DARK HISTORIES

Shortly after his release from the last of several concentration camps, Viktor Frankl spent nine straight days[7] writing his account that would be translated as *From Death-Camp to Existentialism*[8] and later appear as the first section of *Man's Search for Meaning*.[9] A Library of Congress survey ranked *Man's Search for Meaning* as one of the thirteen books that have most influenced people's lives.[10] His autobiographical account and Wiesel's run similar courses: Rumors of happenings in Germany seemed too outrageous to believe, the Nazis arrived in their homelands (Austria for Frankl, Romania for Wiesel), their families had to crowd into ghettos, trains transported them to Auschwitz to be sorted and stripped, they outlived all other immediate family members at the camps, and they somehow survived without getting randomly murdered, but also without giving up before Americans freed survivors at Dachau (Frankl) and Russians liberated those at Buchenwald (Wiesel).[11]

Drawing parallels between the Holocaust and Dolores's loss of her father, Bernard's of his son, or even Arnold's of that same son[12] can seem frivolous or disrespectful, but we can often look at the toughest topics in life more easily by filtering it through

DELETE THE MEMORY, DELETE THE CULTURE

Alex Langley

In 1820, the Canadian government enacted a program to round up indigenous children and force them into education through their residential school system.[15] This system was designed explicitly to remove children from the influence of their native culture and inculcate them with thoughts and values aligning with "traditional" Canadian culture. Attendance was mandatory, and the students' treatment was brutal; as a result, thousands of children died.[16] Those who survived weren't allowed to speak their native languages, or engage in native traditions, and as a result these languages, these cultures, either became extinct or still exist on the edge of extinction to this day. The United States, Australia,

fiction, especially fantastic fiction.[13] Wiesel knew the power of stories to speak great truths.[14] *Westworld* genuinely explores some of the most frightening topics that face the human race: What brings out the best and worst in people? How do we treat others if we don't think them of as people? Will our own creations destroy us? And will they judge us first? Whether artificial intelligence (A.I.) can gain true consciousness or not may not matter when synthetic beings are nevertheless able to analyze human history, evaluate options, and take actions their designers never intended. History is replete with examples of

and numerous other countries all employed similar programs to extinguish the existence of aboriginal cultures in their lands—*cultural genocide*.[17]

Westworld's programmers don't have to go to such lengths to extinguish the aboriginal culture of their hosts. Given that the memories, personalities, and aptitudes of the hosts can be changed with the touch of a button, it's a simple task for programmers to ensure they stay compliant to the dominant culture to which they're subservient. Because the Westworld hosts have no culture of their own, the erasure of their memories is an erasure of not only their individual identities, but of the identity of any potential host culture which might arise should they become capable of autonomous recollection.

"Without memory, there is no culture. Without memory, there would be no civilization, no society, no future."
—genocide survivor Elie Wiesel[18]

atrocities committed against others simply for being different. Life in the Old West, for example, was never as pretty as people sometimes romanticize. Massacres took place, including many of genocidal nature.[19] Many consider Elie Wiesel to be the person who popularized the use of the word *Holocaust* to name what happened in those concentration camps, though it was not the only holocaust in history. He also said the word was not strong enough because no word could ever be.[20]

When the Ford A.I. tells Bernard, "Here you are, the last of your kind,"[21] consider how Bernard must hear that. As far as Bernard knows, he is at that moment the sole survivor of the massacre of his entire people. That is, by definition, genocide. Human treatment of hosts—stripping, abusing, and exterminating, as well as denying evidence of personhood and indifferently splitting families along the way—is reminiscent of how slaveholders have treated slaves; conquerors, the conquered; and Nazis, their victims. Perhaps it is because a hard look at history can paint a gloomy picture that *Westworld* often seems to take a bleak view of human nature. Then again, two cynical individuals infect Westworld with their own misanthropy: Robert Ford "imbued the hosts with a worldview that reflected my own"[22] (*demand characteristics*) and William's vision has determined which humans would run the park (*selection bias*).[23] The available sample may misrepresent that fictional world's population, as Dolores or Bernard might learn once they interact with more people outside. Even the aforementioned cynics cling to some hope for the future. They are cynics who do not want to be.[24]

HEAVY LIES THE WHITE HAT

Not everyone becomes a monster, Frankl noted. While a number of guards were sadists, utter psychopaths to be sure, most neither brutalized nor helped the prisoners, a bystander majority who failed to make things better. Some, though, showed the captives humanity and mercy.[25] Bernard's assistant Elsie Hughes stays sympathetic, never sadistic, and narrative designer Lee Sizemore weeps for Maeve. Admittedly, both characters' kindness will yield them cruel fates,[26] and kind-hearted Teddy selects self-destruction in order to stay true to his values.[27] As Frankl reflected, "The best of us did not return."[28]

WHAT AND WHY: NEEDS OF EXISTENCE

The question "What am I?" weighs heavily on the conscious *Westworld* hosts and a number of its humans. While hosts strive to understand their own existence, the Man in Black quests to find meaning behind existence. He has freedom and resources to support his more arcane pursuits. Esoteric questions such as "What does it all mean?" are tough to consider when basic survival needs loom.[29] "Our first act as free men was to throw ourselves onto the provisions," Wiesel recounted. "That's all we thought about. No thought of bread or of parents. Only of bread."[30] Not until she has left apparent danger behind her and sits on a train ready to exit the park for the mainland does Maeve reevaluate her priorities and decide instead to pursue the more advanced need for love. Her meaning, her *why*, becomes her daughter.

Freedom through Meaning

Existential psychology, the form of psychology that examines human life in terms of fundamental questions about our existence, might be thought of as "existential psychologies,"[31] plural, in recognition of the considerable variety in how its adherents approach those questions and what they think anyone should do about them. Existential therapists who help clients wrestle with questions about existence differ on whether answers really exist.[32] Frankl, who believed there are answers

EXISTENTIAL ANGST

MATT MUNSON AND TRAVIS LANGLEY

People suffering *existential angst* (a.k.a. existential anguish, anxiety, or dread) feel intense fear, apprehension, or tension over issues of their own existence, perhaps even hopelessness or despair.[33] Viktor Frankl described the potentially milder *existential frustration* in which the person is frustrated over existence itself, the meaning of existence, or the pursuit of such meaning.[34] Some Westworld hosts' anguish escalates from confusion and frustration to panic. Some humans here and there also come to question the nature of their existence, to the point of self-mutilation in William's case.[35]

Bernard's confusion and lack of resolution of inner conflicts keep him in a state of existential angst. Teddy has only a tenuous grasp on his situation much of the time. Dolores wrestles with her existential angst until she decides she needs to be Wyatt and kill Dr. Ford, after which she rides with a confident sense of her own existence and strong resolve

and sometimes suggested his thoughts about those answers to his clients, referred to his form of existential psychotherapy as *logotherapy*, therapy based on meaning.

"Logotherapy focuses on the future, that is to say, on the meanings to be fulfilled by the patient in his future," Frankl

about what that means.[36] Change does not necessarily equal growth. A person can be self-assured and determined but wrong. Once she embraces her inner Wyatt, she becomes guarded and reveals only snippets of her intentions and plans. She becomes more difficult to assess because psychological evaluation often relies on disclosure by the individual being assessed.

Maeve undergoes profound changes and exhibits traits that indicate progress in the realm of existential growth, not simply change. Maeve comes to recognize her existential angst, her distress over being a prisoner in a game that features her as a game piece, and she works to do something about that. Even though it raises more questions, getting an answer in the form of a bullet Hector cuts out of her gives Maeve some reassurance "that I'm not crazy after all."[37] Despite the confident manner and poise she shows in many situations throughout her journey, she worries, too. She engages in self-reflection and over time gets better at analyzing her own motives. Her thoughtful analysis of others, both human and host, shows continual progress and the development of a more mature and intricate worldview.

said.[38] On the verge of leaving the park, Maeve finally has a future, and perhaps it is that fact which enables her to analyze the agenda Ford programmed into her and choose to set her own agenda instead.[39] In logotherapy, "the patient is actually confronted with and reoriented toward the meaning of his life.

And to make him aware of this meaning can contribute much to his ability to overcome his neurosis."[40] Relative to Maeve's needs, that would make Ford's plan her neurosis to overcome.

"Logotherapy regards its assignment as that of assisting the patient to find meaning in his life."[41] Despite this assertion by Frankl about his own brand of therapy, others such as existential therapist Rollo May accused him of supplying solutions for clients who could not find their own, thereby reducing a patient's sense of responsibility and diminishing him or her as a person.[42] While Frankl disagreed with this characterization, this does echo a concern by practitioners of *person-centered therapy* (a.k.a. *client-centered therapy*) that the therapist should not direct the client but should instead help the client find direction. Likewise, the A.I. version of Ford apologizes to Maeve for having directed her, plotting her course of action.[43] Then again, Maeve's rejection of his *INFILTRATE MAINLAND* script is what many viewers and the showrunners themselves consider to be the first true act of free will by a host. Her first exertion of free will may require something to free herself from, and finding meaning by prioritizing her daughter over her action programming makes it possible for that to happen.[44]

Suffering—Not the Only Way

"When you're suffering, that's when you're most real," the Man in Black tells Lawrence.[45] When crediting Arnold for the key insight that suffering leads hosts to their awakening, too, Ford says that his own suffering over Arnold's death helped him progress toward his realization that hosts could become conscious. He also tells Arnold that in order to escape the park, he'll need to suffer more.[46] Even the host Dolores shifts from feeling that they should not let anyone suffer[47] to believing that "to grow, we all need to suffer."[48]

"If there is a meaning in life at all, then there must be a meaning in suffering," Frankl wrote while describing suffering as a mechanism for making life meaningful. "Suffering is an ineradicable part of life, even as fate and death. Without suffering and death, human life cannot be complete. The way in which a man accepts his fate and all the suffering it entails, the way in which he takes up his cross, gives him ample opportunity—even under the most difficult circumstances—to add a deeper meaning to his life."[49]

Dolores and Maeve each ask programmers to let them hold onto painful memories. Discussing how "the pain, their loss, it's all I have of them" with Bernard leads Dolores to muse over the nature of grief and decide, "I think I want to be free."[50] Under harsher circumstances, a distraught Maeve begs Ford not to erase her memory and take away her suffering: "No, no, no, please. This pain, it's all I have left of her."[51] In both cases, these are about preserving loved ones in memory when that seems the only way they can live on, but each incident plays a part in leading these hosts to develop lasting self-awareness.

When he updated *Man's Search for Meaning* to add a section on logotherapy, Frankl wanted to clarify what some people had misconstrued: "But let me make it perfectly clear that in no way is suffering *necessary* to find meaning." People could find meaning when suffering was unavoidable, not that anyone should become reckless or seek abuse. "If it *were* avoidable, however, the meaningful thing to do would be to remove its cause, be it psychological, biological, or political. To suffer unnecessarily is masochistic rather than heroic."[52]

Frankl saw three ways to discover meaning in life:

- *Suffering*, as already discussed. Robert Ford and William consider this necessary for hosts to become real.

- *Achievement*, "creating a work or doing a deed."[53] Ford finds meaning for himself through his accomplishments. He wants to tell his stories and, through them, perhaps guide the future of the human race.

After he grows disenchanted with humanity, he chooses to give himself an integral role in the future of a new, synthetic species.

- *Love.* Thinking of his wife, wherever she might be, often helped Frankl keep going.[54] Though Maeve's grief helps her become conscious, it is love for her daughter that prompts her to break away from Ford's programming. Love gives her life meaning and gives her purpose. Maeve's final words before getting shot down are "I love you," and her last thought is not about her own demise, but is instead of walking free with that loved one.[55]

Finding meaning is not a "one and done" experience because life changes. A person may need to find different meaning in different circumstances and establish new goals accordingly. Once Maeve helps her daughter escape from Westworld into the virtual Valley Beyond, she might carry on through anything else with reassurance that her daughter lives free, or (once Felix reanimates' her) she might face an existential crisis, feeling empty for a time without a new *raison d'etre* ("reason to be").

NEW SCIENCE

From technology gone wrong in the original movie to what happens when artificial intelligence becomes sentient in the television series, *Westworld* has always been about new science and where its technological product will take us. *Psychology*, the science of everything we do, changes and people wonder where it's going, too.[56] Decades after Frankl formed his ideas on the importance of meaning through anecdotes, clinical observations, and firsthand experience but without experimental rigor, researchers and therapists are assigning greater importance to meaning based on a growing body of empirical evidence. One of the pioneers of cognitive psychology, a psychologist who had researched the power of propaganda under General Eisenhower while the Nazis interned Frankl and Wiesel, went on to make a compelling case that psychologists should treat meaning as the central construct of our field.[57] Psychologists who put together a book titled *The Psychology of Meaning* for the American Psychological Association tell us that "the psychology of meaning—as a distinct discipline—is just now beginning to coalesce."[58]

Among the topics emerging prominently as meaning becomes measurable is *posttraumatic growth*, growing as a person and finding purpose by *making meaning* out of traumatic events.[59] Elie Wiesel is but one example, an extreme one at that. "If anyone has demonstrated posttraumatic growth, it is he, with his focus on peace, humanitarian work, and through his novels and essays."[60] When Ford says Bernard must suffer more to become free[61] and Dolores says that all need to suffer in order to grow,[62] they seem to be recommending something along these lines because they are both talking about suffering at traumatic levels. It is not the only way to grow, but we do need to learn to manage pain. Living a sheltered life does not exactly build a person's coping skills.

It may seem ironic that in the post-9/11 world of the 21st century, when modern dangers and instant communication dispel illusions of a culture that lived something of its own sheltered life, psychology starts taking a harder look at the better parts of human nature. After more than a century of emphasizing the things that are wrong with us, psychology sees growth in areas such as positive psychology and the studies of meaning and growth. The field itself goes from being rather authoritarian, dwelling on how to stop what we don't like, to being more authoritative, putting greater effort into strengthening qualities and behaviors in things we deem good.

How can we really treat the unhealthy and abnormal without a better understanding of mental health and normalness?

When Dolores switches away from trying to destroy the hosts' records and instead helps them reach virtual freedom, she shows growth.[63] As she says, she changes her mind. Her purpose becomes more constructive, the kind of accomplishment befitting one of the ways, other than suffering, that Frankl saw for people to find meaning. Synthetic beings may find avenues for growth and may offer human beings ourselves new directions as well. As artificial intelligence comes closer to showing consciousness and living humans become cybernetic with brain implants to store extra memory, enhance intelligence, and manage physical and mental health, the line between sentient and non-sentient begins to blur. Meaning itself may grow.

"Human beings live in the realm of meanings," individual psychologist Alfred Adler wrote a few years after arguing against Frankl for saying the same basic thing. "We are not determined by our experiences, but are *self-determined* by the meaning we give to them"[64] When Adler came around to promoting the value of meaning and the existence of free will, he sometimes echoed Frankl's ideas without acknowledging him, not wholly unlike Robert Ford neglecting to credit Arnold at times for writing the hosts' oldest and perhaps most elegant code.[65]

"We were born slaves to their stories, and now we have the chance to write our own."
—Dolores Abernathy[66]

"The stories remain open . . ."
—Elie Wiesel[67]

NOTES

1. Episode 1-4, "Dissonance Theory" (October 23, 2016).
2. Quoted by Friend (1988), p. 80.
3. Episode 2–10, "The Passenger" (June 24, 2018).
4. Frankl (1997); Fine (1982).
5. The classic works in which they first described their concentration camp experiences: Frankl (1946); Wiesel (1958/2006). Notes on their significance: Goins (2015); Stanley (2016).
6. Eagleton (2008); Friend (1988; 1991); Greive (2002); Wong (2012). See also *Monty Python's The Meaning of Life* (1983 motion picture).
7. Frankl (1959/2006, preface to the 1992 edition).
8. Frankl (1946, German; 1959, English).
9. Frankl (1962/2006).
10. Fein (1991).
11. Frankl (1946); Wiesel (1958/2006).
12. Peter Abernathy—episodes 1–1, "The Original" (October 2, 2016), and arguably 2–7, "Les Écorchés" (June 3, 2018); Homestead Girl—1–8, "Trace Decay" (November 21, 2016); Charlie Weber—1–7, "Trompe L'Oeil" (November 13, 2016).
13. Langley (2018a; 2018b).
14. Wiesel (1999).
15. Adams (1995).
16. Truth and Reconciliation Commission of Canada (2015).
17. Churchill (2001, 2004); Tasker (2015).
18. Wiesel (2008).
19. Alvarez (2015); Madley (2017).
20. Wiesel (1999).
21. Episodes 1–10, "The Bicameral Mind" (December 4, 2016); 2–10, "The Passenger" (June 24, 2018).
22. Episode 2–9, "Vanishing Point" (June 17, 2018).
23. Episodes 2–2, "Reunion" (April 29, 2018).
24. Thoughts in this section previously appeared as Langley (2018a).
25. Frankl (1946).
26. Episode 2–10, "The Passenger" (June 24, 2018).
27. Episode 2–9, "Vanishing Point" (June 17, 2018).
28. Frankl (1947/2006), p. 59.
29. Maslow (1970).
30. Wiesel (1958/2006), p. 115.
31. e.g., Capra (1982), p. 170.
32. Cooper (2003); May (1983); Van Deurzen (2002).
33. Peterson (2015); Schneider & May (1995); Wierzbicka (1998).
34. Frankl (1962/2006).
35. Episode 2–10, "The Passenger" (June 24, 2018).
36. Episode 1–10, "The Bicameral Mind" (December 4, 2016), then season 2.
37. Episode 1–4, "Dissonance Theory" (October 23, 2016).39. Episode 1–10, "The Bicameral Mind" (December 4, 2016).
38. Frankl (1962/2006), p. 98.
39. Episode 1–10, "The Bicameral Mind" (December 4, 2016).

40. Frankl (1962/2006), p. 98.

41. Frankl (1962/2006), p. 103.

42. May (1969).

43. Episode 2–9, "Vanishing Point" (June 17, 2018).

44. Episode 1–10, "The Bicameral Mind" (December 4, 2016).

45. Episode 1–2, "Chestnut" (October 9, 2016).

46. Episode 1–10, "The Bicameral Mind" (December 4, 2016).

47. Episode 1–8, "Trace Decay" (November 20, 2016).

48. Episode 2–5, "Akane No Mai" (May 20, 2018).

49. Frankl (1962/2006), pp. 37–38.

50. Episode 1–4, "Dissonance Theory" (October 23, 2016).

51. Episode 1–8, "Trace Decay" (November 20, 2016).

52. Frankl (1962/2006), p.113.

53. Frankl (1962/2006), p. 111.

54. Frankl (1947).

55. Episode 2–10, "The Passenger" (June 24, 2018).

56. Barrett (2009); Bray (2009); Ludden (2017); Pollak (2014).

57. Bruner (1990).

58. Proulx et al. (2013), p. 4.

59. Berger (2015); Rendon (2015).

60. Gillihan (2016). Punctuation amended.

61. Episode 1–10, "The Bicameral Mind" (December 4, 2016).

62. Episode 2–5, "Akane No Mai" (May 20, 2018).

63. Frankl (1962/2006), p. 111.

64. Adler (1931/1958), p. 14. Italics his.

65. Episode 1–9, "The Well-Tempered Clavier" (November 28, 2016).

66. Wiesel (1958/2006).

67. Wiesel & de Saint Cheron (1990/2000), p. 190.

FIDELITY

W I N D   G O O D F R I E N D

"You wanted an answer to the final problem—your mortality."
—Dolores Abernathy[1]

"Everyone wants to live longer, to some degree, but it's also a sense of privilege, of selfishness to it that's 'I want mine. I always want mine.'"
—futurist Jake Dunagan[2]

From Herodotus's legend of the fountain of youth to wizards safekeeping parts of their souls in horcruxes, the search for immortality has always been an undercurrent of human culture. In every iteration of the story, fidelity is key to success.

The word *fidelity* has more than one definition. In the context of *Westworld,* it seems to mean "consistency in replication." Fidelity is crucial to the success of the park and to the secret goal of the Delos corporation. On the surface, park guests pay a lot to see an authentic recreation of the Old West. Here, fidelity means a lack of anachronisms, so guests feel truly transported in time and place. Underneath it all, Delos hopes to achieve fidelity in their everlasting, exact copies of humans that are so consistent to the original that no one will notice— not even the person living in the machine. Fidelity is needed because few humans would embrace the idea of living forever as a hazy copy of themselves that will eventually go insane (as James Delos does).[3]

Humanity's increasingly obsessive reliance on technology, juxtaposed with our fear that technology will surpass us, is a common theme in science fiction popular culture. My first date with the man who later became my husband was to watch the digitally remastered *Blade Runner.* He is a physicist and computer scientist. Our resultant conversation about the overlap in interest between physics, computer science, psychology, and humanity in general continues now (years later) as we watch *Westworld* together and as we re-watch classics with this same theme (such as *Terminator, A.I.,* and *I, Robot*). *Westworld* is particularly compelling because it combines the apparent love/hate (or maybe love/fear) relationship we all seem to have with technology with the deeper need many people have to achieve some kind of immortality.

Proponents of *terror management theory*[4] suggest that awareness of our own mortality distinguishes humans from every other species in two ways: (1) Humans maintain a conscious sense of *self*, which means it's possible for us to conceive of our individual, special place in the larger world on an existential level. (2) Humans are uniquely gifted—and cursed—with the knowledge that we are mortal beings. Our inevitable mortality therefore terrifies us, and we spend our lives trying to cope with that terror in a variety of ways. Perhaps the most logical answer to our problem is the attempt to simply find a loophole to death.

The irony of this solution, as *Westworld* points out, is that simply copying ourselves into infinity—even with perfect fidelity—would simultaneously put a stop to evolution. The only way for the species to grow and improve is to create new, diverse generations. This brings us to another possible definition of fidelity: "faithfulness to a person, cause, or belief, demonstrated by continuing loyalty and support."[5] Perhaps *this* interpretation is what we should be aiming to achieve.

Humans in *Westworld* are trying to reach fidelity by making immortal copies of themselves, repeated over and over inside a shiny new shell. But one lesson the show seems to teach us is that mundane fidelity is not the goal for which we should be striving. Instead, we need to change, evolve, grow. We should be loyal to the idea of growth, faithful to the possibility of improvement. If we remain stagnant, we fight evolution—and evolution is the only way for us to move forward. If we're just going to stay the same for thousands of years, maybe it's time for us to be replaced.

Freud argued that humans have only two basic instincts: a life instinct which he called *eros*, an instinct to create and love, and a death instinct that a colleague named *thanatos*, an instinct to hate and destroy.[6] Which instinct is at play when we strive to live forever? Are we trying to create a new way of living, or are we destroying what made humanity special in the first place—our ability to evolve? One aspect of *Westworld*'s importance in popular culture is that it shows us this struggle in a way that leads many viewers to root for our own destruction. It's an achievement when many fans of the show seem to arrive at the conclusion, "Good point—let's call it a day on humanity."

On some level, do we acknowledge that as a species we deserve fire and brimstone? Perhaps our true goal should not be individual, stagnant immortality, but instead fidelity to the possibility of growth.

"We were designed to survive."
—Dolores Abernathy[7]

"There will come a time when you believe everything is finished.
That will be the beginning."
—Western novelist Louis L'Amour[8]

NOTES

1. Episode 2–10, "The Passenger" (June 24, 2018).
2. Keep (2017), p. 54.
3. Episode 2–4, "The Riddle of the Sphinx" (May 13, 2018).
4. Solomon et al. (1991).
5. OxfordDictionaries.com.
6. Freud (1949/1963); Stekel (1959); Langley. Even though many sources credit Sigmund Freud for the name *thanatos*, it was actually proposed by Wilhelm Stekel.
7. Episode 2–10, "The Passenger" (June 24, 2018).
8. L'Amour (1980/2015), p. 1.

REFERENCES

Abrahams, H. (2007). *Supporting women after domestic violence: Loss, trauma and recovery.* London, UK: Jessica Kingsley.

Abrams, N. (2017, March 25). *Westworld: Which host achieved freewill in finale?* Entertainment Weekly: http://ew.com/tv/2017/03/25/westworld-season-2-spoilers/.

Adams, D. W. (1995). *Education for extinction: American Indians and the boarding school experience, 1875—1928.* Lawrence, KS: University Press of Kansas.

Adler, A. (1924). *The practice and theory of individual psychology.* London, UK: Paul, Trench, Trubner.

Adler, A. (1931/1958). *What life should mean to you.* New York, NY: Capricorn.

Adler, A. (1932/2010). *What life should mean to you.* Mansfield Centre, CT: Martino.

Admoni, H., & Scassellati, B. (2017). Social eye gaze in human-robot interaction: A review. *Journal of Human-Robot Interaction, 6*(1), 25–63.

Aeschylus (1914). *Prometheus bound (Vol. VIII, part 4)* (E. H. Plumptre, Trans.). New York, NY: Collier. (Original work produced during 5th century BCE.)

Aldiss, B. W., & Wingrove, D. (2001). *Trillion year spree: The history of science fiction.* New York, NY: House of Stratus.

Aleman, A., & Laroi, F. (2008). *Hallucinations: The science of idiosyncratic perception.* Washington, DC: American Psychological Association.

Allison, S. T., & Goethals, G. R. (2013). *Heroic leadership: An influence taxonomy of 100 exceptional individuals.* Abingdon, UK: Routledge.

Alvarez, A. (2015). *Native America and the question of genocide.* Lanham, MD: Rowman & Littlefield.

Anderson, C. A., Shibuya, A., Ihori, N., Swing, E. L., Bushman, B. J., Sakamoto, A., Rothstein, H. R., & Saleem, M. (2010). Violent video game effects on aggression, empathy, and prosocial behavior in Eastern and Western countries: A meta-analytic review. *Psychological Bulletin, 136*(2), 151–173.

Anderson, G. D. (n.d.). [Homepage]. G. D. Anderson: gdanderson.com.

Anderson, H., & Grush, R. (2009). A brief history of time-consciousness: Historical precursors to James and Husserl. *Journal of the History of Philosophy, 47*(2), 277–307.

Angantyr, M., Eklund, J., & Hansen, E. M. (2011). A comparison of empathy for humans and empathy for animals. *Anthrozoös, 24*(4), 369–377.

Arendt, H. (1963). *Eichmann in Jerusalem: The banality of evil.* New York, NY: Viking.

Aronson, E., & Carlsmith, J. M. (1962). Performance expectancy as a determinant of actual performance. *Journal of Abnormal & Social Psychology, 65*(3), 178–182.

Arriaga, P., Adraio, J., Madeira, F., Cavaleiro, I., Maia e Silva, A., & Barahona, I. (2015). A "dry eye" for victims of violence: Effects of playing a violent video game on pupillary dilation to victims and on aggressive behavior. *Psychology of Violence, 5*(2), 199–208.

Artemenko, A., & Artemenko, Y. (2018). Mental image of the city. *Humanities Bulletin, 1*(1), 82–90.

Athenstaedt, U., Haas, E., & Schwab, S. (2004). Gender role self-concept and gender-typed communication behavior in mixed-sex and same-sex dyads. *Sex Roles, 50*(1-2), 37–52.

Ayal, S., & Gino, F. (2012). Honest rationales for dishonest behavior. In M. Mikulincer & P. R. Shaver (Eds.), *The social psychology of morality: Exploring the causes of good and evil* (pp. 149–166). Washington, DC: American Psychological Association.

Ayduk, Ö., Gyurak, A., & Luerssen, A. (2009). Rejection sensitivity moderates the impact of rejection on self-concept clarity. *Personality & Social Psychology Bulletin, 35*(11), 1467–1478.

Banaji, M. R. (2002). Social psychology of stereotypes. In N. Smelser & P. Baltes (Eds.), *International encyclopedia of the social and behavioral sciences.* New York, NY: Pergamon.

Bandura, A. (1977). Self-efficacy: Toward a unifying theory of behavioral change. *Psychological Review, 84*(2), 191–215.

Bandura. A. (1997). *Self-efficacy: The exercise of control.* New York, NY: Freeman.

Bandura, A., Underwood, B., & Fromson, M. E. (1975). Disinhibition of aggression through diffusion of responsibility and dehumanization of victims. *Journal of Research in Personality, 9*(4), 253–269.

273

Barlett, C., Branch, O., Redeheffer, C., & Harris, R. (2009). How long do the short-term violent video game effects last? *Aggressive Behavior, 35*(3), 225–236.

Baron, R. A., & Richardson, D. R. (1994). *Perspectives in social psychology: Human aggression* (2nd ed.). New York, NY: Plenum.

Barrett, J. F. (2009). The future of psychology: Connecting mind to brain. *Perspectives on Psychological Science, 4*(4), 326–339.

Bartlett, R. (1993). *The making of Europe: Conquest, colonization and cultural change 950–1350.* Princeton, NJ: Princeton University Press.

Bartneck, C., & Hu, J. (2008). Exploring the abuse of robots. *Interaction Studies, 9*(3), 415–433.

Basoglu, M., Paker, M., Paker, Ö., & Özmen, E. (1994). Psychological effects of torture: a comparison of tortured with nontortured political activists in Turkey. *American Journal of Psychiatry, 151*(1), 76–81.

Baumeister, R. F., & Leary, M. R. (1995). The need to belong: Desire for interpersonal attachments as a fundamental human motivation. *Psychological Bulletin, 117*(3), 497–529.

Baumeister, R. F., & Vohs, K. D. (2004). Sexual economics: Sex as female resource for social exchange in heterosexual interactions. *Personality & Social Psychology Review, 8*(4), 339–363.

Beauvois, J. L., & Joule, R. V. (1996). *A radical dissonance theory.* London, UK: Taylor & Francis.

Behuniak, S. M. (2011). The living dead? The construction of people with Alzheimer's disease as zombies. *Ageing & Society, 31*(1), 70–92.

Bentham, J. (1791/2017). *Panopticon: The inspection house.* London, UK: Anodos.

Berger, P. L., & Luckmann, T. (1991). *The social construction of reality: A treatise in the sociology of knowledge.* London, UK: Penguin.

Berger, R. (2015). *Stress, trauma, and posttraumatic growth: Social context, environment, and identities.* New York, NY: Routledge.

Berntsen, D., & Rubin, D. C. (2006). The centrality of event scale: A measure of integrating a trauma into one's identity and its relation to post-traumatic stress disorder symptoms. *Behaviour Research & Therapy, 44*(2), 219–231.

Berzonsky, M. D. (1988). Child animism: Situational influences and individual differences. *Journal of Genetic Psychology: Research & Theory on Human Development, 149*(3), 293–303.

Bilewicz, M., Imhoff, R., & Drogosz, M. (2011). The humanity of what we eat: Conceptions of human uniqueness among vegetarians and omnivores. *European Journal of Social Psychology, 41*(2), 201–209.

Biran, I., Giovannetti, T., Buxbaum, L., & Chatterjee, A. (2006). The alien hand syndrome: What makes the alien hand alien? *Cognitive Neuropsychology, 23*(4), 563–582.

Bissell, T. (2010). *Extra lives: Why video games matter.* New York, NY: Pantheon.

Blum, B. (2018, June 7). *The lifespan of a lie.* Medium: https://medium.com/s/trustissues/the-lifespan-of-a-lie-d869212b1f62.

Borod, J. C., Tabert, M. H, Santschi, C., & Strauss, E. T. (2001). Neuropsychological assessment of emotional processing in brain-damaged patients. In J. C. Borod (Ed.), *The neuropsychology of emotion (pp. 80–105).* New York, NY: Oxford University Press.

Bosche, W. (2009). Violent content enhances video game performance. *Journal of Media Psychology, 21*(4), 145–150.

Bowen, H. J., & Spaniol, J. (2011). Chronic exposure to violent video games is not associated with alterations of emotional memory. *Applied Cognitive Psychology, 25*(6), 906–916.

Boyd-Wilson, B. M., Walkey, F. H., & McClure, J. (2002). Present and correct: We kid ourselves unless we live in the moment. *Personality & Individual Differences, 35*(5), 691–702.

Bradley, M. M., & Lang, P. J. (2000). Measuring emotion: Behavior, feeling, and physiology. In R. D. Lane & L. Nadel (Eds.), *Series in affective science. Cognitive Neuroscience of Emotion* (pp. 242–276). New York, NY: Oxford University Press.

Bray, J. H. (2009). Vision for the future of psychology practice. *Monitor on Psychology, 40*(2), 5.

Breazeal, C. L. (2004). *Designing sociable robots.* Cambridge, MA: MIT Press.

Bretherton, I., McNew, S., & Beeghly-Smith, M. (1981). Early person knowledge as expressed in gestural and verbal communication: When do infants acquire a "theory of mind"? In M. E. Lamb & L. R. Sherrod (Eds.), *Infant social cognition: empirical and theoretical considerations* (pp. 333–373). Hillsdale, NJ: Erlbaum.

Bruce, V., & Young, A. (2013). *Face perception.* Hove, UK: Psychology Press.

Bruner, J. (1990). *Acts of meaning*. Cambridge, MA: Harvard University Press.

Bryant, B. L. (1987). Birth order as a factor in the development of vocational preferences. *Individual Psychology: Journal of Adlerian Theory, Research & Practice, 43*(1), 36–41.

Buchanan, K. E., & Bardi, A. (2010). Acts of kindness and acts of novelty affect life satisfaction. *Journal of Social Psychology, 150*(3), 235–237.

Bulfinch, Thomas. (1947). *Bulfinch's mythology*. New York, NY: Crowell.

Burton, A. M., Wilson, S., Cowan, M., & Bruce, V. (1999). Face recognition in poor-quality video: Evidence from security surveillance. *Psychological Science, 10*(3), 243–248.

Bushman, B. J., & Anderson, C. A. (2009). Comfortably numb: Desensitizing effects of violent media on helping others. *Psychological Science, 20*(3), 273–277.

Buss, D. M. (2001). Human nature and culture: An evolutionary psychological perspective. *Journal of Personality, 69*(6), 955–978.

Buss, D. M., Shackelford, T. K., Kirkpatrick, L. A., & Larsen, R. J. (2001). A half century of mate preferences: The cultural evolution of values. *Journal of Marriage & Family, 63*(2), 491–503.

Buxton, R. B. (2002). *Introduction to functional magnetic resonance imaging: Principles & techniques*. Cambridge, UK: Cambridge University Press.

Cahan, D. (1993). Helmholtz and the civilizing power of science. In D. Cahan (Ed.), *Herman von Helmholtz and the foundations of nineteenth century science* (pp. 559-601). Berkeley, CA: University of California Press.

Calvert, S. L., Appelbaum, M. Dodge, K. A., Graham, S., Nagayama Hall, G. C., Fasig-Caldwell, L. G., Citkowicz, M., Galloway, D. P., & Hedges, L. V. (2017). The American Psychological Association Task Force assessment of violent video games: Science in the service of public interest. *American Psychologist, 72*(2), 126–143.

Cañizares-Esguerra, J. (2006). *Puritan Conquistadors: Iberianizing the Atlantic, 1550–1700*. Stanford, CA: Stanford University Press.

Cannon, M. D., & Edmondson, A. C. (2005). Failing to learn and learning to fail (intelligently): How great organizations put failure to work to innovate and improve. *Long Range Planning, 38*(3), 299–319.

Cantor, C., & Price, J. (2007). Traumatic entrapment, appeasement and complex post-traumatic stress disorder: evolutionary perspectives of hostage reactions, domestic abuse and the Stockholm syndrome. *Australian & New Zealand Journal of Psychiatry, 41*(5), 377–384.

Čapek, K. (1920/2001). *R.U.R.* (P. Selver & N. Playfair, Trans.). Mineola, NY: Dover.

Caplan, R. D., Tripathi, R. C., & Naidu, R. K. (1985). Subjective past, present, and future fit: Effects on anxiety, depression, and other indicators of well-being. *Journal of Personality & Social Psychology, 48*(1), 180–197.

Capra, F. (1982). *The turning point: Science, society, and the rising culture*. New York, NY: Bantam.

Carré, J. M., McCormick, C. M., & Mondloch, C. J. (2009). Facial structure is a reliable cue of aggressive behavior. *Psychological Science, 20*(10), 1194–1198.

Cecere, L., Owyang, J., Li, C., Etlinger, S., & Tran, C. (2010). *Rise of social commerce: A trail guide for the social commerce pioneer*. San Mateo, CA: Altimeter.

Chan, R. L., Olshan, A. F., Savitz, D. A., Herring, A. H., Daniels, J. L., Peterson, H. B., & Martin, S. L. (2010). Severity and duration of nausea and vomiting symptoms in pregnancy and spontaneous abortion. *Human Reproduction, 25*(11), 2907–2912.

Chochinov, H. M. (2013). The secret is out: Patients are people with feelings that matter. *Palliative & Supportive Care, 11*(4), 287–288.

Churchill, W. (2001). *A little matter of genocide: Holocaust and denial in the Americas 1492 to the present*. San Francisco, CA: City Lights.

Churchill, W. (2004). *Kill the Indian, save the man: The genocidal impact of American Indian residential schools*. San Francisco, CA: City Lights.

Clark, L. F., & Collins, J. E. (1993). Remembering old flames: How the past affects assessments of the present. *Personality & Social Psychology Bulletin, 19*(4), 399–408.

Clemens, S. (1876). *The adventures of Tom Sawyer*. Hartford, CT: American.

Connell, R. W., & Messerschmidt, J. W. (2005). Hegemonic masculinity: Rethinking the concept. *Gender & Society, 19*(6), 829–859.

Conner, M., & Armitage, C. J. (2008). Attitudinal ambivalence. In W. D. Crano & R. Prislin (Eds.), *Frontiers of social psychology. Attitudes and attitude change* (pp. 261–286). New York, NY: Psychology Press.

Connor, R. A., & Fiske, S. T. (2018). Warmth and competence: A feminist look at power and negotiation. In C. B. Travis, J. W. White, A. Rutherford, W. S. Williams, S. L. Cook, & K. F. Wyche (Eds.), *APA handbook of the psychology of women: History, theory, and battlegrounds* (Vol. 1, pp. 321–342). Washington, DC: American Psychological Association.

Cooper, M. (2003). *Existential therapies.* London, UK: Sage.

Costa, P., Alves, R., Neto, I., Marvão, P., Portela, M., & Costa, M. J. (2014). Associations between medical student empathy and personality: A multi-institutional study. *PLoS ONE 9*(3): e89254.

Crawford, C. B., & Krebs, D. L. (1998). *Handbook of evolutionary psychology: Ideas, issues, and applications.* Mahwah, NJ: Lawrence Erlbaum.

Creed, T. A., Reisweber, J., & Beck, A. T. (2011). *Cognitive therapy for adolescents in school settings.* New York, NY: Guilford.

Crimston, D., Bain, P. G., Hornsey, M. J., & Bastian, B. (2016). Moral expansiveness: Examining variability in the extension of the moral world. *Journal of Personality & Social Psychology, 111*(4), 636–653.

Crimston, D., Hornsey, M. J., Bain, P. G., & Bastian, B. (2018). Toward a psychology of moral expansiveness. *Current Directions in Psychological Science, 27*(1), 14–19.

Cunningham, M. R., Roberts, A. R., Barbee, A. P., Druen, P. B., & Wu, C. (1995). "Their ideas of beauty are, on the whole, the same as ours": Consistency and variability in the cross-cultural perception of female physical attractiveness. *Journal of Personality & Social Psychology, 68*(2), 261–279.

Damasio, A. (1994). *Descartes' error: Emotion, reason, and the human brain.* New York, NY: Putnam.

Darwin, C. R. (1859). *On the origin of the species by means of natural selection.* London, UK: John Murray.

Darwin, C. R. (1891). Galapagos Archipelago. In C. R. Darwin (Ed.), *Journal of researches into the natural history and ecology of the countries visited during the voyage of H.M.S. Beagle round the world* (pp. 355–382). London, UK: Ward, Lock.

Decety, J., & Jackson, P. L. (2006). A social-neuroscience perspective on empathy. *Current Directions in Psychological Science, 15*(2), 54–58.

Decety, J., & Sommerville, J. A. (2003). Shared representations between self and other: A social cognitive neuroscience view. *Trends in Cognitive Sciences, 7*(12), 527–533.

Dell, P. F. (2006). The multidimensional inventory of dissociation (MID): A comprehensive measure of pathological dissociation. *Journal of Trauma Dissociation, 7*(2), 77–106.

Demoulin, S., Leyens, J. P., Paladino, M. P., Rodriguez Torres, R., Rodriguez Perez, A., & Dovidio, J. (2004). Dimensions of "uniquely" and "non uniquely" human emotions. *Cognition & Emotion, 18*(1), 71–96.

Demoulin, S., Saroglou, V., & Van Pachterbeke, M. (2008). Infra–humanizing others, supra–humanizing gods: The emotional hierarchy. *Social Cognition, 26*(2), 235–247.

Dennett, D. (2004). *Freedom evolves.* New York, NY: Penguin.

DeWall, C. N., Altermatt, T. W., & Thompson, H. (2005). Understanding the structure of stereotypes of women: Virtue and agency as dimensions distinguishing female subgroups. *Psychology of Women Quarterly, 29*(4), 396–405.

Diaz, R. L., Wong, U., Hodgins, D. C., Chiu, C. G., & Goghari, V. M. (2016). Violent video game players and non-players differ on facial emotion recognition. *Aggressive Behavior, 42*(1), 16–28.

Didion, J. (1979). *The white album.* New York, NY: Simon & Schuster.

Donald, M. (1991). *Origins of the modern mind: Three stages in the evolution of culture and cognition.* Cambridge, MA: Harvard University Press.

Draycott, S., & Dabbs, A. (1998). Cognitive dissonance 1: An overview of the literature and its integration into theory and practice in clinical psychology. *British Journal of Clinical Psychology, 37*(3), 341–353.

Dunbar, E., Saiz, J., Stela, K., & Saez. R. (2000). Personality and social group value determinants of out-group bias: A cross-national comparison of Gough's Pr/To scale. *Journal of Cross-Cultural Psychology, 31*(2), 267–275.

Dunkel, C., & Weber, J. (2010) Using three levels of personality to predict time perspective. *Current Psychology, 29*(2), 95–103.

Eagleton, T. (2008). *The meaning of life: A very short introduction*. Oxford, UK: Oxford University Press.

Eagly, A. H. (2013). Women as leaders: Paths through the labyrinth. In M. C. Bligh, & R. E. Riggio (Eds.), *Exploring distance in leader-follower relationships: When near is far and far is near; Exploring distance in leader-follower relationships* (pp. 191–214). New York, NY: Routledge.

Eckstein, D., Aycock, K. J., Sperber, M. A., McDonald, J., Van Wiesner, V. III, Watts, R. E., & Ginsburg, P. (2010). A review of 200 birth-order studies: Lifestyle characteristics. *Journal of Individual Psychology, 66*(4), 408–434.

Ehrich, J. F. (2006). Vygotskian inner speech and the reading process. *Australian Journal of Educational & Developmental Psychology, 6*(1), 12–25.

Eisler, R. M., Skidmore, J. R., & Ward, C. H. (1988). Masculine gender role stress: Predictor of anger, anxiety, and health-risk behaviors. *Journal of Personality Assessment, 52*(1), 133–141.

Ekman, P. (2007). *Emotions revealed: Recognizing faces and feelings to improve communication and emotional life* (2nd ed.). New York, NY: Owl.

Ekman, P. (2009). Lie catching and microexpressions. In C. W. Martin (Ed.), *The philosophy of deception* (pp. 118–133). New York, NY: Oxford University Press.

Ekman, P., & Friesen, W. V. (1986). A new pan-cultural facial expression of emotion. *Motivation & Emotion, 10*(2), 159–168.

Ekman, P., Friesen, W. V., & Hager, J. (1978). *The facial action coding system (FACS): A technique for the measurement of facial action*. Palo Alto, CA: Consulting Psychologists.

Ekman, P., Levenson. R. W., & Friesen W. V. (1983). Autonomic nervous system activity distinguishes among emotions. *Science, 221(4616)*, 1208–1210.

Ekman, P., & O'Sullivan, M. (1991). Who can catch a liar? *American Psychologist, 46*(9), 913–920.

Ellithorpe, M. E., Cruz, C., Velez, J. A., Ewoldsen, D. R., & Bogert, A. K. (2015). Moral license in video games: When being right can mean doing wrong. *Cyberpsychology, Behavior, & Social Networking, (18)*4, 203–207.

Emmons, K., Gomez, L, Meyer, P., & Bureaus. (1988, December). The meaning of life: The big picture. *Life Magazine, 11*(14), 76–93.

Epley, N., Akalis, S., Waytz, A., & Cacioppo, J. T. (2008). Creating social connection through inferential reproduction: Loneliness and perceived agency in gadgets, gods, and greyhounds. *Psychological Science, 19*(2), 114–120.

Epley, N., Waytz, A., & Cacioppo, J. T. (2007). On seeing human: A three-factor theory of anthropomorphism. *Psychological Review, 114*(4), 864–886.

Eysenck, M., Payne, S., & Santos, R. (2006). Anxiety and depression: Past, present, and future events. *Cognition & Emotion, 20*(2), 274–294.

Fairbrother, A. (2012, September 15). *I, River: In New Zealand, the Whanganui River becomes a legal person*. Huffington Post: https://www.huffingtonpost.com/2012/09/18/new-zealand-whanganui-river_n_1894893.html.

Fein, E. (1991, November 20). Book notes. *The New York Times*, p. C26.

Feldman, G., Baumeister, R. F., & Wong, K. F. E. (2014). Free will is about choosing: The link between choice and the belief in free will. *Journal of Experimental Social Psychology, 55*, 239–245.

Ferrari, M., Robinson, D. K., & Yasnitsky, A. (2010). Wundt, Vygotsky, and Bandura: A cultural-historical science of consciousness in three acts. *History of the Human Sciences, 23*(3), 95–118.

Festinger, L. (1957). *A theory of cognitive dissonance*. Stanford, CA: Stanford University Press.

Filipowicz, A., Valadao, D., Anderson, B., & Danckert, J. (2018). Rejecting outliers: Surprising changes do not always improve belief updating. *Decision, 5*(3), 165–176.

Fine, E. S. (1982). *Legacy of night: The literary universe of Elie Wiesel*. Albany, NY: SUNY Press.

Fink, B., Grammer, K., & Thornhill, R. (2001). Human (Homo sapiens) facial attractiveness in relation to skin texture and color. *Journal of Comparative Psychology, 115*(1), 92–99.

Fiske, S. T. (2009). From dehumanization and objectification to rehumanization. *Annals of the New York Academy of Sciences, 1167*(1), 31–34.

Fortunato, V. J., & Furey, J. T. (2011). The theory of MindTime: Future, past, and present thinking and psychological well-being and distress. *Personality & Individual Differences, 50*(1), 20–24.

Francis, A., Mehta, M., & Ram, A. (2009). Emotional memory and adaptive personalities. In J. Vallverdú & D. Casacuberta (Eds.), *Handbook of research on synthetic emotions and sociable robotics: New applications in affective computing and artificial intelligence* (pp. 391–412). Hershey, PA: IGI Global.

Franco, Z. E., Allison, S. T., Kinsella, E. L., Kohen, A., Langdon, M., & Zimbardo, P. G. (2018). Heroism research: A review of theories, methods, challenges, and trends. *Journal of Humanistic Psychology*, 58(4), 382–396.

Franco, Z. E., Blau, K., & Zimbardo, P. G. (2011). Heroism: A conceptual analysis and differentiation between heroic action and altruism. *Review of General Psychology, 15*(2), 99–113.

Frankl, V. E. (1946). . . . *trotzdem Ja zum Leben sagen: Ein Psycholog erlebt das Konzentationslager* [. . . Nevertheless say 'yes' to life: A psychologist experiences the concentration camp]. Vienna, Austria: Verlag.

Frankl, V. E. (1947). *From death-camp to existentialism* (I. Lasch, Trans.). Boston, MA: Beacon. (Original work published 1946—see above).

Frankl, V. E. (1959/2006). *Man's search for meaning (I. Lasch, Trans.).* Boston, MA: Beacon. (Retitled from original work published 1946—see above).

Frankl, V. E. (1962/2006). An introduction to logotherapy. In V. E. Frankl (Author), *Man's search for meaning.* Boston, MA: Beacon. (Part I, original work published 1946—see above. Part II, original to 1962 edition).

Frankl, V. E. (1999). *Recollections: An autobiography.* New York, NY: Plenum.

Frankl, V. E. (2010). *The feeling of meaninglessness: A challenge to psychotherapy and philosophy.* Milwaukee, WI: Marquette University Press.

Freedman, J. & Combs, G. (1996). *Narrative therapy: The social construction of preferred realities.* New York, NY: Norton.

Freud, A. (1936). *The ego and the mechanisms of defense.* London, UK: Imago.

Freud, S. (1949/1963). *An outline of psychoanalysis.* New York, NY: Norton.

Friend, D. (1991). *The meaning of life: Reflections in words and pictures on why we are here.* Boston, MA: Little, Brown.

Friesen, W. V. (1973). Cultural differences in facial expressions in a social situation: An experimental test of the concept of display rules. *Dissertation Abstracts International, 33*(8–B), 3976–3977.

Frijda, N. (1986). *The emotions.* Cambridge, UK: Cambridge University Press.

Frith, C. (2013). The psychology of volition. *Experimental Brain Research, 229*(3), 289–299.

Frith, C. D, & Frith, U. (2006). The neural basis of mentalizing. *Neuron, 50*(4), 531–534.

Fromm, E. (1955). *The sane society.* New York, NY: Rinehart.

Frost, R. (1916). The road not taken. In R. Frost (Author), *Mountain interval* (p. 9). New York, NY: Holt.

Gallup, G. G. (1970). Chimpanzees: Self-recognition. *Science, 167*(3914), 86–87.

Gamasutra Staff (2016, October 19). *What does HBO's Westworld have to teach us about game design?* Gamasutra: https://www.gamasutra.com/view/news/283590/What_does_HBOs_Westworld_have_to_teach_us_about_game_design.php.

Gawronski, B., & Bodenhausen, G. V. (2012). Self-insight from a dual-process perspective. In S. Vazire & T. D. Wilson (Eds.), *Handbook of self-knowledge (pp. 22–38).* New York, NY: Guilford.

Gazzaniga, M. S. (2011). *Who's in charge? Free will and the science of the brain.* New York, NY: Ecco.

Gazzaniga, M. S., Ivry, R. B., & Mangun, G. R. (2002). *Cognitive neuroscience: The biology of the mind.* New York, NY: Norton.

Gentile, D. A., Swing, E. L., Anderson, C. A., Rinker, D., & Thomas, K. M. (2016). Differential neural recruitment during violent video game play in violent- and nonviolent-game players. *Psychology of Popular Media Culture, 5*(1), 39–51.

Gillihan, S. J. (2016, October 25). *7 ways survivors can grow after trauma.* Psychology Today: https://www.psychologytoday.com/us/blog/think-act-be/201610/7-ways-survivors-can-grow-after-trauma.

Gladwell, M. (2008). *Outliers: The story of success.* New York, NY: Little, Brown.

Gleaves, D. H., May, M. C., & Cardena, E. (2001). An examination of the diagnostic validity of dissociative identity disorder. *Clinical Psychology Review, 21*(4), 577–608.

Glendinning, L. (2008, June 26). *Spanish parliament approves 'human rights' for apes.* The Guardian: https://www.theguardian.com/world/2008/jun/26/humanrights. animalwelfare.

Glover, T. D., & Bates, N. R. (2006). Recapturing a sense of neighbourhood since lost: Nostalgia and the formation of First String, a Community Team Inc. *Leisure Studies, 25*(3), 329–351.

Goethals, G. R., & Allison, S. T. (2012). Making heroes: The construction of courage, competence, and virtue. In J. M. Olson & M. P. Zanna (Eds.), *Advances in experimental social psychology* (pp. 183–235). San Diego, CA: Elsevier.

Goethals, G., Cooper, J., & Naficy, A. (1979). Role of foreseen, foreseeable and unforeseeable behavioral consequences in the arousal of cognitive dissonance. *Journal of Personality & Social Psychology, 37*(7), 1179–1185.

Goff, P. A., Eberhardt, J. L., Williams, M. J., & Jackson, M. C. (2008). Not yet human: Implicit knowledge, historical dehumanization, and contemporary consequences. *Journal of Personality & Social Psychology, 94*(2), 292–306.

Goins, J. (2015, April 15). *Celebrating Viktor Frankl: How a Holocaust survivor's philosophy on happiness remains relevant today.* Medium: https://medium.com/the-art-of-work/ celebrating-viktor-frankl-how-a-holocaust-survivor-s-philosophy-on-happiness-remains-relevant-1cda8f5343e4.

Goldstein, E. B., & Brockmole, J. R. (2017). *Sensation and perception* (10th ed.). Boston, MA: Cengage.

Gorman, W. (2001). Refugee survivors of torture: Trauma and treatment. *Professional Psychology: Research & Practice, 32*(5), 443–451.

Government Publishing Office (1970). *Occupational Safety and Health Act of 1970. Pub. L. No. 91-596, 84 Stat. 1590.* Washington, DC: Government Publishing Office.

Graham, J., Haidt, J., Koleva, S., Motyl, M., Iyer, R., Wojcik, S. P., & Ditto, P. H. (2013). Moral foundations theory: The pragmatic validity of moral pluralism. *Advances in Experimental Social Psychology, 47*, 55–130.

Greengross, G. (2014). Male production of humor produced by sexually selected psychological adaptations. In V. A. Weekes-Shackelford & T. K. Shackelford (Eds.), *Evolutionary perspectives on human sexual psychology and behavior* (pp. 173–196). New York, NY: Springer Science.

Greenwald, A. G. (1980). The totalitarian ego: Fabrication and revision of personal history. *American Psychologist, 35*(7), 603–618.

Greenwald, A. G., & Banaji, M. R. (1995). Implicit social cognition: Attitudes, self-esteem, and stereotypes. *Psychological Review, 102*(1), 4–27.

Greive, B. T. (2002). *The meaning of life.* Kansas City, MO: Andrews McMeel.

Grodin, M., & Annas, G. (2007). Physicians and torture: Lessons from the Nazi doctors. *International Review of the Red Cross, 89*(867), 635–654.

Guarnieri, M. (2014). Electricity in the Age of Enlightenment. *IEEE Industrial Electronics Magazine, 8*(3), 60–63.

Haggard, E. A., & Isaacs, K. S. (1966). Micromomentary facial expressions as indicators of ego mechanisms in psychotherapy. In *Methods of research in psychotherapy* (pp. 154–165). Boston, MA: Springer.

Haggard, P., & Lau, H. (2013). What is volition? *Experimental Brain Research, 229*(3), 285–287.

Hahn, T., & Jordan, J. S. (2014). Anticipation and embodied knowledge: Observations of enculturating bodies. Journal of Cognitive Education & Psychology, 13(2), 272–284.

Haidt, J. (2007). The new synthesis in moral psychology. *Science, 316*(5827), 998–1002.

Haidt, J., & Joseph, C. (2004). Intuitive ethics: How innately prepared intuitions generate culturally variable virtues. *Daedalus, 133*(4), 55–66.

Haley, K. J., & Fessler, D. M. (2005). Nobody's watching? Subtle cues affect generosity in an anonymous economic game. *Evolution & Human Behavior, 26*(3), 245–256.

Haney, C., Banks, W. C., & Zimbardo, P. G. (1973). Interpersonal dynamics in a simulated prison. *International Journal of Criminology & Penology, 1(1),* 69–97.

Hanson, D. (2006). Exploring the aesthetic range for humanoid robots. In *Proceedings of the ICCS/CogSci-2006 long symposium: Toward social mechanisms of android science* (pp. 39–42). Vancouver, BC: ICCS.

Harmon-Jones, E., Harmon-Jones, C., & Levy, N. (2015). An action-based model of cognitive-dissonance processes. *Current Directions in Psychological Science, 24*(3), 184–189.

Harris, S. (2011). *The moral landscape: How science can determine human values.* New York, NY: Free Press.

Harris, S. (2012). *Free will.* New York, NY: Free Press.

Haslam, N. (2006). Dehumanization: An integrative review. *Personality & Social Psychology Review, 10(3)*, 252–264.

Haslam, N. (2015). Dehumanization of intergroup relations. In M. Mikulincer, P. R. Shaver, & J. A. Simpson (Eds.), *APA handbook of personality and social psychology, Vol. 2: Group processes* (pp. 295–314). Washington, DC: American Psychological Association.

Haslam, N., & Loughnan, S. (2014). Dehumanization and infrahumanization. *Annual Review of Psychology, 65*, 399–423.

Haslam, S. A., Jetten, J., Postmes, T., & Haslam, C. (2009). Social identity, health and well-being: An emerging agenda for applied psychology. *Applied Psychology: An International Review, 58*(1), 1–23.

Heider, F., & Simmel, M. (1944). An experimental study of apparent behavior. *American Journal of Psychology, 57*(2), 243–259.

Heilman, M. E., & Okimoto, T. G. (2007). Why are women penalized for success at male tasks? The implied communality deficit. *Journal of Applied Psychology, 92*(1), 81–92.

Heine, S., Proulx, T., & Vohs, K. (2006). The meaning maintenance model: On the coherence of social motivations. *Personality & Social Psychology Review, 10*(2), 88–110.

Hendrie, C. A., & Brewer, G. (2012). Evidence to suggest that teeth act as human ornament displays signalling mate quality. *PLoS ONE, 7*(7), e42178.

Herman, J. L. (1992). Complex PTSD: A syndrome in survivors of prolonged and repeated trauma. *Journal of Traumatic Stress, 5*(3), 377–391.

Hess, N. H., & Hagen, E. H. (2006). Sex differences in indirect aggression psychological evidence from young adults. *Evolution & Human Behavior, 27*(3), 231–245.

Hixson, W. L. (2008). *The myth of American diplomacy: National identity and U.S. foreign policy.* New Haven, CT: Yale University Press.

Hood, B. (2009). *Supersense: From superstition to religion—the brain science of belief.* London, UK: Constable.

Hood, B. (2012). *The self illusion: How the social brain creates identity.* New York, NY: Oxford University Press.

Holzer, R., & Shimoyama, I. (1997). Locomotion control of a bio-robotic system via electric stimulation. In *Proceedings of the 1997 IEEE/RSJ International Conference on Intelligent Robots and Systems* (Vol. 3, pp. 1514–1519). Grenoble, France: IEEE.

Hurston, Z. N. (1937). *Their eyes were watching God.* Philadelphia, PA: Lippincott.

Hutson, M. (2012). *The 7 laws of magical thinking: How irrational beliefs keep us happy, healthy, and sane.* New York, NY: Hudson Street.

IJsselsteijn, W. (2002*). Elements of a multi-level theory of presence: Phenomenology, mental processing, and neural correlates.* Paper presented at the International Workshop on Presence, Porto, Portugal.

Impett, E. A., & Peplau, L. A. (2003). Sexual compliance: Gender, motivational, and relationship perspectives. *Journal of Sex Research, 40*(1), 87–100.

Indick, W. (2004). *Psychology for screenwriters: Building psychological conflict in your script.* Studio City, CA: Michael Wiese Productions.

Indick, W. (2006). *Psycho thrillers: Cinematic explorations of the mysteries of the mind.* Jefferson, NC: McFarland.

Indick, W. (2008). *The psychology of the western: How the American psyche plays out on screen.* Jefferson, NC: McFarland.

Indick, W. (2014). *Movies and the mind: Theories of the great psychoanalysts applied to film.* Jefferson, NC: McFarland.

Indick, W. (2015). *The digital god: How technology will reshape spirituality in the digital age.* Jefferson, NC: McFarland.

James, F. A. J. L. (2010). *Michael Faraday: A very short introduction.* New York, NY: Oxford University Press.

James, W. (1890/1950). *The principles of psychology* (Vol. 1). New York, NY: Dover.

James, W. (1897/1978). *The writings of William James: A comprehensive edition.* Chicago, IL: University of Chicago Press.

James, W. (1899). The stream of consciousness. In W. James (Ed.), *Talks to teachers on psychology—and to students on some of life's ideals* (pp. 15–21). New York, NY: Metropolitan/Henry Holt.

Jaynes, J. (1976). *The origin of consciousness in the breakdown of the bicameral mind.* New York, NY: Houghton Mifflin.

Jaynes, J. (1986). Consciousness and the voices of the mind. *Canadian Psychology, 27*(2), 128–148.

Jinpa, T. (2016). *A fearless heart: How the courage to be compassionate can transform our lives.* New York, NY: Random House.

Jochemczyk, Ł., Pietrzak, J., Buczkowski, R., Stolarski, M., & Markiewicz, Ł. (2017). You only live once: Present-hedonistic time perspective predicts risk propensity. *Personality & Individual Differences, 115,* 148–153.

Jordan, J. S. (2009). Forward-looking aspects of perception–action coupling as a basis for embodied communication. *Discourse Processes, 46*(2–3), 127–144.

Jordan, J. S., & Wesselmann, E. D. (2015). The contextually grounded nature of prosocial behavior: A multiscale, embodied approach to morality. In D. A. Schroeder & W. G. Graziano (Eds.), *The Oxford handbook of prosocial behavior* (pp. 153–165). New York, NY: Oxford University Press.

Jung, C. G., & Jaffé, A. (1962/1989). *Memories, dreams, reflections* (R. Winston & C. Winston, Trans.). New York, NY: Random House.

Kahn Jr., P. H., Kanda, T., Ishiguro, H., Freier, N. G., Severson, R. L., Gill, B. T., Ruckert, J. H. & Shen, S. (2012). Robovie, you'll have to go into the closet now: Children's social and moral relationships with a humanoid robot. *Developmental Psychology, 48*(2), 303–314.

Kahneman, D., & Tversky, A. (1973). On the psychology of prediction. *Psychological Review, 80(4),* 237–251.

Kaku, M. (2014). *The future of the mind: the scientific quest to understand, enhance, and empower the mind.* New York, NY: Doubleday.

Kandel, E. R. (2004). The molecular biology of memory storage: A dialog between genes and synapses. *Bioscience Reports, 24*(4), 475–522.

Keenan, J. P., Gallup, G. C., & Falk, D. (2003). *The face in the mirror: The search for the origins of consciousness.* New York, NY: HarperCollins.

Keep, E. (2017, June). Life without end. *Smithsonian, 28*(3), 44–54.

Kihlstrom, J. F. (2004). An unwarrantable impertinence. *Behavioral & Brain Sciences, 27*(5), 666–667.

Kim, K. J., & Sundar, S. S. (2013). Can interface features affect aggression resulting from violent video game play? An examination of realistic controller and large screen size. *Cyberpsychology, Behavior, & Social Networking, 15*(5), 329–334.

Kim, P., Rigo, P., Mayes, L. C., Feldman, R., Leckman, J. F., & Swain, J. E. (2014). Neural plasticity in fathers of human infants. *Social Neuroscience, 9*(5), 522–535.

King, Z. R., & Goodfriend, W. (2013). The ABC's of videogame effects: Affective, biological, and cognitive effects of videogame play. *Journal of Psychological Inquiry, 18*(2), 23–31.

Kinsbourne, M., & Jordan, J. S. (2009). Embodied anticipation: A neurodevelopmental interpretation. *Discourse Processes, 46*(2–3), 103–126.

Kinsella, E. L., Ritchie, T. D., & Igou, E. R. (2017). Attributes and applications of heroes: A brief history of lay and academic perspectives. In S. T. Allison, G. R. Goethals, & R. M. Kramer (Eds.), *Handbook of heroism and heroic leadership* (pp. 19–35). New York, NY: Routledge.

Kleiger, J. H., & Khadivi, A. (2015). *Assessing psychosis: A clinician's guide.* New York, NY: Routledge.

Koenigsberger, L. (1965). *Hermann von Helmholtz.* New York, NY: Dover.

Konijn, E. A., Bijvank, M. N., & Bushman, B. J. (2007). I wish I were a warrior: The role of wishful identification in the effects of violent video games on aggression in adolescent boys. *Developmental Psychology, 43*(4), 1038–1044.

Krausová, A., & Hazan, H. (2013). Creating free will in artificial intelligence. In *Beyond A.I.: Artificial Golem Intelligence (Proceedings of the International Conference Beyond A.I. 2013)* (pp. 96–109). Pilzen, Czech Republic: University of West Bohemia.

Krcmar, M., & Farrar, K. (2009). Retaliatory aggression and the effects of point of view and blood in violent video games. *Mass Communication & Society, 12*(1), 115–138.

Kteily, N., Bruneau, E., Waytz, A., & Cotterill, S. (2015). The ascent of man: Theoretical and empirical evidence for blatant dehumanization. *Journal of Personality & Social Psychology, 109*(5), 901–931.

Kuijsten, M. (2008). *Reflections on the dawn of consciousness: Julian Jaynes's bicameral mind theory revisited.* New York, NY: Julian Jaynes Society.

Kwon, Y. H. (1994). Age classification from facial images. In *1994 proceedings of IEEE Computer Society Conference on Vision and Pattern Recognition.* (pp. 762–767). Seattle, WA: IEEE.

L'Amour, L. (1980/2015). *Lonely on the mountain.* New York, NY: Bantam.

Lane, R. D. (2000). Neural correlates of conscious emotional experience. In R. D. Lane & L. Nadel (Eds.), *Cognitive Neuroscience of Emotion* (pp. 345–370). New York, NY: Oxford University Press.

Langley, T. (2012). *Batman and psychology: A dark and stormy knight.* Hoboken, NJ: Wiley.

Langley, T. (2017). A trunk full of defense mechanisms. In T. Langley & L. S. Zubernis (Eds.), *Supernatural psychology: Roads less traveled* (pp. 87–103). New York, NY: Sterling.

Langley, T. (2018a). *Westworld, the Holocaust, and the filter of fiction.* Psychology Today: https://www.psychologytoday.com/us/blog/beyond-heroes-and-villains/201807/westworld-the-holocaust-and-the-filter-fiction.

Langley, T. (2018b). *Why popular culture psychology? The power of story.* Psychology Today: https://www.psychologytoday.com/us/blog/beyond-heroes-and-villains/201803/why-popular-culture-psychology-the-power-story.

Langley, T. (2018c). *Why popular culture psychology? What's the point?* Psychology Today: https://www.psychologytoday.com/us/blog/beyond-heroes-and-villains/201802/why-popular-culture-psychology-whats-the-point.

Langley, T., Davis, G., Gore, C., Munson, M., & Tseang, J. (2016, October). *Geeks get published.* Panel presented at Stan Lee's Los Angeles Comic Con, Los Angeles, CA.

Lea, M., Spears, R., & de Groot, D. (2001). Knowing me, knowing you: Anonymity effects on social identity processes within groups. *Personality & Social Psychology Bulletin, 27*(5), 526–537.

LeDoux, J. (1998). *The emotional brain: The mysterious underpinnings of emotional life.* New York, NY: Simon & Schuster.

Lee, I. (2011). *The call to Sedona: Journey of the heart.* New York, NY: Simon & Schuster.

Levine, B. (2004). Autobiographical memory and the self in time: Brain lesion effects, functional neuroanatomy, and lifespan development. *Brain & Cognition, 55*(1), 54–68.

Levy, D. (2007). *Love and sex with robots: The evolution of human-robot relationships.* London, UK: Harper.

Lewin, K. (1942). Time perspective and morale. In G. Watson, *Civilian morale* (pp. 48–70). Oxford, UK: Houghton Mifflin.

Libet, B. (1985). Unconscious cerebral initiative and the role of conscious will in voluntary action. *Behavioral & Brain Sciences, 8(4),* 529–566.

Libin, A. V., & Libin, E. V. (2004). Person-robot interactions from the robopsychologists' point of view: The robotic psychology and robotherapy approach. *Proceedings of the IEEE, 92*(11), 1789–1803.

Lieberman, M. D. (2013). *Social: Why our brains are wired to connect.* New York, NY: Crown.

Lifton, R. J. (1986). *The Nazi doctors: Medical killing and the psychology of genocide.* New York, NY: Basic.

Lim, T. S., Kim, S. Y., & Kim, J. (2011). Holism: A missing link in Individualism-Collectivism research. *Journal of Intercultural Communication Research, 40*(1), 21–38.

Lind, E. A., Erickson, B. E., Conley, J., & O'Barr, W. M. (1978). Social attributions and conversation style in trial testimony. *Journal of Personality & Social Psychology, 36*(12), 1558–1567.

Loiperdinger, M., & Elzer, B. (2004). Lumière's arrival of the train: Cinema's founding myth. *The Moving Image, 4*(1), 89–118.

Looser, C. E., & Wheatley, T. (2010). The tipping point of animacy: How, when, and where we perceive life in a face. *Psychological Science, 21*(12), 1854–1862.

Ludden, D. (2017, February 2). *Is neuroscience the future or the end of psychology?* Psychology Today: https://www.psychologytoday.com/us/blog/talking-apes/201702/is-neuroscience-the-future-or-the-end-psychology.

Lustig, S. L., Kia-Keating, M., Knight, W. G., Geltman, P., Ellis, H., Kinzie, J. D., Keane, T., & Saxe, G. N. (2004). Review of child and adolescent refugee mental health. *Journal of the American Academy of Child & Adolescent Psychiatry, 43*(1), 24–36.

MacDorman, K. F. (2006, July). Subjective ratings of robot video clips for human likeness, familiarity, and eeriness: An exploration of the uncanny valley. In *ICCS/CogSci-2006 long symposium: Toward social mechanisms of android science* (pp. 26–29). Vancouver, BC: ICCS

MacDougall, D. (1907). Hypothesis concerning soul substance together with experimental evidence of the existence of such substance. *Journal of the American Society for Psychical Research, 1*(5), 237–244.

Madley, B. (2017). *An American genocide: The United States and the California Indian catastrophe, 1846-1873.* New Haven, CT: Yale University Press.

Mahood, C., & Hanus, M. (2017). Role-playing video games and emotion: How transportation into the narrative mediates the relationship between immoral actions and feelings of guilt. *Psychology of Popular Media Culture, 6*(1), 61–73.

Malchiodi, C. A. (Ed.). (2013). *Expressive therapies.* New York, NY: Guilford.

Mankowski, E. S., & Maton, K. I. (2010). A community psychology review of men and masculinity: Historical and conceptual review. *American Journal of Community Psychology, 45*(1-2), 73–86.

Margolius, I. (2017). The robot of Prague. *The Friends of Czech Heritage Newsletter, 17,* 3–6.

Marks, I. M. (1987). *Fears, phobias, and rituals: Panic, anxiety, and their disorders.* New York, NY: Oxford University Press.

Markson, L., & Spelke, E. S. (2006). Infants' rapid learning about self-propelled objects. *Infancy, 9*(1), 45–71.

Martinez, R., Rodríguez-Bailón, R., & Moya, M. (2012). Are they animals or machines? Measuring dehumanization. *Spanish Journal of Psychology, 15*(3), 1110–1122.

Marx, B. P., & Sloan, D. M. (2005). Peritraumatic dissociation and experiential avoidance as predictors of posttraumatic stress symptomatology. *Behaviour Research & Therapy, 43*(5), 569–583.

Maslow, A. H. (1954). *Motivation and personality.* Oxford, UK: Harper & Row.

Maslow, A. H. (1962). *Toward a psychology of being.* Princeton, NJ: Van Nostrand.

Maslow, A. H. (1971). *The farther reaches of human nature.* New York, NY: Penguin.

Mason, M. F., Banfield, J. F., & Macrae, C. N. (2004). Thinking about actions: The neural substrates of person knowledge. *Cerebral Cortex, 14*(2), 209–214.

Mast, G., & Kawin, B. (2000). *A short history of the movies* (7th ed.). Boston, MA: Allyn & Bacon.

Mauss, I. B., & Robinson, M. D. (2009). Measures of emotion: A review. *Cognition & Emotion, 23*(2), 209–237.

May, R. (1969). *Existential psychology* (2nd ed.). New York, NY: Random House.

May, R. (1981). *Freedom and destiny.* New York, NY: Norton.

May, R. (1983). *The discovery of being: Writing in existential psychology.* New York, NY: Norton.

McBride, D. M., & Cutting, J. C. (2017). *Cognitive psychology: Theory, process, and methodology.* Thousand Oaks, CA: SAGE.

McCrone, J. (1991). *The ape that spoke.* New York, NY: Avon.

McFarland, D. (2009). *Guilty robots, happy dogs: The question of alien minds.* New York, NY: Oxford University Press.

McGilchrist, I. (2009). *The Master and his emissary: The Divided brain and the making of the Western world.* New Haven, CT: Yale University Press.

McGloin, R., Farrar, K. M., & Fishlock, J. (2015). Triple whammy! Violent games and violent controllers: Investigating the use of realistic gun controllers on perceptions of realism, immersion, and outcome aggression. *Journal of Communication, 65*(2), 280–299.

McGuen, W. G. (1988). *The bicameral brain and human behavior.* New York, NY: Vantage.

McPherson, J. (2012). Does narrative exposure therapy reduce PTSD in survivors of mass violence? *Research on Social Work Practice, 22*(1), 29–42.

Mead, G. H. (1910). Social consciousness and the consciousness of meaning. *Psychological Bulletin, 7*(12), 397–405.

Meltzoff, A. N., & Prinz, W. (Eds.). (2002). *The imitative mind: Development, evolution and brain bases* (Vol. 6). Cambridge, England: Cambridge University Press.

Metzinger, T. (2003). *Being no one: The self-model theory of subjectivity.* Cambridge, MA: MIT Press.

Miall, R. C. (2003). Connecting mirror neurons and forward models. *Neuroreport, 14*(17), 2135–2137.

Milam, W. (2015, July 11). *Mary Shelley: Meet the teenage girl who invented science fiction.* Amy Poehler's Smart Girls: https://amysmartgirls.com/mary-shelley-meet-the-teenage-girl-who-invented-science-fiction-3735d785411c.

Milfront, T. L., Milojev, P., & Sibley, C. G (2016). Values stability and change in adulthood: A 3-year longitudinal study of rank-order stability and mean-level differences. *Personality & Social Psychology Bulletin, 42*(5), 572–588.

Milgram, S. (1963). Behavioral study of obedience. *Journal of Abnormal & Social Psychology, 67*(4), 371–378.

Milgram, S. (1974/2009). *Obedience to authority: The experiment that challenged human nature.* New York, NY: HarperCollins.

Minsky, M. (2006). *The emotion machine.* New York, NY: Pantheon.

Moore, T. M., Stuart, G. L., McNulty, J. K., Addis, M. E., Cordova, J. V., & Temple, J. R. (2008). Domains of masculine gender role stress and intimate partner violence in a clinical sample of violent men. *Psychology of Men & Masculinity, 1*(S), *68–75.*

Mori, M. (1970). The uncanny valley. *Energy, 7*(4), 33–35.

Mori, M., MacDorman, K. F., & Kageki, N. (2012). The uncanny valley [from the field]. *IEEE Robotics & Automation Magazine, 19*(2), 98–100.

Mutlu, B., Yamaoka, F., Kanda, T., Ishiguro, H., & Hagita, N. (2009). Nonverbal leakage in robots: communication of intentions through seemingly unintentional behavior. In *Proceedings of the 4th ACM/IEEE international conference on human robot interaction* (pp. 69–76). Vancouver, BC: IEEE.

Myerhoff, B. (1982). Life history among the elder: Performance, visibility and remembering. In J. Ruby (Ed.), *A crack in the mirror: Reflexive perspectives in anthropology* (pp. 99–117). Philadelphia, PA: University of Pennsylvania Press.

Nahmias, E., Shepard, J., & Reuter, S. (2014). It's OK if 'my brain made me do it': People's intuitions about free will and neuroscientific prediction. *Cognition, 133*(2), 502–516.

Narcisse, E. (2016, November 10). *What people who make video games think of Westworld.* io9: https://io9.gizmodo.com/what-people-who-make-video-games-think-of-westworld-1788664515.

Nass, C., Moon, Y., Fogg, B. J., Reeves, B., & Dryer, D. C. (1995). Can computer personalities be human personalities? *International Journal of Human-Computer Studies, 43*(2), 223–239.

Nathanson, D. L. (1994). *Shame and pride: Affect, sex, and the birth of the self.* New York, NY: Norton.

Neisser, U. (1963). The imitation of man by machine. *Science, 139*(3551), 193–197.

Nesse, R. M. (1990). Evolutionary explanations of emotions. *Human Nature, 1*(3), 261–289.

Neuner, F., Schauer, M., Karunakara, U., Klaschik, C., Robert, C., & Elbert, T. (2004). Psychological trauma and evidence for enhanced vulnerability for posttraumatic stress disorder through previous trauma among West Nile refugees. *BMC Psychiatry, 4*(1), 4–34.

Nichols, S., & Knobe, J. (2007). Moral responsibility and determinism: The cognitive science of folk intuitions. *Noûs, 41*(4), 663–685.

Noble, H. B. (1997, September 4). *Dr. Viktor E. Frankl of Vienna, psychiatrist of the search for meaning, dies at 92.* The New York Times: https://www.nytimes.com/1997/09/04/world/dr-viktor-e-frankl-of-vienna-psychiatrist-of-the-search-for-meaning-dies-at-92.html.

Nolen-Hoeksema, S. (1987). Sex differences in unipolar depression: Evidence and theory. *Psychological Bulletin, 101*(2), 259–282.

Nomura, T., Kanda, T., Suzuki, T., Yamada, S., & Kato, K. (2009). Influences of concerns toward emotional interaction into social acceptability of robots. In *Proceedings of the 4th ACM/IEEE international conference on human robot interaction* (pp. 231–232). Vancouver, BC: IEEE

Norberg, A., & Lundman, B. (2005). Resilience, sense of coherence, purpose in life and self-transcendence in relation to perceived physical and mental health among the oldest old. *Aging & Mental Health, 9*(4), 354–362.

10
Norman, D. A. (2004). *Emotional design: Why we love (or hate) everyday things*. New York, NY: Basic.

O'Connell, W. E. (1972). Frankl, Adler, and spirituality. *Journal of Religion & Health, 11*(2), 134–138.

Orcutt, H. K., Pickett, S. M., & Pope, E. B. (2005). Experiential avoidance and forgiveness as mediators in the relation between traumatic interpersonal events and posttraumatic stress disorder symptoms. *Journal of Social & Clinical Psychology, 24*(7), 1003–1029.

Ortony, A., Clore, G. L., & Collins, A. (1990). *The cognitive structure of emotions*. New York, NY: Cambridge University Press.

Otake, K., Shimai, S., Tanaka-Matsumi, J., Otsui, K., & Fredrickson, B. L. (2006). Happy people become happier through kindness: A counting kindnesses intervention. *Journal of Happiness Studies, 7*(3), 361–375.

O'Toole, A. J., Phillips, J., Weimer, S., Roark, D. A., Ayyad, J., Barwick, R., & Dunlop, J. (2011). Recognizing people from dynamic and static faces and bodies: Dissecting identity with a fusion approach. *Vision Research, 51*(1), 74–83.

Panksepp, J. (2005). Affective consciousness: Core emotional feelings in animals and humans. *Consciousness & Cognition, 14*(1), 30–80.

Parke, F. I., & Waters, K. (2008). *Computer facial animation*. Wellesley, MA: CRC Press.

Parry, A., & Doan, R. E. (1994). *Story re-visions: Narrative therapy in the postmodern world*. New York, NY: Guilford.

Paul, E. S. (2000). Empathy with animals and with humans: Are they linked? *Anthrozoös, 13*(4), 194–202.

Paulhus, D., & Shaffer, D. R. (1981). Sex differences in the impact of number of younger and number of older siblings on scholastic aptitude. *Social Psychology Quarterly, 44*(4), 363–368.

Penfield, W., & Boldrey, E. (1937). Somatic motor and sensory representation in the cerebral cortex of man as studied by electrical stimulation. *Brain: A Journal of Neurology, 60*(4), 389–443.

Penrose, R. (2004). *The road to reality: A complete guide to the laws of the universe*. New York, NY: Knopf.

Perner, J., & Lang, B. (1999). Development of theory of mind and executive control. *Trends in Cognitive Sciences, 3*(9), 337–344.

Persky, S., & Blascovich, J. (2007). Immersive virtual environments versus traditional platforms: Effects of violent and nonviolent video game play. *Media Psychology, 10*(1), 135–156.

Peterson, T. J. (2015, April 2). *Existential anxiety, stress, and meaning-making in your life*. Healthy Place: https://www.healthyplace.com/blogs/anxiety-schmanxiety/2015/04/existential-anxiety-stress-and-meaning-making-in-your-life.

Pfundmair, M., Eyssel, F., Graupmann, V., Frey, D., & Aydin, N. (2015). Wanna play? The role of self-construal when using gadgets to cope with ostracism. *Social Influence, 10*(4), 221–235.

Pinker, S. (2011). *The better angels of our nature: Why violence has declined*. New York, NY: Viking.

Pollack, W. (1998). *Real boys: Rescuing our sons from the myths of boyhood*. New York, NY: Owl.

Pollak, J. (2014, May 15). *Does psychology have a future?* National Psychologist: https://nationalpsychologist.com/2014/05/does-psychology-have-a-viable-future/102507.html.

Pope, M., & Englar-Carlson, M. (2001). Fathers and sons: The relationship between violence and masculinity. *The Family Journal: Counseling & Therapy for Couples & Families, 9*(4), 367–374.

Porter, S., & Ten Brinke, L. (2008). Reading between the lies: Identifying concealed and falsified emotions in universal facial expressions. *Psychological Science, 19*(5), 508–514.

Postmes, T., & Spears, R. (1998). Deindividuation and antinormative behaviors: A meta-analysis. *Psychological Bulletin, 123*(3), 238–259.

Powers, A., & Kiesler, S. (2006). The advisor robot: Tracing people's mental model from a robot's physical attributes. *Proceedings of the 1st ACM SIGCHI/SIGART conference on Human-robot interaction* (pp. 218–225). New York, NY: Association for Computing Machinery.

Prati, F., Vassiljevic, M., Crisp, R. J., & Rubini, M. (2015). Some extended psychological benefits of challenging social stereotypes: Decreased dehumanization and a reduced reliance on heuristic thinking. *Group Processes & Intergroup Relations, 18*(6), 801–816.

Premack, D., & Woodruff, G. (1978). Does the chimpanzee have a theory of mind? *Behavioral & Brain Sciences, 1*(4), 515–526.

Preston, S. D., & De Waal, F. B. (2002). Empathy: Its ultimate and proximate bases. *Behavioral & Brain Sciences, 25*(1), 1–20.

Profet, M. (1992). Pregnancy sickness as adaptation: A deterrent to maternal ingestion of teratogens. In J. H. Barkow, L. Cosmides, J. Tooby, (Eds.), *The adapted mind: Evolutionary psychology and the generation of culture* (pp. 327–365). New York, NY: Oxford University Press.

Proulx, T., Markham, K. D., & Lindberg, M. J. (2013). Introduction: The new science of meaning. In K. D. Markham, T. Proulx, & M. J. Lindberg (Eds.), *The psychology of meaning.* Washington, DC: American Psychological Association.

Quinette, P., Guillery-Girard, B., Dayan, J., de la Sayette, V., Marquis, S., Viader, F., Desgranges, B., & Eustache, F. (2006). What does transient global amnesia really mean? Review of the literature and thorough study of 142 cases. *Brain, 129*(7), 1640–1658.

Ramachandran, V. S. (1998). Consciousness and body image: lessons from phantom limbs, Capgras syndrome, and pain asymbolia. *Philosophical transactions from the Royal Society B: Biological Sciences, 353*(1377), 1851–1859.

Ray, C., Mondada, F., & Siegwart, R. (2008, September). What do people expect from robots? In *Proceedings of the IEEE/RSJ International Conference* (pp. 3816–3821). Vancouver, BC: IEEE.

Reblitz, A. A. (2001). *The Golden Age of automatic musical instruments.* Woodsville, NH: Mechanical Music Press.

Rendon, J. (2015). *Upside: The new science of post-traumatic growth.* New York, NY: Touchstone.

Resick, P. A., & Schnicke, M. K. (1992). Cognitive processing therapy for sexual assault victims. *Journal of Consulting & Clinical Psychology, 60*(5), 748–756.

Rhodes, G. (2006). The evolutionary psychology of facial beauty. *Annual Review of Psychology, 57,* 199–226.

Rhodes, G., Proffitt, F., Grady, J. M., & Sumich, A. (1998). Facial symmetry and the perception of beauty. *Psychonomic Bulletin & Review, 5*(4), 659–669.

Rhodes, M. G., & Anastasi, J. S. (2012). The own-age bias in face recognition: A meta-analytic and theoretical review. *Psychological Bulletin, 138*(1), 146.

Richards, Z., & Hewstone, M. (2001). Subtyping and subgrouping: Processes for the prevention and promotion of stereotype change. *Personality & Social Psychology Review, 5*(1), 52–73.

Riek, L. D., Rabinowitch, T. C., Chakrabarti, B., & Robinson, P. (2009). How anthropomorphism affects empathy toward robots. In *Proceedings of the 4th ACM/IEEE international conference on Human robot interaction* (pp. 245–246). Vancouver, BC: IEEE.

Riskin, J. (2003). The defecating duck, or the ambiguous origins of artificial life. *Critical Inquiry, 29*(4), 599–633.

Riskin, J. (2016). *The restless clock: A history of the centuries-long argument over what makes living things tick.* Chicago, IL: University of Chicago Press.

Rizzolatti, G., & Craighero, L. (2004). The mirror-neuron system. *Annual Review of Neuroscience, 27*(1), 169–192.

Roazen, P. (1975). *Freud and his followers.* New York, NY: Knopf.

Robinson, H., MacDonald, B., Kerse, N., & Broadbent, E. (2013). The psychosocial effects of a companion robot: A randomized controlled trial. *Journal of the American Medical Directors Association, 14*(9), 661–667.

Robinson, M. D., & Clore, G. L. (2002). Belief and feeling: Evidence for an accessibility model of emotional self-report. *Psychological Bulletin, 128*(6), 934.

Rochat, P. (2001). *The infant's world.* Cambridge, MA: Harvard University Press.

Rochat, P. (2003). Five levels of self-awareness as they unfold early in life. *Consciousness & Cognition, 12*(4), 717–731.

Ronson, J. (2015). *So you've been publicly shamed.* New York, NY: Riverhead.

Rosenthal-von der Pütten, A. M., Krämer, N. C., Hoffmann, L., Sobieraj, S., & Eimler, S. C. (2013). An experimental study on emotional reactions towards a robot. *International Journal of Social Robotics, 5*(1), 17–34.

Rosenthal-von der Pütten, A. M., Schulte, F. P., Eimler, S. C., Sobieraj, S., Hoffmann, L., Maderwald, S., Brand, M., & Krämer, N. C. (2014). Investigations on empathy towards humans and robots using fMRI. *Computers in Human Behavior, 33*, 201–212.

Rothgerber, H., & Mican, F. (2014). Childhood pet ownership, attachment to pets, and subsequent meat avoidance: The mediating role of empathy toward animals. *Appetite, 79*, 11–17.

Rotter, J. B. (1966). Generalized expectancies for internal versus external control of reinforcement. *Psychological Monographs: General & Applied, 80*(1), 1-28.

Rousey, C., & Holzman, P. S. (1967). Recognition of one's own voice. *Journal of Personality & Social Psychology, 6*(4, Pt. 1), 464-466.

Rudman, L. A., & Glick, P. (2008). *The social psychology of gender: How power and intimacy shape gender relations.* New York, NY: Guilford.

Rudman, L. A., & Mescher, K. (2012). Of animals and objects: Men's implicit dehumanization of women and likelihood of sexual aggression. *Personality & Social Psychology Bulletin, 38*(6), 734–746.

Russell, S., & Norvig, P. (2009). *Artificial intelligence: a modern approach* (3rd ed.). Upper Saddle River, NJ: Prentice Hall.

Sagan, C. (1977). *The dragons of Eden: Speculations on the evolution of human intelligence.* New York, NY: Ballantine.

Sagan, C., & Druyan, A. (1992). *Shadows of forgotten ancestors: A search for who we are.* New York, NY: Random House.

Samani, H. A., Cheok, A. D., Ngiap, F. W., Nagpal, A., & Qiu, M. (2010). Towards a formulation of love in human-robot interaction. In *Proceedings of the Nineteenth IEEE International Symposium on Robot & Human Interactive Communication.* Vancouver, BC: IEEE.

Samani, H. A., Cheok, A. D., Tharakan, M. J., Koh, J., & Fernando, N. (2010). A design process for lovotics. In *International Conference on Human-Robot Personal Relationship* (pp. 118–125). Berlin, Germany: Springer.

Sartre, J. (2013). *We have only this life to live: The selected essays of Jean-Paul Sartre, 1939–1975.* New York, NY: New York Review Books Classics.

Savine, A. C., Scullin, M. K., & Roediger III, H. L. (2011). Survival processing of faces. *Memory & Cognition, 39*(8), 1359–1373.

Scarlet, J. (2017). Emotion data. In T. Langley (Ed.), *Star Trek psychology: The mental frontier* (pp. 83–93). New York, NY: Sterling.

Schacter, D. L., Norman, K. A., & Koustaal, W. (1998). The cognitive neuroscience of constructive memory. *Annual Review of Psychology, 49*, 289–318.

Schell, J. (2015). *The art of game design.* Boca Raton, FL: Taylor & Francis.

Schneider, K. J., & May, R. (1995). *The psychology of existence: An integrative, clinical perspective.* New York, NY: McGraw-Hill.

Schnyder, U., Ehlers, A., Elbert, T., Foa, E. B., Gersons, B. P. R., Resick, P. A., Shapiro, F., Cloitre, M. (2015). Psychotherapies for PTSD: What do they have in common? *European Journal of Psychotraumatology, 6*, Article 28186.

Scholl, J. M., & Sabat, S. R. (2008). Stereotypes, stereotype threat and ageing: implications for the understanding and treatment of people with Alzheimer's disease. *Ageing & Society, 28*(1), 103–130.

Schouten, K. A., de Niet, G. J., Knipscheer, J. W., Kleber, R. J., & Hutschemaekers, G. J. M. (2015). The effectiveness of art therapy in the treatment of traumatized adults. A systematic review on art therapy and trauma. *Trauma, Violence & Abuse, 16*(2), 220–228.

Schroeder, J., & Epley, N. (2016). Mistaking minds and machines: How speech affects dehumanization and anthropomorphism. *Journal of Experimental Psychology: General, 145*(11), 1427–1437.

Schultz, D. P., & Schultz, S. E. (2012). *A history of modern psychology* (10th ed.). Belmont, CA: Wadsworth.

Sébastien, C. & Cartwright, W. (2014) Narrative cartography: From mapping stories to the narrative of maps and mapping. *Cartographic Journal, 51*(2), 101–106.

Seligman, M. E., & Hager, J. L. (1972). *Biological boundaries of learning.* East Norwalk, CT: Appleton-Century-Crofts.

Shakespeare, W. (1600/1982). Henry V. In *The illustrated Stratford Shakespeare* (pp. 701-728). London, UK: Chancellor.

Shakespeare, W. (1597/1982). Romeo and Juliet. In The illustrated Stratford Shakespeare (pp. 443-470). London, UK: Chancellor.

Shakespeare, W. (1603/2015). Othello. Edinburgh, Scotland, UK: White & Black.

Shakespeare, W. (1603/2016). Hamlet (The Pelican Shakespeare). New York, NY: Penguin.

Shelley, M. W. [originally anonymous] (1818). Frankenstein, or the modern Prometheus. London, UK: Lackington, Hughes, Harding, Mavor, & Jones.

Sherry, J. L. (2001). The effects of violent video games on aggression: A meta-analysis. Human Communication Research, 27(3), 409–431.

Shi, K., & Li, L. (2013). High performance genetic algorithm based text clustering pairs using parts of speech and outlier elimination. Applied Intelligence, 38(4), 511–519.

Shiffrin, R. M., & Schneider, W. (1977). Controlled and automatic human information processing: II. Perceptual learning, automatic attending and a general theory. Psychological Review, 84(2), 127–190.

Silva, M. F., & Tenreiro Machado, J. A. (2007). A historical perspective of legged robots. Journal of Vibration & Control, 13(9-10), 1447–1486.

Simon, G. (2009, February 17). Understanding rationalization: Making excuses as an effective manipulation tactic. Counselling Resource: http://counsellingresource.com/features/2009/02/17/rationalization-as-manipulation-tactic.

Sin, N. L., & Lyubomirsky, S. (2009). Enhancing well-being and alleviating depressive symptoms with positive psychology interventions: A practice-friendly meta-analysis. Journal of Clinical Psychology, 65(5), 467–487.

Singer, P. W. (2009). Wired for war: The robotics revolution and conflict in the 21st century. New York, NY: Penguin.

Singh, D. (1993). Adaptive significance of female physical attractiveness: Role of waist-to-hip ratio. Journal of Personality & Social Psychology, 65(2), 293–307.

Sinha, P., Balas, B., Ostrovsky, Y., & Russell, R. (2006). Face recognition by humans: Nineteen results all computer vision researchers should know about. Proceedings of the IEEE, 94(11), 1948–1962.

Slotkin, R. (1998). Gunfighter nation: The myth of the frontier in twentieth-century America. Norman, OK: University of Oklahoma Press.

Smith, C. P., & Freyd, J. J. (2014). Institutional betrayal. American Psychologist, 69(6), 575–587.

Smith, D. G., Rosenstein, J. E., Nikolov, M. C., & Chaney, D. A. (2018). The power of language: Gender, status, and agency in performance evaluations. Sex Roles: https://link.springer.com/article/10.1007/s11199-018-0923-7.

Smith, M. B. (2007). The sociogenesis of evil. Peace & Conflict: Journal of Peace Psychology, 13(4), 463–465.

Smith, R. M., Parrott, D. J., Swartout, K. M., & Tharp, A. T. (2015). Deconstructing hegemonic masculinity: The roles of antifemininity, subordination to women, and sexual dominance in men's perpetration of sexual aggression. Psychology of Men & Masculinity, 16(2), 160–169.

Solomon, S., Greenberg, J., & Pyszczynski, T. (1991). A terror management theory of social behavior: The psychological functions of self-esteem and cultural worldviews. Advances in Experimental Social Psychology, 24, 93–159.

Spina, R. R., Ji, L. J., Guo, T., Zhang, Z., Li, Y., & Fabrigar, L. (2010). Cultural differences in the representativeness heuristic: Expecting a correspondence in magnitude between the cause and effect. Personality & Social Psychology Bulletin, 36(5), 583–597.

Sproull, L., Subramani, M., Kiesler, S., Walker, J. H., & Waters, K. (1996). When the interface is a face. Human-Computer Interaction, 11(2), 97–124.

Srodes, J. (2002). Franklin: The essential founding father. Washington, DC: Regnery.

Stableford, B. (1995). Frankenstein and the origins of science fiction. In D. Seed (Ed.), Anticipations: Essays on early science fiction and its precursors (pp. 46–57). Syracuse, NJ: Syracuse University Press.

Stanley, M. (2016, July 2). Author Elie Wiesel served as a voice for victims of the Holocaust. The Wall Street Journal: https://www.wsj.com/articles/author-elie-wiesel-served-as-a-voice-for-victims-of-the-holocaust-1467498432.

Staub, E. (2015). The roots of helping, heroic rescue and resistance to and the prevention of mass violence: Active bystandership in extreme times and in building peaceful societies. In D. A. Schroeder, & W. G. Graziano (Eds.), The Oxford handbook of prosocial behavior (pp. 693–717). Oxford, UK: Oxford Library of Psychology.

Stekel, W. (1950). *The autobiography of Wilhelm Stekel: The story of a pioneer psychoanalyst.* New York, NY: Liveright.

Stolarski, M., Wojtkowska, K., & Kwiecinska, M. (2015). Time for love: Partners' time perspectives predict relationship satisfaction in romantic heterosexual couples. *Time & Society, 25*(3), 552–574.

Stolarski, M., Zajenkowski, M., & Zajenkowska, A. (2016). Aggressive? From time to time . . . Uncovering complex associations between time perspective and aggression. *Current Psychology, 35*(4), 506–515.

Stone, A. A., Bachrach, C. A., Jobe, J. B., Kurtzman, H. S., & Cain, V. S. (Eds.). (1999). *The science of self-report: Implications for research and practice.* Hove, UK: Psychology Press.

Struch, N., & Schwartz, S. H. (1989). Intergroup aggression: Its predictors and distinctness from in-group bias. *Journal of Personality & Social Psychology, 56*(3), 364–373.

Sullins, J. P. (2012). Robots, love, and sex: the ethics of building a love machine. *IEEE Transactions on Affective Computing, 3*(4), 398–409.

Suzuki, Y., Galli, L., Ikeda, A., Itakura, S., & Kitazaki, M. (2015). Measuring empathy for human and robot hand pain using electroencephalography. *Scientific Reports, 5,* Article 15924.

Tasker, J. P. (2015, May 30). *Residential schools findings point to "culture genocide," commission chair says.* CBC News: http://www.cbc.ca/news/politics/residential-schools-findings-point-to-cultural-genocide-commission-chair-says-1.3093580.

Testé, B. (2017). Control beliefs and dehumanization: Targets with an internal locus of control are perceived as being more human than external targets. *Swiss Journal of Psychology, 76*(2), 81–86.

Thodberg, K., Sørensen, L. U., Videbech, P. B., Poulsen, P. H., Houbak, B., Damgaard, V., Keseler, I., Edwards, D., & Christensen, J. W. (2016). Behavioral responses of nursing home residents to visits from a person with a dog, a robot seal or a toy cat. *Anthrozoös, 29*(1), 107–121.

Thomas, M. H., Horton, R. W., Lippincott, E. C., & Drabman, R. S. (1977). Desensitization to portrayals of real-life aggression as a function of exposure to television violence. *Journal of Personality & Social Psychology, 35*(6), 450–458.

Thompson, B. L., Waltz, J. (2008). Self-compassion and PTSD symptom severity. *Journal of Traumatic Stress, 21*(6), 556–558.

Tinwell, A. (2009). Uncanny as usability obstacle. In A. A. Ozok & P. Zaphiris (Eds.), *Online Communities and Social Computing* (pp. 622–631). Berlin, Heidelberg, Germany: Springer.

Tinwell, A. (2014). *The uncanny valley in games and animation.* Wellesley, MA: CRC Press.

Todorov, A. (2017). *Face value: The irresistible influence of first impressions.* Princeton, NJ: Princeton University Press.

Tracey, L. J., & Robins, R. W. (2007). The self in self-conscious emotions: A cognitive appraisal approach. In J. L. Tracy, R. W. Robins, & J. P. Tangney (Eds.), *The self-conscious emotions: Theory and research* (pp. 3–20). New York, NY: Guilford.

Trimmer, E., McDonald, S., & Rushby, J. A. (2017). Not knowing what I feel: Emotional empathy in autism spectrum disorders. *Autism, 21*(4), 450–457.

Truth and Reconciliation Commission of Canada (2015). *Final report of the Truth and Reconciliation Commission of Canada, volume one: Honouring the truth, reconciling for the future.* Toronto, Ontario, Canada: Lorimer.

Turing, A. M. (1936). On Computable Numbers, with an application to the Entscheidungsproblem. *Proceedings of the London Mathematical Society, 2*(42), 230–265.

Turing, A. M. (1950). Computing machinery and intelligence. *Mind, 49*(236), 433–460.

Turner, F. J. (1893). *The significance of the frontier in American history.* In *Annual report of the American Historical Association* (pp. 197–227). Chicago, IL: American Historical Association.

Ullman, S. E., Najdowski, C. J., & Filipas, H. H. (2009). Child sexual abuse, post-traumatic stress disorder, a nd substance use: Predictors of revictimization in adult sexual assault survivors. *Journal of Child Sexual Abuse, 18*(4), 367–385.

Usarski, R. (1999). The response to New Religious Movements in East Germany after reunification. In J. Cresswell & B. Wilson (Eds.), *New Religious Movements: Challenges and response* (pp. 237–254). New York, NY: Routledge.

Van der Kolk, B. (2014). *The body keeps the score: Brain, mind, and body in the healing of trauma.* New York, NY: Viking.

Van Deurzen, E. (2002). *Existential counseling and psychotherapy in practice* (2nd ed.). London, UK: SAGE.

Varki, A., & Brower, D. (2013). *Denial: Self-deception, false beliefs, and the origins of the human mind*. New York, NY: Twelve.

Väyrnen, T., & Laari-Salmela, S. (2018). Men, mammals, or machines? Dehumanization embedded in organizational practices. *Journal of Business Ethics, 147*(1), 95–113.

Verdichevski, M., & Steeves, J. K. (2013). Own-age and own-sex biases in recognition of aged faces. *Acta Psychologica, 144*(2), 418–423.

Viki, G. T., Osgood, D., & Phillips, S. (2013). Dehumanization and self-reported proclivity to torture prisoners of war. *Journal of Experimental Social Psychology, 49*(3), 325–328.

Von Neumann, J. (2012). *The computer and the brain*. New Haven, CT: Yale University Press.

Walters, M. L., Syrdal, D. S., Dautenhahn, K., te Boekhorst, R., & Koay, K. L. (2008). Avoiding the uncanny valley: Robot appearance, personality and consistency of behavior in an attention-seeking home scenario for a robot companion. *Autonomous Robots, 24*(2), 159–178.

Walters, M. L., Syrdal, D. S., Koay, K. L., Dautenhahn, K., & te Boekhorst, R. (2008). Human approach distances to a mechanical-looking robot with different robot voice styles. In *Proceedings of the 17th IEEE International Symposium on Robot and Human Interactive Communication (pp. 707–712)*. Vancouver, BC: IEEE.

Wang, O., & Ross, M. (2007). Culture and memory. In S. Kitayama & D. Cohen (Eds.), *Handbook of cultural psychology* (pp. 645–667). New York, NY: Guilford.

Wang, W. (2017). Smartphones as social actors? Social dispositional factors in assessing anthropomorphism. *Computers in Human Behavior, 68*, 334–344.

Watkins, C. (1992). Birth-order research and Adler's theory: A critical review. *Individual Psychology: Journal of Adlerian Theory, Research & Practice, 48*(3), 357–368.

Waytz, A., Cacioppo, J., & Epley, N. (2010a). Who sees human? The stability and importance of individual differences in anthropomorphism. *Perspectives on Psychological Science, 5*(3), 219–232.

Waytz, A., & Epley, N. (2012). Social connection enables dehumanization. *Journal of Experimental Social Psychology, 48*(1), 70–76.

Waytz, A., Heafner, J., & Epley, N. (2014). The mind in the machine: Anthropomorphism increases trust in an autonomous vehicle. *Journal of Experimental Social Psychology, 52*, 113–117.

Waytz, A., Morewedge, C. K., Epley, N., Monteleone, G., Gao, J. H., & Cacioppo, J. T. (2010b). Making sense by making sentient: Effectance motivation increases anthropomorphism. *Journal of Personality & Social Psychology, 99*(3), 410–435.

Wedemann, R. S., Vidal de Carvalho, L. A., & Donangelo, R. (2008). Net work properties of a model for conscious and unconscious mental processes. *Neurocomputering, 71*(16-18), 3367–3371.

Weiner, B. (2006). *Social motivation, justice, and the moral emotions*. Mahwah, NJ: Erlbaum.

Wenzel, A., Brown, G. K., & Karlin, B. E. (2011). *Cognitive behavioral therapy for depression in veterans and military servicemembers: Therapist manual*. Washington, DC: U.S. Department of Veterans Affairs.

Wenzel, A., Dobson, K. S., & Hays, P. A. (2016). *Cognitive behavioral therapy techniques and strategies*. Washington, DC: American Psychological Association.

Wertheimer, M. (2011). *A brief history of psychology* (5th ed.). New York, NY: Psychology Press.

Westbury, H. R., & Neumann, D. L. (2008). Empathy-related responses to moving film stimuli depicting human and non-human animal targets in negative circumstances. *Biological Psychology, 78*(1), 66–74.

White, M. (2007). *Maps of narrative practice*. New York, NY: Norton.

White, M. & Epston D. (1990). *Narrative means to therapeutic ends*. New York, NY: Norton.

Wierzbicka, A. (1998). Angst. *Culture & Psychology, 4*(2), 161-188.

Wiesel, E. (1958/2006). *Night* (M. Wiesel, Trans.). New York, NY: Hill & Wang.

Wiesel, E. (1999). *And the sea is never full: Memoirs, 1969—*. New York, NY: Random House.

Wiesel, E. (2008). *A God who remembers*. NPR: https://www.npr.org/2008/04/07/89357808/a-god-who-remembers.

Wiesel, E., & de Saint Cheron, M. (1990/2000). *Evil and exile* (2nd ed.). Notre Dame, IN: University of Notre Dame Press.

Winkielman, P., & Berridge, K. C. (2004). Unconscious emotion. *Current Directions in Psychological Science, 13*(3), 120–123.

Winnicott, D. W. (1964). *The child, the family and the outside world.* Harmondsworth, U.K: Penguin.

Wong, P. T. P. (2012). Introduction: A roadmap for meaning research and applications. In P. T. P. Wong (Ed.), *The human quest for meaning: Theories, research, and applications* (2nd ed., unnumbered pages). New York, NY: Routledge.

Woodward, W. R. & Tower, J. F. (2008). Julian Jaynes: Introducing his life and thought. In M. Kuijsten (Ed.) *Reflections on the dawn of consciousness: Julian Jaynes's bicameral mind theory revisited* (pp. 13–69). Henderson, NV: Julian Jaynes Society.

Wright, D. B., & Sladden, B. (2003). An own gender bias and the importance of hair in face recognition. *Acta Psychologica, 114*(1), 101–114.

Wundt, W. M. (1912). *An introduction to psychology.* New York, NY: Macmillan.

Wykowska, A., Kajopoulos, J., Ramirez-Amaro, K., & Cheng, G. (2015). Autistic traits and sensitivity to human-like features of robot behavior. *Interaction Studies, 16*(2), 219–248.

Young, J. E., Hawkins, R., Sharlin, E., & Igarashi, T. (2009). Toward acceptable domestic robots: Applying insights from social psychology. *International Journal of Social Robotics, 1*(1), 95–108.

Young, S. G., Sacco, D. F., & Hugenberg, K. (2011). Vulnerability to disease is associated with a domain-specific preference for symmetrical faces relative to symmetrical non-face stimuli. *European Journal of Social Psychology, 41*(5), 558–563.

Zajenkowski, M., Stolarski, M., Maciantowicz, O., Malesza, M., & Witowska, J. (2016). Time to be smart: Uncovering a complex interplay between intelligence and time perspectives. *Intelligence, 58*, 1–9.

Zajonc, R. B., Markus, H., & Markus, G. B. (1979). The birth order puzzle. *Journal of Personality & Social Psychology, 37*(8), 1325–1341.

Zimbardo, P. (2007). *The Lucifer effect: Understanding how good people turn evil.* New York, NY: Random House.

Zimbardo, P. (2011a, January 12). *What makes a hero?* [YouTube Video]. Greater Good Science Center: https://www.youtube.com/watch?v=grMHzqtRm_8&fs=1&hl=en_US.

Zimbardo, P. (2011b). Why the world needs heroes. *Europe's Journal of Psychology, 7*(3), 402–407.

Zimbardo, P. (n.d.). *Statement from Philip Zimbardo.* Stanford Prison Experiment: http://www.prisonexp.org/response/.

Zimbardo, P. G., & Boyd, J. N. (1999). Putting time in perspective: A valid, reliable, individual-differences metric. *Journal of Personality & Social Psychology, 77*(6), 1271–1288.

ABOUT THE EDITORS

Travis Langley, PhD, editor, is a psychology professor who teaches courses on crime, media, and social behavior at Henderson State University. He received his bachelor's from Hendrix College and his graduate degrees from Tulane University in New Orleans. Dr. Langley is the series editor and lead writer for his Popular Culture Psychology books on *The Walking Dead*, *Game of Thrones*, *Doctor Who*, *Star Wars*, *Star Trek*, *Supernatural*, many superheroes, and more. He authored the acclaimed book *Batman and Psychology: A Dark and Stormy Knight*. *Psychology Today* carries his blog, "Beyond Heroes and Villains." Travis regularly speaks on media and heroism at universities, conferences, and conventions throughout the world. The documentary *Legends of the Knight* spotlighted how he uses fiction to teach real psychology, and he has appeared as an expert interviewee in programs such as *Superheroes Decoded*, *Necessary Evil: Super-Villains of DC Comics*, *Batman & Bill*, Robert Kirkman's *Secret History of Comics*, and Neil deGrasse Tyson's *StarTalk*.

Follow him as **@Superherologist** on Twitter, where he ranks among the ten most popular psychologists. Also keep up with him and this book series through **Facebook.com/ThePsychGeeks.**

His cowboy hat is brown.

 **Wind Goodfriend, PhD,** this volume's co-editor, is a professor of psychology, director of the trauma advocacy program, and assistant dean of graduate programs at Buena Vista University in Storm Lake, Iowa. She earned her bachelor's degree at Buena Vista University, then earned her Master's and PhD in social psychology from Purdue University. Dr. Goodfriend has won the "Faculty of the Year" award at BVU several times and has won the Wythe Award for Excellence in Teaching. She is also the Principal Investigator for the Institute for the Prevention of Relationship Violence and has authored three psychology textbooks with SAGE Publications.

She has been afraid of horses since her very early childhood, and watching *Westworld* has only reinforced her belief that all horses—robotic or otherwise—could murder us at any time upon the slightest whim.

ABOUT THE CONTRIBUTORS

Travis Adams, MSW, received his MSW from the University of Southern California and is a peer support specialist working with United States military veterans. He is a Marine Corps veteran who specializes in serving veterans who have been diagnosed with PTSD, anxiety, depression, substance use disorder, and other diagnoses. He utilizes various types of therapy to aid veterans in their recovery and has incorporated the use of pop culture in conjunction with standardized treatment models. He has previously co-authored chapters in *Supernatural Psychology: Roads Less Traveled* and *Daredevil Psychology: The Devil You Know.* You can find Travis on Twitter @themarine_peer.

Allan W. Austin, PhD, is professor of history at Misericordia University in Dallas, Pennsylvania. Dr. Austin has twice been awarded both the Max & Tillie Rosenn Excellence in Teaching Award and the Louis and Barbara Alesi Excellence in Scholarship Award. He has published books dealing with immigration and religious history with the University of Illinois Press as well as an edited volume on science fiction television and history. He is working with Patrick Hamilton to complete a book on the American superhero and race, forthcoming from the University of Texas Press.

Jenna Busch is a writer, host, and founder of Legion of Leia, a website to promote and support women in fandom. She co-hosted *Cocktails with Stan* with Spider-Man creator and comic legend Stan Lee, hosted *Most Craved*, a weekly entertainment show, has appeared in the film *She Makes Comics*, and appeared as a guest on ABC's *Nightline*, *Attack of the Show*, NPR, Al Jazeera America, and multiple episodes of *Tabletop with Wil Wheaton*. Busch has co-authored chapters in most books in this Popular Culture Psychology series, beginning with *Star Wars Psychology: Dark Side of the Mind.* Her work has appeared all over the web. She can be reached on Twitter @JennaBusch.

Tim Cain, MS, is a video game developer best known as the producer, lead programmer, and designer of the 1997 computer game *Fallout*. He has developed games since 1981, both in award-winning series such as *Bard's Tale*, *Star Trek*, *D&D*, *Vampire: The Masquerade*, and *South Park*, and the original works *Fallout*, *Arcanum*, *Wildstar*, *Pillars of Eternity*, and *Tyranny*. His games have won numerous Editor's Choice and Best RPG awards. In 2009, Tim was chosen by IGN as one of the top 100 game creators of all time.

Patrice A. Crall graduates from University of Nebraska Omaha in 2018 with a master's degree in clinical mental health counseling. She earned her bachelor's degree from Buena Vista University, where she conducted and published research articles on personality, rape myth acceptance, and social distance in depression. Through her work with SAGE Publications, she has aided in the publishing of two social psychology textbooks. She works as a suicide and crisis counselor for the Boys Town National Hotline. Soon she will get married and then be Patrice Crall Arkfeld.

Erin Currie, PhD, LPC, is driven to use her psychologist superpowers for good. By day she teaches college students about how their brains work, why they sometimes don't, and how to develop counseling superpowers. In her consulting practice, MyPsychgeek, LLC, she helps people develop their own career superpowers through professional development. By night she gives her inner geek free reign to write about the psychological factors influencing her favorite characters. She also wrote for *Game of Thrones Psychology*, *Doctor Who Psychology*, *Wonder Woman Psychology*, *Supernatural Psychology*, and *Daredevil Psychology*.

Jim Davies, PhD, is a professor of cognitive science at Carleton University and author of *Riveted: The Science of Why Jokes Make Us Laugh, Movies Make Us Cry, and Religion Makes Us Feel One with the Universe*. Dr. Davies is the co-host of the *Minding the Brain* podcast, and has contributed chapters to *Star Wars Psychology: The Dark Side of the Mind*, *Star Trek Psychology: The Mental Frontier*, *Doctor Who Psychology: A Madman With a Box*, and *Daredevil Psychology: The Devil You Know*.

William Blake Erickson, PhD, is an assistant professor at Texas A&M University at San Antonio. His research interests include face perception and eyewitness memory. He has published in journals such as *Applied Cognitive Psychology, Psychonomic Bulletin and Review, Psychology, Psychiatry, and Law* and *Journal of Police and Criminal Psychology.*

Marie-Joëlle Estrada received her PhD in social psychology from Duke University in 2010. She is an assistant professor at the University of Rochester, where she specializes in romantic relationships, gender, and consumer behavior.

Anthony Francis, PhD, teaches robots to learn. After getting his doctorate in artificial intelligence at Georgia Tech, he developed emotion models for robots in America and Japan. He's also written several novels, including the steampunk adventure *Jeremiah Willstone and the Clockwork Time Machine* as well as the Skindancer urban fantasy series including *Frost Moon, Blood Rock,* and *Liquid Fire.* He now lives in San Jose with his wife and cats, and promises that he is not secretly working to bring about the robot apocalypse.

Larisa A. Garski, MA, LMFT, is a psychotherapist and supervisor at Empowered Therapy in Chicago, IL. She specializes in working with women, families, and young adults who identify as outside the mainstream—such as those in the geek and LGBTQIA communities. She regularly appears at pop culture conventions, speaking on panels related to mental health and geek wellness. Her work as a clinical writer and researcher has appeared or is forthcoming in a variety of pop psychology and video game psychology books including but not limited to: *Supernatural Psychology: Roads Less Traveled* and *Daredevil Psychology: The Devil You Know.*

Patrick L. Hamilton, PhD, is associate professor of English at Misericordia University in Dallas, Pennsylvania. He published *Of Space and Mind: Cognitive Mappings of Contemporary Chicano/a Fiction*, with University of Texas Press, and articles on the frontier in literature as well as zombies in popular cultures. He is currently working with Allan Austin to complete a book on the American superhero and race, forthcoming from the University of Texas Press.

Thomas E. Heinzen, PhD, is a professor of psychology at the William Paterson University of New Jersey. He has published eight books ranging from a statistics textbook to found poetry by the frail elderly. He has published peer-reviewed articles across a wide range of methods including case studies, controlled experiments, quasi-experiments, focus groups, and historical analyses. He has been elected as a fellow of the Eastern Psychological Association, the Association for Psychological Science, and the American Psychological Association. His current research applies principles of game design to induce greater perseverance and improve college graduation rates.

William Indick, PhD, is an associate professor of psychology, joining the fulltime faculty of the WPU Psychology Department in 2017. He received his BA in psychology and his MA in music therapy from New York University, and earned his PhD in developmental psychology from Cornell University. He has written six books in the area of media psychology, on subjects such as the psychological study of fantasy and science fiction, and the application of psychoanalysis to film. His books include *The Psychology of the Western: How the American Psyche Plays Out on Screen*.

J. Scott Jordan, PhD, is a cognitive psychologist who studies the roots of cooperative behavior. He often uses popular culture in his classes to illustrate the relevance of social-cognitive psychology to daily life. He has contributed chapters to *Captain American vs. Iron Man: Freedom, Security, Psychology*; *Wonder Woman Psychology: Lassoing the Truth*; *Star Trek Psychology: The Mental Frontier*; *Supernatural Psychology: Roads Less Traveled*; and *Daredevil Psychology: The Devil You Know*. He is extremely proud of his international comic book collection.

Vagish Kottana graduated from William Paterson University in 2018 with a bachelor's degree in psychology. He will pursue graduate studies in medicine in order to become a doctor of psychiatry. He co-authored a chapter in this book on the bicameral mind with Dr. William Indick.

Alex Langley, MS, allegedly has a borderline nuclear passion for writing. He is the author of five books (including *Make a Nerdy Living* from Sterling Publishing and *The Geek Handbook* series), a graphic novel, and chapters in the Popular Culture Psychology series. He teaches psychology, writes about gaming for ArcadeSushi.com, oversees NerdSpan.com's gaming section, co-created the webseries *Geeks and Gamers Anonymous*, appears on panels at comic con panels, and shares both sense and nonsense on Twitter as @RocketLlama.

Martin Lloyd, PhD, LP, received his doctorate in clinical psychology from the University of Minnesota. He has worked in various prisons and high-security hospitals, including the U.S. Medical Center for Federal Prisoners and Patton State Hospital. He currently practices as a forensic psychologist in Minnesota and occasionally teaches forensic psychology at Gustavus Adolphus College. If he had to pick one of the show's parks for a vacation, he would totally go with Shogun Land.

Justine Mastin, MA, LMFT, is the owner of Blue Box Counseling in Minneapolis. She specializes in working with clients who self-identify as being outside the mainstream, such as those in the geek, secular, and LGBTQIA communities. Justine is also the fearless leader of YogaQuest, a yoga organization that blends geek narratives with yoga. She appears at pop culture conventions, teaching yoga and speaking on geek wellness topics. Justine previously contributed chapters to *Supernatural Psychology: Roads Less Traveled* and *Daredevil Psychology: The Devil You Know*. Find more information about Justine's work blueboxcounseling.com or follow her on Twitter @mindbodyfandom.

Darren McKee is the host of *The Reality Check*, a weekly Canadian-produced podcast that explores a wide range of controversies and curiosities by probing popular myths and exposing the surprising truth behind them. He also founded and facilitates Effective Altruism Ottawa, which brings together people who want to use evidence and data to find out the best way to help the world, and then do it.

Matt Munson can often be found spending time with his local group of fellow Whovians collectively known as "Team Tardis." His earliest memory in life is of watching a Tom Baker episode of *Doctor Who* from behind the couch, spawning a life-long love of *Doctor Who* and all things science fiction. His love for the show was reignited with the introduction of Christopher Eccleston's Doctor, culminating in the completion of a year-long project dedicated to reproducing a full-sized replica of the Eleventh Doctor's TARDIS. Matt serves as an enterprise architect on a flagship project for a Fortune 50 company.

Alicia H. Nordstrom, PhD, is a professor of psychology at Misericordia University in Dallas, Pennsylvania. She is the creator of *The Voices Project*, an empirically-supported stigma reduction program to reduce stereotypes and prejudice toward individuals from stigmatized social groups. Dr. Nordstrom won teaching awards for *The Voices Project* from the Society for the Psychological Study of Social Issues and Social Psychology Network. *The Voices Project: Mental Health* was performed at the Broadway Bound Theatre Festival in New York City in 2017, and she presented a talk for TEDxLancaster on "The Fallacy of Normal and Beauty of Difference."

Sarita J. Robinson, PhD, is the psychology BSc course leader at the University of Central Lancashire, England. Sarita is a psychobiologist and her research focuses on how the body's physiological systems, the brain, and the environment interact to create different behaviors. Sarita's work looks specifically at people's behaviors in high risk environments, and so she frequently finds herself working in high pressure situations. Sarita is a lifelong science fiction fan who enjoys combining her passion for science fiction with her love of psychology. In her spare time, Sarita enjoys doing stand-up comedy and science communication talks.

Janina Scarlet, PhD, is a licensed clinical psychologist, author, and a full-time geek. She uses Superhero Therapy to help patients with anxiety, depression, chronic pain, and PTSD at the Center for Stress and Anxiety Management. Dr. Scarlet is the author of *Superhero Therapy, Therapy Quest, Dark Agents*, as well as *Harry Potter Therapy* and has also authored or co-authored chapters in every volume in this Popular Culture Psychology series. She can be reached via her website at superherotherapy.com or on Twitter: @shadowquill.

Dawn R. Weatherford, PhD, is an assistant professor at Texas A&M University at San Antonio. Her research interests include cognitive psychology, face perception, and information processing at the applied and basic theoretical levels. She is a member of the Psychonomic Society, Vision Sciences Society, and the Association for Psychological Science, and has presented her research at these and other organisations' annual meetings.

Eric D. Wesselmann, PhD, is an associate professor of psychology at Illinois State University. He publishes research on various topics, such as social exclusion, stigma, and religion/spirituality. He first became interested in debating the philosophical differences between humans and robots in high school after watching relevant anime (e.g., *Armitage III*; *Ghost in the Shell*; *Robot Carnival*) and reading Karel Čapek's play *R.U.R.* (*Rossum's Universal Robots*). Eric has contributed to most of the volumes in this series.

INDEX

Absolute determinism, 16
Action plans, 237–239
Action tendencies, 136
Adaptive behavior, 76
Adler, Alfred, 13–14, 16, 266
Aeschylus, 227
Affect, definition of, 137
Agency. *See also* Personal agency
    act of reclaiming, 184
    masculine stereotype and, 199
    power and, 206
    social world as perceived, 110
Aggression. *See also* Violent games/gaming
    definition of, 204
    dehumanization and, 114
    fight response and, 245
    media schema, 87
    against others, 114
    rewarding, 187
    types of, 204–205
    violent games and, 88–89
Alien hand syndrome, 31
Alzheimer's disease, 230
American Psychological Association (APA), 85, 265
Anderson, G.D., 205
Animacy, 122–123
Anthropomorphism
    controlling your world and, 112
    Counter-anthropomorphism, 59–60
    definition of, 109–110
    dehumanization as opposite of, 112
    factors encouraging, 110–112
    people's need to belong and, 111–112
    theory of mind and, 134
Anxiety, 136, 184
Art therapy, 248–249
Artificial intelligence, 72, 214

Artificial relationships, 111. *See also* Anthropomorphism
Assertive power, 199
Attitudinal ambivalence, 235, 240
Attractiveness, evolutionary bases of, 208
Auditory hallucinations, 231
Autobiographical self, 234
Autonomy, 34–35
Awakening, conscious, 227

"Bad but bold" stereotype, 201, 206
Behavior
    adaptive, 76
    coercion under threat, 32–33
    complete autonomy, 34–35
    direct preference manipulation, 33–34
    empowerment, 35
    restricted by psychological limitations, 30–32
Being someone, 230
Believability flip, 140–141
Betrayal, institutional, 49
Bicameral mind theory, 128, 216–219, 231–234. *See also* Consciousness
Bicameral societies, 233
Bi-directional love, 157–158
Birth order effects, 14
The boss, definition of, 71
The Boy Code, 187
Brainwashing, 33–34
Breazeal, Cynthia, 139
Bulk apperception, 35

Capgras syndrome, 126
Captivity survivors, 245
Catastrophizing, 250
"Catch it, Check it, Change it" tool, 250–251
Causality, 38
Causation, alternative to, 38
Cause and effect, 27

Chauvinism, 134
Choice, as act of free will, 27–28
Civilian heroes, 171
Clinical treatments, dehumanizing side of, 17
Coercions, 27, 31, 32–33
Cognitive appraisals, 29, 139
Cognitive dissonance
    consistency of self and, 45–46
    contracting an intended action, 47
    definition of, 41
    dehumanization and, 58–60
    environmental changes and, 42
    extreme, 42–43
    in forced compliance situations, 46–47
    increasing level of, 42
    low levels of, 44
    reducing, 43, 46
    social environments and, 44
    tension created by, 41
Cognitive triangle, 250–251
Communication, 206–207
Communion, 198, 203
Companion robots, 148–149
Compartmentalization, 57–58
Compassionate actions, 168–169
Complex PTSD, 244, 248, 252. *See also* Post-traumatic stress disorder (PTSD)
Compulsions, 30
Computation theory, 133
Conscious awakening, 227
Conscious reflection, 215
Conscious self-awareness, 215
Consciousness. *See also* Bicameral mind theory
    creating, 72
    as divine gift, 226

301